MEN AND SPEED

Also by G. Wayne Miller

Thunder Rise (1989)
The Work of Human Hands (1993)
Coming of Age (1995)
Toy Wars (1998)
King of Hearts (2000)

*MEN*AND*SPEED*

A **WILD RIDE** THROUGH
NASCAR'S
BREAKOUT SEASON

G. WAYNE MILLER

 PUBLICAFFAIRS   *New York*

Book design and composition by Mark McGarry, Texas Type & Book Works, Inc.
Set in Meridien

Library of Congress Cataloging-in-Publication data
Miller, G. Wayne.
Men and speed: a wild ride through NASCAR's breakout season: a fast-paced liter-
ary narrative of NASCAR's breakthrough 2001 season, reflecting unprecedented and
exclusive access inside America's largest auto racing operation / G. Wayne Miller.
p. cm.
Includes index.
ISBN 1-58648-096-0 (hb)
1. Stock car racing—United States.
2. NASCAR (Association). I Title.
GV1029.9.S74 M55 2002
796.72'0973—dc21
2002018980

FIRST EDITION
10 9 8 7 6 5 4 3 2 1

To Kay McCauley,
My dear friend and trusted agent all these years.

CONTENTS

THE 2001 WINSTON CUP SCHEDULE

FEBRUARY 18	Daytona 500, Daytona International Speedway, Daytona Beach, Florida
FEBRUARY 25	Dura-Lube 400, North Carolina Speedway, Rockingham, North Carolina
MARCH 4	UAW-Daimler Chrysler 400, Las Vegas Motor Speedway
MARCH 11	Cracker Barrel Old Country Store 500, Atlanta Motor Speedway, Hampton, Georgia
MARCH 18	Carolina Dodge Dealers 400, Darlington (South Carolina) Raceway
MARCH 25	Food City 500, Bristol (Tennessee) Motor Speedway
APRIL 1	Harrah's 500, Texas Motor Speedway, Fort Worth
APRIL 8	Virginia 500, Martinsville (Virginia) Speedway
APRIL 22	Talladega 500, Talladega (Alabama) Superspeedway
APRIL 29	NAPA Auto Parts 500, California Speedway, Fontana, California
MAY 5	Pontiac Excitement 400, Richmond (Virginia) International Raceway
MAY 19	The Winston, Lowe's Motor Speedway, Concord, North Carolina
MAY 27	Coca-Cola 600, Lowe's Motor Speedway
JUNE 3	MBNA Platinum 400, Dover Downs International Speedway, Dover, Delaware
JUNE 10	Kmart 400, Michigan International Speedway, Brooklyn, Michigan
JUNE 17	Pocono 500, Pocono Raceway, Long Pond, Pennsylvania

JUNE 24   Dodge/Save Mart 350, Sears Point Raceway, Sonoma, California

JULY 7   Pepsi 400, Daytona International Speedway

JULY 15   Tropicana 400, Chicagoland Speedway, Joliet, Illinois

JULY 22   New England 300, New Hampshire International Speedway, Loudon, New Hampshire

JULY 29   Pennsylvania 500, Pocono Raceway

AUGUST 5   Brickyard 400, Indianapolis Motor Speedway

AUGUST 12   Global Crossing@The Glen, Watkins Glen (New York) International

AUGUST 19   Pepsi 400 presented by Meijer, Michigan International Speedway

AUGUST 25   Sharpie 500, Bristol Motor Speedway

SEPTEMBER 2   Mountain Dew Southern 500, Darlington Raceway

SEPTEMBER 8   Chevrolet Monte Carlo 400, Richmond International Raceway

SEPTEMBER 16   rescheduled to November 23

SEPTEMBER 23   MBNA Cal Ripken Jr. 400, Dover Downs International Speedway

SEPTEMBER 30   Protection One 400, Kansas Speedway, Kansas City, Kansas

OCTOBER 7   UAW-GM Quality 500, Lowe's Motor Speedway

OCTOBER 14   Old Dominion 500, Martinsville Speedway

OCTOBER 21   EA Sports 500, Talladega Superspeedway

OCTOBER 28   Checker Auto Parts 500 presented by Pennzoil, Phoenix International Raceway

NOVEMBER 4   Pop Secret 400, North Carolina Speedway

NOVEMBER 11   Pennzoil Freedom 400, Homestead-Miami Speedway, Homestead, Florida

NOVEMBER 18   NAPA 500, Atlanta Motor Speedway

NOVEMBER 23   New Hampshire 300, New Hampshire International Speedway

NOVEMBER 30   Annual banquet, Waldorf-Astoria Hotel, New York

Until one day in the spring of 2001, I thought I understood speed. For more than a year, I'd been traveling NASCAR's elite Winston Cup circuit, which features some of America's most exciting automobile racing. I'd experienced the sensation of racecars whizzing by at over 200 miles per hour. I'd gotten to know drivers, mechanics, and builders of cars. I'd spent many days with Jack Roush, an engineer, ex-racer, and racecar owner who had built a $250 million empire on speed. Roush raced four cars in Winston Cup competition, more than anyone.

That spring day, Jack handed me the keys to one of the Stage 3 Mustang convertibles he sells on the open market. It wasn't a racecar—but it was close, a low-slung, super-charged street machine that top ends at some 170 miles per hour and hits sixty in an astonishing 4.3 seconds. The sedan I ordinarily drive was a slug compared to it, a fact that was evident from the moment I gave it the gas.

One touch and the Mustang rocketed forward, pushing me back into my seat. It felt good, and inviting: What would this car do if I put the pedal to the floor? Perhaps I would learn. I had joined Jack on an early leg of The History Channel's Great Race, a cross-country competition involving antique cars. His new Mustang obviously couldn't enter, but Jack was sending it along as a VIP vehicle—and he'd given me the wheel for an entire day, a trip that would take us on a winding route from Knoxville, Tennessee, to Lexington, Kentucky.

Tempted though I was, I exercised caution as we started off through the morning commute. I didn't want to risk damaging Jack's car, which retails for more than $50,000—nor embarrass myself with a man who had won many racing championships. But the sun shone, the traffic thinned, and we started down a long stretch of open highway. Almost unconsciously, I began to lean into the gas, until we were doing eighty. The car handled like the proverbial dream, and I experienced a flutter inside my chest whenever I passed someone. And even if they were booking it, I passed, without a whisper of protest from Jack's 360-horsepower V-8 engine.

Our route took us from highway to narrow mountain roads. This was wild country: steep inclines, precipitous ravines, dead-man's curves, a place better suited to moonshining than automobiling. We came up behind one of the antique cars, traveling at a sober speed, and I backed off; the road hooked abruptly to the left, and I had only about a hundred yards of clearance. Anything could have been around that corner.

"You can pass him, you know," said Jack, a twinkle in his eye. His friend, Victor Vojcek, another ex-racer, who was riding in back, agreed.

I stood on the gas. We shot from twenty to sixty in about two seconds—and blew by the old classic with room to spare. The flutter intensified to an adrenaline rush and I craved more. I was entering the zone.

I had a few close calls on those mountain roads, including nearly running us into a ditch—but instead of slowing me down, flirting with disaster produced the opposite effect. By now, I felt invincible. Other defining characteristics of my life (a wife and three dependent children, for example) had lost relevance. My world now was a cool car and blacktop, and what a glorious world it was.

Late afternoon found us on the highway again, specifically, an interstate that leads into Lexington. Rush hour traffic was building. I asked Jack, who married a Kentucky woman, if the state police here were tough—and he said they were worse than in Ohio, notorious for handing out speeding tickets. Deciding to be vigilant but not dawdling, I started passing again. I was back in the zone.

Suddenly, we were alongside a shiny black Pontiac Firebird—a fast car, but surely no match for a Roush Stage 3. A man in his early twenties was driving, and he grinned over at us. Jack surmised that he was a street racer who probably had something other than an assembly-line engine under his innocent-looking hood. I only knew that when I attempted to pass, he powered up.

I stood on the gas. For an instant, we led—but the young man roared ahead. I leaned into the gas a little deeper and we took him. Back and forth, trading the lead, until we'd hit ninety. I'd reached my limit. I eased off, and the young man disappeared in the traffic ahead of me.

"You didn't have to let him take you," Jack said. "You had fifty horsepower on him."

I felt humiliated. We were about ten miles outside of Lexington now and the highway was clogged, but I silently vowed to hunt down that Firebird—I couldn't get the image of the young man's triumphant smile as he'd zoomed away out of my head. Jack could see what I was up to, but he figured we were done.

Jack was wrong. Taking chances a man of forty-seven never should, I tore through the traffic—and there was the Firebird, on my right door.

I punched the gas and we shot ahead. Caught off guard, the young man lagged—but only momentarily. I wove through the commuters, now left, now right, the young man all the while gaining. Damn if he didn't have some kind of engine under his hood.

I was totally in the zone now—knuckles white, sweat on my forehead, the flutter in my chest a narcotic pounding. I could see with a clarity I'd never before experienced, and my reflexes were dangerously sharp—but sound had virtually ceased, as if they'd dropped the soundtrack out of the movie. I think Jack said something about showing no mercy now, but I didn't need Jack to light the way. I punched the pedal to the floor, and we finally smoked the Firebird. The speedometer read 120, or so Jack later informed me.

Thank God the Stage 3 was equipped with race brakes and race suspension—traffic had slowed to a clot, and I was about to wreck us. I slammed on the brakes, and we came back from 120 faster than we'd gotten there, with nary a wiggle. Jack gave me a high-five, and I allowed as how you'd become a millionaire if you could bottle the feeling I had right then. I hadn't just gone fast— I'd won, and the high of winning our brief contest was more blissful than any drug.

We exited the highway shortly thereafter, and as we stopped at a red light like the good citizens we were once again, the Firebird pulled up next to us. As it happened, the young man had his teenage brother along for the ride, and they both congratulated me on an excellent race. I asked if they were into NASCAR, and they said they were. But they hadn't made careful note of the man sitting beside me—and when I introduced Jack Roush, they went crazy. "No way!" shouted the brother. "We raced Jack Roush!" said the driver. Turns out the boys liked Mark Martin, Jack's most popular Winston Cup driver.

Jack invited them to follow us into downtown Lexington, where a crowd of several thousand awaited the Great Race cars. The twenty-four-year-old driver, Jeremiah Staab, told us about his Firebird, which he had indeed configured to street race, and his eighteen-year-old brother, Jakob, let on as how he'd just graduated from high school. Jack autographed some Roush Racing hats for the boys, who lived in the hills of eastern Kentucky, and then we all posed for pictures. I had returned to my calm and rational self, but I could still feel a trace of something mighty good inside my body. I later asked Jack about the effect of introducing such a substance into a young person's veins.

"When the sap is high in the tree, oh man!" he said. "It's something that really drives you. It's just incredible. It spins you off into that business."

Speed entices, and for the characters in this book, it proved a potent addiction from the earliest taste.

G. WAYNE MILLER
Pascoag, Rhode Island
January 27, 2002

CHAPTER 1

THE GURU AND THE KID

On the afternoon of Saturday, July 8, 2000, a man who looked barely old enough to drive climbed into an automobile designed to race at almost a third the speed of sound. Kurt Busch and thirty-three other drivers fired up their engines. Bone-rattling noise rocked New Hampshire International Speedway and the air smelled suddenly burnt.

From the grandstands, the luxury boxes, and atop the campers and motor homes lining the hill behind the backstretch of the mile-long track, a sellout crowd of some ninety thousand fans watched. Most were getting their first glimpse of Busch, a tall, slender twenty-one-year-old with a boyish face who only eight months earlier had earned his living fixing broken pipes. If they knew anything about the kid, it was that he drove ferociously and with uncommon skill—and that his talent, while still raw, had earned him the backing of one of the most powerful men in American motorsports. Only last week, Busch had won his first big race, at a track in Milwaukee.

Polite and impeccably mannered off the track, and gifted with an easy humor, Busch became transformed when he took the wheel of a racecar. He drove at the edge—out in that rarefied zone between fearlessness and craziness, the place where speed kings thrive. No track intimidated Busch. No race seemed unwinnable at the green flag, regardless of where he started.

He was starting in fifth place today in this NASCAR Craftsman Truck Series race—behind the series leader and three racing veterans, two of whom had begun their careers before he was born. As Busch fastened his belts, checked his gauges, and otherwise connected with his machine, he reviewed his strategy, which involved conserving his tires, which could give him track advantage, and a commitment to racing clean. Busch would go eyeball-to-eyeball with an opponent—would crawl to within an inch of someone's bumper to bully him out of the way, if need be—but he was determined to avoid contact.

Contact preoccupied everyone that July afternoon in Loudon, a small town in central New Hampshire. NASCAR racing is among the most violent of the motorsports: Virtually no race passes without cars wrecking, often in fiery collisions that thrill fans. Protective gear, custom seats, and steel caging ordinarily protect drivers—but concrete and speed can be lethal. Just twenty-six hours earlier, popular driver Kenny Irwin Jr. had died while practicing at this track, whose nickname, The Magic Mile, now seemed a cruel joke. The throttle on his 720-horsepower engine stuck at full speed, rendering meaningful braking impossible, and Irwin hit the Turn Three wall head-on at some 160 miles per hour. The impact destroyed Irwin's vehicle and fractured the base of his skull, destroying his brain. A virtually identical crash on Turn Three had killed another well-known young driver, Adam Petty, grandson of stockcar legend Richard Petty, only two months earlier.

Busch and his competitors circled the track behind the pace car, swerving in and out of file like hornets startled from a nest—a maneuver that warms tires, improving grip. The field took the green flag and now the noise, fueled by 110-octane gas and the absence of mufflers, exceeded a jet on takeoff. For the moment, Busch pushed Turn Three from his mind. The race known as the thatlook.com 200 had begun. Half a million dollars was at stake.

Standing with Busch's crew on pit road, owner Jack Roush watched his young protégé blister the mile-long oval.

A short man who favored button-down shirts, cuffed khaki pants, and a straw fedora—an outfit that made him an eccentric in a world of oil and grease—Roush had built the largest motorsports operation in America. But Roush, fifty-eight, was renowned for more than his racing achievements. Bearer of a master's degree in mathematics, he had taught college physics. He had founded and remained the chairman of a $250 million engineering firm, Roush Industries, of which Roush Racing was a subsidiary. He enjoyed piloting his own corporate jet, and he was about to purchase three 727 airliners to move his race teams around the country—but he felt deeper passion for his P-51 Mustang, a World War II fighter plane that he'd bought, restored, and now used to perform aerobatics, frequently with someone he wanted to thrill riding expectantly (if not nervously) in back.

Before one such adventure, Roush talked to the home office on his cell phone while conducting a preflight inspection of his plane, which was parked at an airport near his racecar-building shops in Concord, North Carolina, just outside of Charlotte. Freshly painted in its original colors and sporting its original name—Old Crow, bestowed by Bud Anderson, the war hero who'd flown it in combat—the P-51 sparkled in the midday sun. Roush shed his fedora and pulled a flight suit over his shirt and pants, then removed two parachutes from the trunk of his Lincoln and handed one to his passenger.

"Only two reasons you'd need it," said Roush. "One is if we catch fire. The other is a midair collision."

After explaining the basics of operation as he understood

them, Roush noted that he had never used a parachute. "I don't believe in practicing for something you must do correctly the first time," he said, grinning.

The plane rattled and shook as it sped down the runway, and, after a final shudder, lifted like an eagle into the blue. Roush cruised northwest, turning the plane upside-down as he passed over the business headquarters of Roush Racing, where the mahogany walls glisten and the employees wear suits. A few moments later, having determined that he had the airspace all to himself, Roush executed maneuvers that he described in an animated monologue over the plane's intercom: a barrel roll, an aileron roll, a four-point victory roll, an enormous loop. At this point, having repeatedly achieved five Gs, a force that can flood the body with adrenaline, Roush leveled off and headed toward a friend's farm, which he buzzed at treetop level. Only then did Roush confide that he'd never taken lessons in aerobatics, but had figured things out himself.

But automobiles, not aircraft, had remained Roush's foremost obsession since childhood, when he got his first taste of speed. Son of a housewife and an intermittently successful mechanic and entrepreneur who raised their family in small-town Ohio, Roush owned a bicycle not long after he learned to walk. Pedaling by itself couldn't propel him fast enough—so he sought out steep hills to increase the speed.

"I was a junkie for it," he said. "You can become addicted, you know."

Motors promised bigger doses, and by the age of ten Roush had remade his red wagon into a go-cart powered by a lawn-mower engine he'd figured out how to tear down and rebuild. Then came the mid-1950s, when America's highways growled with cast-iron V-8s, the muscle of high Industrial Age Detroit. Lacking wealth but overflowing with ambition, the teenage Roush scoured junkyards and fields for rusted hulks that he transformed into fast, powerful machines. He then raced his creations: against friends on dusty back roads at first, and later on organized drag strips, which feature straight-line duels. Too slight to prevail in sports played with a ball, Roush had found one where ingenuity and nerve counted for more than brawn—a sport where he could win, which mattered deeply from an early age. "I've always been competitive," Roush said, "maybe because I'm small."

Business demands kept him from racing full-time as he took employment at Ford Motor Company and, later, established the Michigan-based Roush Industries. But he could build engines and cars, and he became an owner, with his racers competing on circular tracks, road courses, and twenty-four-hour endurance events. The actor Paul Newman and the Olympian Bruce Jenner are among those who drove for Roush in the 1970s and 1980s, when his teams won national championships in leagues with acronyms such as NHRA and IMSA.

Impressive in their own right, Roush's titles came in the relative obscurity of the racing purist's universe. But by the late 1980s, that universe was expanding; NASCAR was pulling away from all other forms of automobile racing to become one of America's most popular spectator sports.

William H. G. France was operating a service station in Daytona Beach, Florida, in 1947 when he founded the National Association for Stock Car Auto Racing, a sanctioning body for a sport that to that point had been loosely organized. France had been competing part-time on the hard-packed sands of the beach— the so-called Birthplace of Speed, home to auto racing since the turn of the century. He raced American stockcars: vehicles that an ordinary fellow with a degree of mechanical aptitude and a compulsion to go fast could buy off the showroom floor, then soup up with modified engines and racing suspensions. France believed that fans would relate better to cars that looked like the ones they themselves drove than funny-looking purebred racing machines, such as those in Grand Prix racing. His marketing instincts were sound, and people listened. France was called Big Bill—for his stature, six-foot-five, and his commanding personality.

Although NASCAR racing took root in the rural south, where moonshiners skilled at outrunning federal agents ranked among the best early competitors, France envisioned a sport that would rival the big three of football, baseball, and basketball in national prominence—and profit, which he and his family would share since he controlled NASCAR. Big Bill and his sons Bill Jr., who became president in 1972, and Jim, executive vice president and secretary, worked ambitiously at broadening NASCAR's regional base. They arranged live national network coverage of the 1979 Daytona 500, an exciting race that Richard Petty won, and two years later the new cable network ESPN began televising stockcar racing. The Frances moved their annual banquet to New York's Waldorf-Astoria Hotel, and in 1985 a NASCAR driver, Bill Elliott, graced the cover of *Sports Illustrated*. A sport perceived as the exclusive province of rednecks was going mainstream.

Bill France Jr., chairman since his father died in 1992, credited a simple formula for NASCAR's success. "We work hard," he said. "We get up every morning and hit the ground running. That's what we expect of our people and they deliver."

But hard work minus a good product hardly created a phenomenon. Part of NASCAR's appeal derived from the raw excitement of its brand of racing, in which tens of thousands of spectators surround dozens of racecars circling for three hours or more at speeds that can approach 200 miles per hour. The unrelenting thunder of so many high-powered machines, the strangely intoxicating smells of burning rubber and high-octane exhaust, the hurricane-like feel of air suddenly cleft by iron—a TV tube cannot adequately convey the sensation, which thrills on a primal level. Another attraction, of course, was danger—and the danger was real, unlike in professional wrestling. Drivers died in stockcar racing, untold dozens of them over the years.

The corporate suites were always full at Winston Cup races, but a larger, more colorful spectacle also unfolded: Thousands of predominantly blue-collar fans turned the race into a long weekend of partying, and they filled the infields and outlying areas with their recreational vehicles, tents, and, some of them, their Confederate flags. A fleeting look at any NASCAR speedway on a race weekend, and one might wonder if the clock had been turned back to the 1950s, when fuel crises, ozone alerts, and Surgeon Generals' warnings were years in the future. By noon, fans were already drinking (domestic beer, mostly), many were smoking cigarettes, and hot dogs and meats cooked over barbecue grilles. It was OK at a NASCAR race to drop your chicken bones and beer cans wherever you were—and also for men, and even women, to remove their T-shirts to be turned lobster-red in the midday sun.

As NASCAR grew, the Frances created new divisions within their sport. Lesser ones were regionally and locally based. The big action was in NASCAR's three national leagues, which roughly paralleled the structure of professional baseball. The equivalent of Double A ball, NASCAR's Sears, Roebuck and Co.–sponsored Craftsman Truck Series featured a mix of veteran drivers and rookies like Kurt Busch. The next level up—Triple A, as it were—was the Busch Grand National Series, sponsored by the brewer Anheuser-Busch (whose controlling family was no relation to Kurt Busch). NASCAR's top level was the Winston Cup series, in which America's best stockcar racers, about four dozen in all, competed.

With growth came bigger purses—enough, when supplemented by licensing revenues and other income, to make even moderately successful Winston Cup drivers millionaires. Inevitably, costs rose, too. No longer could a guy tinker with his car weekdays in his garage, then go racin' on Saturday night; at the Winston Cup level, stock cars evolved into $150,000 hand-built machines that were designed with computers, tested in wind tunnels, and only vaguely resembled a Ford, Chevrolet, Pontiac, or Dodge that a consumer could buy off the lot. A close look at a stockcar revealed that the lights were decals and the tires lacked tread, a smooth surface providing better grip. Stock-cars also had no windshield wipers or doors (drivers crawled in and out through a narrow window). And the interior—with its fire extinguisher, toggle switches on the dash, single cocoonlike seat, and steering wheel that detaches to let a driver in—looked nothing like a regular automobile.

Personnel costs rose along with the costs of the vehicles. A support crew that once might have included a driver's brother-in-law and a good drinking buddy became a highly specialized team of more than a dozen men who had to be paid, housed, fed, and transported around the country for most of a year. Only corporate America could bankroll such an expensive enterprise, and NASCAR's popularity attracted Fortune 500 companies such as Coca-Cola, McDonald's, and Kellogg's. For $10 million or more a year, a primary car sponsor bought the right to put its name on cars, uniforms, hats, Web sites, and just about anywhere else a logo might fit. NASCAR also sold the rights to individual races and series, and companies like R. J. Reynolds Tobacco Holdings Inc., the maker of Winston cigarettes, took advantage.

Unlike with football, baseball, and basketball, where team owners collectively control the sanctioning body—and thus their sport—the France family ran NASCAR as a benevolent dictatorship, maintaining sole control of its finances, rules, and participants. No drivers' unions existed, nor did car owners have formal representation. "My way or the highway" was a phrase used to describe the management style of Big Bill and Bill Jr.

It happened to be the way to fabulous wealth. The Frances earned income from TV rights, sanctioning fees, licensing, and their controlling interest in the publicly traded International Speedway Corporation—a profitable entity comprising a radio network, a merchandise business, and thirteen large tracks, including Daytona International Speedway, stockcar racing's crown jewel. *Forbes* magazine described Bill Jr. and his brother Jim as billionaires, tied at 236 on its list of America's 400 wealthiest people.

The growing prestige of Winston Cup racing attracted car owners with some of the most famous names in racing: Penske, Foyt, Yates. Other owners, like the Super Bowl-champion Washington Redskins coach Joe Gibbs, came to NASCAR from outside motorsports. But few had succeeded like Jack Roush, who by the year 2000 fielded five drivers in Winston Cup, two in Grand National, and two in Craftsman Truck. Since Roush's first NASCAR entry in 1988, his drivers had won $62.5 million in Cup racing alone, second on the all-time list only to owner Rick Hendrick, who counted the incomparable Jeff Gordon in his stable.

Only a Winston Cup championship had eluded Jack Roush.

Mark Martin, the Arkansas native who drove the No. 6 Viagra Ford Taurus, had come the closest to bringing him one. Roush's original NASCAR driver, Martin had finished second or third seven times in his twelve years of Winston Cup racing with the owner—and he would have been the 1990 champion if not for a controversial penalty that gave Dale Earnhardt the title in one of the closest finishes in NASCAR history. This July 2000 found Martin in sixth place, within striking distance of leader Bobby Labonte.

Jeff Burton, the driver of the No. 99 CITGO Supergard Ford Taurus, had raced for Roush since 1996, finishing fifth or better in the Cup standings each of the previous three years. A leading safety advocate and arguably NASCAR's most cerebral driver, Burton, a Virginian, had won two of the seventeen points races so far in 2000 and had placed second three times, including at the season-opening Daytona 500. Burton held fourth in the standings.

Matt Kenseth, Roush's third driver, was in his first full year of

Winston Cup racing. A quiet Wisconsinite, Kenseth was competing for Rookie of the Year with Earnhardt's son, Dale Junior, who
drove the No. 8 Budweiser Beer car. Kenseth had already won a
Cup race, a rare achievement for a rookie. He drove Roush's No.
17 DeWALT Industrial Tools Ford Taurus.

Two other drivers raced for Roush on the Cup circuit—but
neither had met the owner's expectations. Barring sudden
improvement, Roush would let Kevin Lepage go at the end of the
season and mothball his No. 16 FamilyClick.com car.

Time had already run out for Chad Little, who drove the No.
97 John Deere car. Within weeks, Roush intended to replace him
with a twenty-one-year-old kid who'd never taken the wheel of a
Winston Cup car.

Trouble arrived early in the thatlook.com 200.

On lap 3, on the same turn where Petty and Irwin had lost
their lives, a driver suffered a broken shoulder blade in a four-car
pileup. Kurt Busch was close by—but he managed to avoid
wrecking, a tribute to uncanny prescience and superior reflexes.
He dodged mayhem again on lap 39, when two second-rate drivers, perhaps settling an old grudge, mixed it up in a smoking tan-
gle that sent both of them home early.

As the race continued, Busch stayed near the front of the
pack, waiting to challenge for the lead. Patience was a virtue
Roush had tried to impress upon the kid.

"Thirty laps to go. Pace yourself, pal," radioed Rich Reichenbach, Busch's spotter, who had worked for Roush for 20 years.
Perched on a speedway's high point, often atop the press box,
spotters radio the position of nearby competitors to their racers,
who have limited visibility to the side and rear.

Busch had advanced to second place now; his tire strategy had
prevailed, and he was turning perfect laps. Irwin came to mind
when he ripped through Turn Three, but Busch, whose own

worst racing injury had been a bruised knee, maintained his concentration. His most urgent concern was the race leader, an experienced driver who figured he knew how to keep a rookie in his rearview. Busch figured otherwise.

But before he could make his move, fate smiled: The leader blew a tire and limped back to pit road, leaving Busch in first.

"Twenty to go," Reichenbach said. "You're doing a good job. Just keep squeezing it like that, kid."

But now Busch was sitting in the crosshairs: Another seasoned driver was crawling up his rear bumper. The veteran tried to pass high—on the outside, or right of the car—and Busch boxed him out. He went low, there on deadly Turn Three—and Busch hit the brakes, which slowed the pack and put the third-place driver on the veteran's tail. Busch then stood on the gas and sprinted to the checkered flag, winning by just a few feet. One race after his first win in the Craftsman Truck Series, Busch had won his second.

On pit road, his crew erupted. Under his signature fedora, Jack Roush was all grin.

"Good job, Buschster!" Reichenbach radioed. "Get to Victory Lane!"

But Busch couldn't find it. Like most of the tracks this year, he'd never raced at Loudon before.

"You missed the exit!" Reichenbach shouted. "Back up! Follow the 17! Turn right! Good job, kid! Remember to talk about Goodyear!"

Busch drove through the mob of reporters and photographers and parked his racecar, which bore a passing similarity to a pickup truck, the type of vehicle NASCAR featured in its Craftsman Truck Series (passenger sedans served as the models in the Winston Cup and Grand National series). Busch dropped the safety webbing on his window, crawled out of his car, and jumped onto the stage as someone sprayed Coke like champagne. The young driver thanked his crew and his owner, and then a public relations specialist guided him through a succession of poses in which he wore hats with the names of NASCAR, the race sponsor thatlook.com, and the primary and many associate sponsors of his No. 99 stockcar. To sponsors, winning was everything.

Facing the press in the media room after Victory Lane, Busch initially acted overwhelmed, as if his confidence had evaporated when he walked into the glare of the TV lights; he didn't even acknowledge his girlfriend, Melissa Schaper, a high school senior from his hometown, Las Vegas, who stood shyly behind the cameras at the back of the room.

But Busch soon regained his composure. He attributed his second Craftsman Truck victory to the hard work of his crew and his crew chief, Matt Chambers, a bespectacled, studious young man who looked like he belonged behind a college lectern, not with his head inside the engine compartment of a racecar. Busch also paid tribute to a dead colleague he'd never met.

"I think Kenny Irwin was with us today and he guided me through," Busch said. "And it was really a troublesome spot over there in Three. I might have thrown away a bunch over there just because of the thoughts."

Only eight months ago, Busch had been competing in the desert Southwest, which had given stockcar racing no great champions. He lived with his parents and worked as a common laborer on the Las Vegas Valley Water District's graveyard shift, an arrangement that allowed him time and money for his passion—speed. Busch had claimed several victories on NASCAR's regional circuits, but back East virtually no one had heard of him, certainly not Jack Roush.

Roush had not created racing's biggest operation on luck—although luck, he would be the first to tell you, was always one of the factors when men joined to machines competed. An engineering mind proceeds deliberately, and Roush had decided that open auditions were a productive way to recruit new talent. He called his tryouts "Gong Shows," after the 1970s TV program. Busch won the 1999 show, and Roush signed him to compete in the Craftsman Truck Series. A promising racer ordinarily might spend two or three years there, and then another couple of years in Grand National before being considered for a Cup car. A promising racer might never get an invitation. The story of stockcar racing was written with broken dreams.

Kurt Busch debuted as a Roush driver in February 2000 at Daytona International Speedway.

He hardly inspired instant confidence. On the third lap of the first round of practice for the Daytona 250, the Craftsman Truck counterpart to the longer and more prestigious Daytona 500, he wrecked his car. Jack Roush's mechanics could not repair it at the track, and Busch was forced into a back-up vehicle. He drove it during qualifying competition, the time-trial laps that determine the starting order of a race—and his engine blew. Unable to complete qualifying, Busch was forced to start the race 34th of 36. Now a third engine was powering his backup car.

But Busch was not deterred. Thirty laps into the race, he had charged to second place when his Truck Series teammate, Greg Biffle, accidentally bumped him—sending him sideways through the infield grass. Amazingly, Busch regained control, and he returned to the race having lost only a few positions. But somewhat later, another racer touched Busch, pushing him into a third car and precipitating a wreck the likes of which few had ever seen.

Thirteen cars collided—and one, driven by the fifty-year-old Geoffrey Bodine, flipped, cartwheeled, and erupted into a screaming fireball. Blinded by smoke and scorching flame, driver after driver crashed into the charred remains of Bodine's vehicle, reducing it in seconds to a battered skeleton of roll cage. Flying debris injured nine spectators. Bodine suffered a broken back and wrist, and also cuts, bruises, and abrasions, but from his hospital bed he vowed to someday race again. A born-again Christian, Bodine credited God with saving him from his gasoline-stoked inferno—and he maintained that as he lay trapped unconscious in his smoldering heap, his dead father had appeared to foretell his survival. "No, it's not your time," Bodine claimed his late father told him. "You have more to do."

Busch reacted somewhat less profoundly. "I was just thinking, 'Friends today and try not to make any enemies,'" he told reporters. "I think I may have done the opposite."

Unscathed in the maelstrom he'd unwittingly ignited, Busch went on to place second in the Daytona 250—a finish no one except Busch and his new boss had imagined possible. Less than four months later—at the Sears DieHard 200 in Milwaukee, one week before the thatlook.com 200—Busch recorded his first Truck Series win.

But Roush hadn't waited for that win to conclude that Busch, young as he was, had what it took to someday be a Winston Cup champion. In late June, having decided to replace Chad Little, Roush had asked Busch if he wanted to take the wheel of the No. 97 car when the summer was over.

"From a talent potential point of view," Roush said later, "Kurt has been quicker to adapt to changes and to new things than anybody that I've ever worked with as a driver. This guy is just incredible."

That July afternoon in New Hampshire, only Roush's inner circle knew what the owner had in mind. Come autumn, Busch would compete in seven Cup races, the maximum NASCAR allows a first-time driver before running a full rookie year. Beginning with the Daytona 500 in February 2001, Busch would run the complete Cup schedule. He would become a racing celebrity, featured on the covers of magazines and profiled on national TV. With his Roush Racing salary, his winnings, and his income from endorsements and royalties, he could soon become rich. His could truly be a rags-to-riches story—assuming, of course, that he could handle the pressure of a life at extreme speed.

Facing reporters after the thatlook.com 200, Roush, who never praised lightly, spoke of his delight at the young driver's performance so far in the Craftsman Truck Series. "I honestly hadn't expected that he would win two races this year," he said. "I hadn't expected that he would be able to win as early as he has. And it's been just a really pleasant surprise that he hasn't torn up more equipment—that he's been able to adapt to the racetracks. He's going to have a great future."

When they learned what he really meant by the future, some would wonder if Roush had gone soft. Few, if any, NASCAR racers had so quickly traveled the path he'd set out for Kurt Busch.

CHAPTER 2

BLACK SUNDAY

On the day that Dale Earnhardt died, the rookie Kurt Busch awoke refreshed. His girlfriend Melissa Schaper cooked him a breakfast of bacon and eggs, and then he dressed in shirt, jeans, and a comfortable pair of shoes he'd worn since high school. In five hours, he would compete in one of the world's most famous auto races.

It was a wonder he wasn't consumed with worry.

Busch had never driven in the Daytona 500, the opening race of the 2001 Winston Cup season. He barely had any experience in a Winston Cup car, the fastest of all stockcars. But speed by itself wasn't what might have unnerved Busch—it was the manner in which racecars circled Daytona International Speedway, a steeply banked track two-and-a-half miles long. Separated by inches, the cars traveled in packs three wide and ten or more deep—a parking lot at nearly 200 miles per hour. Daytona punished mistakes cruelly: Since its opening in 1959, more than two dozen racers had lost their lives there.

Rookie drivers rarely found friends among the veterans at Daytona—but Busch would find at least one sworn enemy. Last fall, driving in one of his seven novice Cup races, Busch had accidentally bumped Dale Earnhardt Jr., spinning him out and dashing his hopes for that day. Junior, a soft-spoken young man, forgave. Junior's father did not. Word was that Dale Earnhardt, nicknamed "The Intimidator" for his uniquely ruthless style of racing, intended to teach Busch a lesson—perhaps today.

Whatever happened, Busch knew, a nation would be watching. NASCAR had just signed a $2.8 billion television deal with Fox, NBC, and Turner Broadcasting to bring Winston Cup races into America's living rooms. Television executives had heavily promoted the race, and they anticipated a record audience.

Busch finished his breakfast and left his motor coach, parked alongside those of the other drivers in a fenced area of the track infield that was patrolled by guards. After a stop at the Ford Motor Company hospitality tent, where he addressed some of the people who provided him technical assistance, Busch entered the garage area, where racecars are serviced and tuned. He conferred with the crew of his No. 97 car, whose rear bumper carried a strip of yellow tape that NASCAR mandated to alert competitors to a driver's rookie status. Then he strolled out onto pit road, where crews refuel, change tires, and adjust suspensions during a race.

Busch confided that he was anxious, but not paralyzingly so. "This is something that we've built toward over the whole winter," he said. "I'm ready to go. It's time to start racing."

Busch's parents, Tom and Gaye, were worrying after him when he arrived at his hauler, an eighteen-wheel truck that transports racecars, equipment, and supplies, and which features a small kitchen and a lounge outfitted with computers and a television set. During their free time at the track, drivers often seek the air-conditioned privacy of their lounge.

"I'm ready to start my crying thing," said Gaye. "I hate this race. I don't care where he finishes, just bring him home."

Gaye greeted Kurt, the older of their two sons. Kurt's younger brother, Kyle, only fifteen, also raced, back home in Las Vegas.

"Ready?" said Gaye.

"Yeah," said Busch. "I relaxed for a while."

Said Gaye: "He always tells me: 'Calm down, Mom.'"

But Gaye couldn't settle her nerves before a race. She prayed for her son's safety, starting with the warm-up laps.

Busch hugged his father, and then hugged and kissed his mother, who by now was in tears. In a moment, the older Busches would leave to join the 200,000 or so others at Daytona International Speedway, a crowd almost double that for any Super Bowl. They would watch from the stands.

"I love you, Mom," said Busch. "Hang in there."

Jack Roush arrived at the garage shortly after the gates opened at 6 A.M. that Sunday, February 18. Dawn had yet to break.

Roush had felt anxious when he awoke. The Daytona 500 was by its nature an unpredictable race, one where even a great driver could finish last through no fault of his own. But fans expected wins and top-five finishes from Roush drivers. Roush fielded Ford cars and the manufacturer also had high expectations. So did Roush's sponsors, for whom a win would bring the kind of advertising no money could buy.

"It's an inconvenient and inappropriate time from the teams' point of view to have the biggest race of the year," said Roush. "We go into the first race of the year with the unknowns of the technical balance of the cars from a rules point of view—and then try to deliver back to our sponsors and to our manufacturer and to our fans a performance that is credible, something that would justify their investment and their support."

Roush this year also had another pressing concern. During the off-season, he had not attracted a sponsor for Kurt Busch's No. 97 car, which subsequently was painted white, not with some corporation's colors. A potential sponsor with deep pockets had traveled to Daytona to hear Roush and his people pitch the kid, and a good showing today would help in reaching a deal. A bad run might send this prospect to another owner. Fortune 500 companies never lacked choices in NASCAR racing.

But Roush had not flourished by surrendering to anxieties, and by the time he'd entered the garage area, he'd pushed financial concerns aside. He strode to Mark Martin's hauler, which he used as his trackside headquarters—and which featured a small machine shop, in which a row of carburetors awaited him this morning. Roush had built his empire on a genius for designing and building internal-combustion engines with unsurpassed power, fuel economy, and durability. Many of his innovations had made their way into production automobiles, but Roush was best known for his race engines, which he used in his own race-cars—and which he sold or leased to other NASCAR teams, as well as competitors in other auto racing leagues. What Roush didn't offer others was his personal carburetor tunings. Only his drivers got those.

Carburetor by carburetor, Roush went to work: first Martin's, then Jeff Burton's, then Matt Kenseth's. Squinting through a magnifying glass, he individually examined the eight spark plugs from each carburetor's engine, looking for the subtle differences in color and condition that provided insight into performance during the engine's last run. He consulted a mechanic's log, blew dust away, hammered this throttle plate and tightened that screw, changed the carburetor jets, cleaned and lubricated using two types of oil, held the carburetor to the light, reexamined each spark plug with his glass, and tinkered some more. Looking at his face, which showed engrossment and a glimmer of joy, you could almost see the ten-year-old boy from small-town Ohio, enchanted by an old lawnmower engine he hoped would power him faster than any bicycle could.

"And then there was one," said Roush, moving to Busch's carburetor.

Crew members had retrieved the carburetors to Roush's other

three cars, but after tuning Kurt Busch's, Roush decided to return it to the No. 97 car himself. Finding dirt on a part of the carburetor where no dirt should have been, Roush had concluded that the air-cleaner cover was improperly attached, and he wanted to ensure that it was positioned properly for the race. "Is that a big thing?" said Roush. "No. But this is a game of inches."

Racing also was a game where old-fashioned ingenuity had its place alongside wind tunnels and computers. Said Roush: "There's still an element of alchemy and blacksmithing and witchcraft in this." And not with racecar chassis and engines only. Drivers themselves sometimes seemed influenced by forces they did not entirely understand, much less control.

The sun was up now, and the garage area was becoming crowded with fans and corporate executives. Roush left Martin's hauler and started toward the bay that held Busch's car. He hadn't gotten far when a middle-aged man asked him to autograph his program. Roush signed it. A few steps later, and a woman asked if her companion could take a picture of her with Roush. Roush posed. A rookie like Kurt Busch could still move largely unnoticed through a race throng, but not the boss.

"Good luck, Jack," another fan said.

Roush thanked him and hurried on to the No. 97 car. Roush possessed a wicked humor and when the mood fit, he told entertaining stories—but he was all business today. He hoped this would be the year one of his drivers finally captured the Winston Cup.

It was approaching 9 A.M. when Roush account manager Becky Hanson, whose duties included public relations, knocked on the door to Jeff Burton's motor coach. Burton was about to take out the trash; back in the bedroom area of the coach, Kim, Burton's wife of nine years, tended to their five-year-old daughter and their baby son.

Burton and Hanson boarded a golf cart and headed off through the infield, a massive space that contained parking lots, the garage, a man-made lake (on which a boat racer had been killed in Daytona's early days), and several villages of motor homes and campsites. The speedway was coming alive. Spectators were filling the luxury boxes and grandstands, red meats cooked on barbecue pits, and many fans, including a pot-bellied man wearing a plastic penis on his nose, had resumed drinking after a long night of debauchery. Seventies southern rock music blasted from many stereos, and overhead a plane pulled a banner advertising a strip joint on the beach. A driver couldn't contemplate this spectacle moving at almost 200 miles per hour, but Burton did note that at the slower Watkins Glen International raceway, a road course in New York, women baring their breasts could be a significant, if not unpleasant, distraction.

Burton's golf cart left the infield, crossed the asphalt, and departed the speedway for the hospitality-tent city outside. Fans seeking autographs mobbed Burton at every turn, but eventually the cart made it to a big top decorated with red, white, and blue balloons. Cans of motor oil festooned with tinsel composed the centerpieces at the tables inside; sitting at them, the hundreds of employees and friends of CITGO Petroleum Corporation, Burton's primary sponsor, could behold one of Burton's red, white, and blue No. 99 racecars parked in front.

As Burton waited in the wings, the emcee recounted highlights of his record: fifteen career Cup wins (38th on the all-time list) and a third-place finish in the overall standings last season (a mere 29 points behind second-place Dale Earnhardt and 294 points behind the champion, Bobby Labonte). The emcee did not mention another impressive number: Burton's nearly $19 million in career Cup winnings. Nor did the emcee need to point out to this crowd, most of whom wore No. 99 caps and T-shirts, that many motorsports journalists and even some Las Vegas oddsmakers had picked Burton to win this year's Winston Cup.

Unlike Busch, Burton, thirty-three, had spent years on NASCAR's lesser circuits before reaching stockcar racing's highest level. Now he indeed seemed destined to bring Roush the one trophy he lacked. Blessed like all great drivers with the ability to concentrate for hours under conditions of intense motion, confinement, noise, and heat, he had achieved a rare union of man to machine—and a zenlike comfort in that treacherous place between catastrophe and control. Racetracks come in different lengths, shapes, and surfaces, and Burton knew precisely which cars from Roush's extensive inventory drove best on each—indeed, he'd helped design the cars. He knew, after driving just a few laps on any track, what subtle changes in suspension or tire pressure that his car of the day needed to deliver that extra tenth or two of a mile per hour it took to prevail. In the prime of his career, Burton had mastered existence at the edge.

Rousing music burst from a loudspeaker as Burton appeared on stage. The driver was animated when he took the microphone. "It's gonna be a great race," he said, in the silky tones of his native state. "It's gonna be really exciting to watch."

Burton outlined his admittedly simple strategy for the race—essentially, positioning himself to prevail in the usual mad dash at the end—and he professed satisfaction with the way his car had handled during the previous week's practices. In the question-and-answer session that followed, a fan asked Burton if he wanted to be leading the Daytona 500 halfway through. "I want to be leading at the end!" he replied, to great laughter.

Another fan asked Burton how many spotters he used.

"We only have one spotter," said Burton.

"With really good eyesight," said the fan.

"Well, we hope he has really good eyesight!" said Burton. "We haven't determined that yet!"

Burton worked a crowd masterfully—blending down-home humor with wit and insight. These talents would serve him well if someday he sought to achieve his grand ambition. Few people knew, but Burton wanted be a United States senator after his racing career ended.

"We're ready to kick off the 2001 season," the driver said. "We'll do our best to make you proud."

Leaving the CITGO breakfast, Burton traveled to a separate tent to address employees of Coca-Cola, an associate sponsor of his car. Returning on his golf cart to the speedway, where pre-race ceremonies would soon begin, Burton talked about safety, which was often on his mind. The way racecars tended to bunch up at Daytona spooked him.

"I'm sure there will be a big wreck today," Burton said. "I just hope we're not in it."

After Kurt Busch's parents left for the grandstands, the rookie driver changed into his race shoes and fire suit, which was white, like his car. Jack Roush had given Busch proprietorship of almost twenty of his hand-built vehicles for this season—more than his other drivers would use on the many speedways they all visited on the tour, for it was assumed that an aggressive young man required a surplus as he ascended the steep side of the learning curve. With the cars came a crew of mechanics—some seasoned in Cup racing, others new to the series, including crew chief Matt Chambers, who had been with Busch in the Craftsmen Truck Series.

It was noon, an hour before the Daytona 500 was to begin.

Chambers had assembled the crew for a final pre-race meeting, and the No. 97 hauler was jammed. The meeting had just started when Jack Roush stepped inside. Roush stood listening, at first.

"This is our first race together," said Chambers, "so everybody be smart. I always try to think of the worst-case scenario that could happen, so everybody do that and kind of be prepared for a flat tire, or if we run into somebody, or running out of gas, or needing to put water in it."

Chambers began to advise a team member on filling a radiator, no artless task during the frenzy of a pit stop, where a fraction of a second advantage can bring victory in a close race. Roush interrupted Chambers—with a discourse on water pressure, water temperature, and the necessity of keeping a clean grille, through which cooling air reaches the engine. Cooling weighed on Roush's mind: One of his cars had overheated during the final race of the 2000 season, so infuriating him that he had vaulted the pit wall to personally refill the radiator—an unusual, perhaps unprecedented, move for a millionaire car owner.

After telling the crew that he would monitor their radio during the race and would be available immediately should they need him, Roush addressed the relative importance of the Daytona 500 for Busch and his crew. With the addition this year of two races (one near Chicago, and one at Kansas City, Kansas), the Winston Cup season now consisted of thirty-six races that extended, with only three weekends off, from mid-February until the Sunday before Thanksgiving—the longest season of any major American sport. Under a system that awarded a driver a maximum of 185 points for a single race, the eventual champion would amass something on the order of 5,000 points—but he probably would win only four or five races, for the competition was intense at this level. A rookie would be lucky to win a single race, and it was unlikely to be the biggest one of all, the Daytona 500.

"If we get out of here in the top twenty," Jack Roush said, "we're good. If we get out of here in the top ten, we just won the World Series. This is the first race of a really long season—don't go out there and do yourself in on this one. Don't wreck yourself out. Don't get yourself nervous. Do what you can do and you'll be fine. Have a good day."

Then Roush left, to check on his other drivers.

It was Busch's turn to speak. He knew about the long season, which consumed not only most weekends, but also most weekdays, when cars are built, tested, tuned, and maintained—a schedule that would leave him and most of his crew precious few days off until almost Christmas. Morale was critical under these conditions, and so, before leaving the Roush home base near Charlotte, North Carolina, for Daytona, Busch had treated his crew and their girlfriends and wives to a Saturday night of beers and karaoke. He'd also bought everyone matching athletic shoes, to further the camaraderie.

"The only thing I got," Busch said, "is everybody's total focus for the whole 200 laps. We're going to be riding around for a while, hanging out on the outside lane, might go the inside lane to learn a little bit. But we're making friends. We're searching for a sponsor, so we need to run hard. Everybody do good pit stops every time, just on and off, just solid—nothing out of control. That's the way I'm going to be out there on the track: just solid."

"Good luck out there, guys," said Chambers. "Let's do it."

As his crew monkeyed at the last minute with his car, Dale Earnhardt sat in the shade alongside his motor coach, which was situated near Jeff Burton's.

A high school dropout from the old mill town of Kannapolis, North Carolina, Earnhardt, forty-nine, had parlayed rare driving skill into one of the most successful businesses in all of sports. With his winnings and income from endorsements, licenses, and the three Cup teams that he owned (though he himself drove for another owner, Richard Childress, his longtime friend), Earnhardt had amassed a fortune worth tens of millions of dollars. Only the likes of Michael Jordan and Tiger Woods had ever played in his league.

Feet up, an ultimately cool pose, Earnhardt was wearing his signature wraparound sunglasses and his customary smirk when a TV camera moved in. A Fox broadcaster asked him about the upcoming race.

"I think it's going to be some exciting racing," Earnhardt said. "Gonna see something you probably haven't never seen on Fox."

The TV interview over, Earnhardt departed his motor coach for pit road, where forty-three shiny new racecars awaited their drivers. Earnhardt walked holding the hand of his third wife and business partner, Teresa. Their only child together, twelve-year-old Taylor Nicole, walked on his other side, smiling.

Earnhardt passed Kurt Busch, who was waiting with Melissa at the back of the stage where the drivers were about to be introduced. When he was four or five years old and just starting to discover racing, Busch had rooted for Earnhardt. He'd hung posters of Earnhardt on his bedroom wall and fantasized about doing what Earnhardt did when he grew up.

"Good luck, Mr. Earnhardt," Busch said.

The Intimidator brushed past him without a word.

With other drivers, though, Earnhardt was more sociable. He embraced his son, Dale Jr., twenty-six, who was beginning his sophomore Cup season and running in only his second Daytona 500. He talked to Kyle Petty, son of Richard Petty, the most successful stockcar driver ever. Kyle had lost his nineteen-year-old son, Adam, the previous May when the teenager was practicing for a race at New Hampshire International Speedway. Unable to find the words that might console Kyle, Earnhardt had avoided him in the months following Adam's death, but today he comforted the still-grieving father with a hug.

An official introduced each of the forty-three drivers, the maximum allowed in any Cup race, and they walked to their vehicles. Earnhardt was starting next to Jeff Burton, and in the moments before they climbed into their cars, the two men and their wives chatted. For some time now, Burton had hungered to buy a yacht, on which he hoped periodically to escape the crush of racing stardom, which all but imprisoned him and his family during race weekends. On the brief vacations his schedule allowed, Burton had leased boats—but Kim, who managed the family finances, had resisted buying one. A boat owner himself, Earnhardt liked to tease her.

"Hey, when you gonna buy that boat?" Earnhardt said.

"Well, we don't make the kind of money you make, you know?" Kim joked.

Cordial though they were, Earnhardt and Burton had their professional differences. Nothing was more menacing, the saying went, than seeing Earnhardt's black No. 3 car in your rearview mirror in the closing laps of a race, for Earnhardt would do anything to win, including wreck an opponent. Burton, on the other hand, always drove clean. "I really don't want to spin somebody else out on the last lap to win a race," he said. "We didn't win the race if we did that—we knocked the guy out of the way. Anybody can knock somebody out of the way."

Except for once during Burton's rookie year, he and Earnhardt had never tangled on the track; Earnhardt respected Burton, who lacked only a title now to ensure an honored place in racing history. But off the track, the two men disagreed on safety, which had become a volatile issue following Adam Petty's death and the death two months later of Kenny Irwin. While they agreed that racing was inherently dangerous, Earnhardt believed that NASCAR had done about all it should to protect drivers' lives, short of reducing speeds to the point where fans wouldn't care to watch nor racers want to race. Burton, who counted a broken back among his racing injuries, believed that NASCAR and track owners could accomplish more without diminishing the appeal of their sport—and in the weeks following the deaths of Petty and Irwin, he had emerged as the most publicly outspoken of all Cup drivers on the issue of safety. Unlike drivers who toed the NASCAR line, Burton never held his tongue.

Earnhardt was no shrinking violet, either. He'd let it be known that he was irked by Burton's insistence that NASCAR slow its cars before the Cup tour returned to New Hampshire. "I've heard some drivers saying, 'We're going too fast at Charlotte, we're going too fast here,'" Earnhardt told a reporter. "Get the hell home—if you're not a racecar driver and not a racer, stay home. Don't come here and grumble about going too fast. Get out of the racecar if you've got feathers on your legs or butt. Put a kerosene-soaked rag around your ankles so the ants won't climb up there and eat your candy ass."

The made-for-TV band O-Town sang the National Anthem, four U.S. Air Force jets buzzed the crowd, and wives and girlfriends kissed drivers as they fidgeted in their cars. A minister recited the invocation and then grand marshal James P. Kelly, chairman and chief executive officer of United Parcel Service, which sponsored the No. 88 Ford Taurus of Dale Jarrett, the 1999 champion, spoke the words everyone had been waiting for: "Gentlemen, start your engines!"

"Let's kick ass for this championship," Earnhardt told his crew over his radio. "It's a new year and we know we can do it." Having won the Winston Cup championship seven times, Earnhardt was seeking a record eighth title.

The pace car led the field through the warmup laps and then the flagman waved the green flag. The cars powered up. Bunched together, they circled the speedway, a tidal wave of sound, motion, and gut-penetrating vibration. Only one accident marred the early going. A car driven by Jeff Purvis, a forty-one-year-old who'd never succeeded in Winston Cup racing, hit the wall, alone, bringing out a yellow caution flag, which slowed the race while a speedway crew cleared the debris from the pavement.

Busch had started 26th, in the middle of the field, but he moved methodically toward the front—to 18th by lap 26. Jeff Burton was tenth, and Roush's two other Cup drivers, Mark Martin and Matt Kenseth, were also running in the top twenty. Earnhardt had advanced to first. The acknowledged master of superspeedway racing, Earnhardt had won more races than anyone on this famed track—but only one Daytona 500, in 1998.

The race continued and other drivers took the lead. But Earnhardt never fell far back—and Busch continued to advance.

"You know who I got in front of me?" Busch radioed to his spotter, Bruce Hayes, on lap 62, shortly after drivers had made their first pit stops of the day.

It was Earnhardt.

"He's the heat, man," Hayes radioed back. "Stay with him. Nice and smooth. Use your head. Hang with him."

Hayes wanted Busch to take advantage of an aerodynamic phenomenon known as draft, in which one car following another at high speed is essentially sucked along by the one in front. He wanted Busch on Earnhardt's bumper, for he believed it was only a matter of time before Earnhardt regained the lead. "If he goes off the track for a hot dog," Hayes radioed, "you go get that hot dog with him."

Busch clung to Earnhardt's bumper. They were inches apart, with cars to either side—and more cars to the front and rear of those cars. If The Intimidator still bore a grudge for the rookie, he'd either forgotten or was biding his time.

Once again, the field shuffled. Martin found the lead, and Burton, who'd been running second, fell back to seventh.

Busch was fourth.

Two laps later, he was second.

"Hang on, just be patient," Hayes radioed. "There you go, nice and smooth. Just take your time."

Busch never did get the lead—but over the next eighty or so laps, he was rarely lower than tenth. This was an astonishing debut. From his customary perch atop Martin's pit cart, Roush was impressed, but hardly surprised.

Nor was he surprised with what happened two-thirds of the way through the race. Coming off Turn Four, Earnhardt snuck up on Busch's left—then banged him, metal-to-metal, door-to-door. Busch didn't spin out, but in case the rookie had missed the message, Earnhardt extended his middle finger as they headed into the front stretch, past the grandstands and the TV cameras.

Turn Four of the Daytona International Speedway is not for the faint-hearted: It is sharp and steeply banked, and drivers negotiating it are focused on steering hard left while preparing to accelerate into the straighter stretch just ahead. With less than a quarter of the race to go, Busch was coming off Turn Four when he decided to go high—go to the right of another car. Spotter Hayes had cleared him, but Busch did not see the nose of Joe Nemechek's car tickling his rear bumper. The cars kissed, but at extreme speed, a kiss invites trouble. Busch spun sideways across the infield grass. Miraculously, he kept his car from overturning and he was unhurt, but the accident broke a part of the undercarriage of his car.

Busch coasted back to pit road, but his car was unraceable. He sat silently in his cockpit as his crew pushed him back to the garage, where they frantically began repairs.

Minus the white car with the yellow bumper, the Daytona 500 resumed. Fewer than thirty laps remained now.

After nearly three hours of concentration so terrific that three-time champion Jeff Gordon later said his eyeballs hurt, the drivers were wearying. And yet, the race was entering its most crucial phase. The winner would receive $1.3 million from a purse of more than $11 million, one of the richest in all of auto racing, and his winning car would be enshrined at NASCAR's popular Daytona museum. From Florida, he would embark on a national media tour that would delight sponsors and please Bill France Jr., who cherished such grand promotional opportunities for the sport that had made him one of the 400 wealthiest people in the nation. For one week, at least, the winner of the Daytona 500 would hold first place in the Winston Cup standings.

And for a short while, he would experience the sensation of winning at speed—a sensation, found nowhere else, that was so pleasurable that Mark Martin declared he would walk one hundred miles barefoot through snow to achieve. "It feels like the best drug ever been made," Martin said. "Incredible. No words to describe it."

For anyone desiring all that, it was now or never.

The pack roared through the backstretch, a 3,000-foot straightaway on which drivers reached maximum speed.

Then it happened, the big wreck Jeff Burton had predicted. Robby Gordon, who'd finished the 2000 season in 43rd place, hit the car driven by Ward Burton, Jeff's older brother. It was as if a bomb had been detonated. Cars spun, smashed, and smoked. They spewed metal, oil, boiling water, and hot grease. Tony Stewart's car launched into the air, barrel-rolling and bouncing off the tops of two other cars before gravity pulled its mangled carcass back to earth. Nineteen cars wrecked, including both of the Burtons', Mark Martin's, Jeff Gordon's, Dale Jarrett's, and Bobby Labonte's. Incredibly, only Stewart required an ambulance.

"I know it was exciting to watch," Jeff Burton said later, "but exciting and dangerous are two different things."

The red flag flew and the race stopped for sixteen minutes while speedway workers carted off the rubble. The most damaged cars did not return when the race resumed. Others came back minus body panels, bumpers, and hoods; under NASCAR's points system, even a hobbled lap could be worth something. His car crippled, Jeff Burton made it back—but not Mark Martin, who was done for the day. Matt Kenseth now was the only Roush driver who had not been involved in an accident—but he'd lost precious laps to a broken shock absorber.

Busch's team, meanwhile, managed to repair his No. 97 car, and with fifteen laps left, Busch rejoined the field.

"Sorry about that, Bruce," he radioed his spotter regarding his accident. "I should have known better."

"It's just as much my fault as yours, pal," said Hayes, whose weekday job was lead fabricator—the man in charge of building the bodies for Busch's racecars. "We're one big team, man. We win together, we lose together."

Busch took his place at the end of the field, now thinned by about a third. At the front, an emotional finish was developing as the last lap neared. Dale Earnhardt was running third—behind Michael Waltrip and Dale Jr. Earnhardt owned his son's car—and also Waltrip's. As the pack thundered down the backstretch for the last time, several drivers maneuvered to get by Earnhardt, but he blocked all of them. Ordinarily, this was the point in a race when The Intimidator would do anything to win—but for the first time anyone could remember, he was letting others stay ahead: his son and Waltrip.

The pack was rounding Turn Four in the final seconds of the race when Sterling Marlin nipped Earnhardt. Earnhardt's black car spun, and Ken Schrader unavoidably hit it. Earnhardt crashed into the wall, then bounced back to the bottom of the bank, where it finally stopped.

Meanwhile, Waltrip had crossed the finish line, a whisker ahead of Junior, who placed second. Delirious with excitement, Waltrip headed to Victory Lane.

What a storybook ending! In 462 Winston Cup points races over sixteen years, Michael Waltrip had never finished first—had craved but never tasted the sensation that Mark Martin likened to a narcotic. For 462 races, an entire career, he had lived in the shadow of his brother Darrell, a three-time champion who had retired after the 2000 season and who was one of the broadcasters working the race for Fox TV. Overcome with emotion, Darrell had called the final laps of his brother's fairy-tale victory.

For the moment, Earnhardt was all but forgotten. Anyone paying attention assumed that, at worst, he had been knocked unconscious in the crash. Certainly, he'd be OK; like virtually every veteran Cup driver, Earnhardt had wrecked bad before and lived to race another day. In 1976, he flipped his car five times in a race in Atlanta—and walked away. In 1979, he broke both collarbones at Pocono Speedway—and missed just four races. In the 1997 Daytona 500, he hit the wall, flipped, went airborne, and was in an ambulance when he discovered his car was still drivable—so he returned to drive it, to a 31st-place finish.

Earnhardt wasn't also called Ironhead for nothing.

Nielsen ratings would show that the record audience that television executives had banked on had materialized: more than 30 million viewers in the United States alone. But a rookie who finished 41st of forty-three attracted scant media attention, and Kurt Busch returned to his hauler accompanied only by his girlfriend. He acted subdued, but not distraught.

"Good job, honey," Melissa said. "You proved yourself today."

"I just came up short," Busch said.

Busch had changed out of his fire suit when Jack Roush walked in. All around, this was far from the opening day he had desired: His best driver in the race, Burton, had finished 19th, followed by Kenseth at 21st and Martin at 33rd. Roush was disappointed, but not angry or defeated; four decades of racing had taught him many lessons, first among them racing's unending capacity for breaking hearts. And the year was still new.

"You could have won that race today," Roush said.

"Yes, I could have," said Busch.

"I want you to dwell on that."

Busch, who dreamed of being named Rookie of the Year, would.

Meanwhile, rescue workers had reached Earnhardt's car, where they found The Intimidator slumped over the wheel. When a paramedic raised his head, he stared into vacant eyes.

"We need 99 and the tool," another paramedic called on his radio. He wanted a doctor and the track's extrication crew.

The crew cut the roof off Earnhardt's car as the medical personnel attempted cardiopulmonary resuscitation, an unenviable task when it involves a large, helmeted man harnessed into a car without doors. Once the roof was off, Earnhardt was carried to an ambulance, which took him to nearby Halifax Medical Center.

Inside the speedway media center, brimming with journalists from around the world, the minutes ticked away. Those who had been in New Hampshire when Adam Petty and Kenny Irwin Jr. died began to get the same eerie feeling—and some remembered the scene at Daytona during the 500 race week back in 1994, when drivers Rodney Orr, a rookie, and Neil Bonnett, a future member of the Motorsports Hall of Fame, both died during prerace qualifying and practice runs. Bonnett, Earnhardt's best friend, was attempting a comeback after a wreck three years earlier that had injured his brain, rendering him temporarily unable to remember the names of his children or his hometown.

"Earnhardt's dead," some reporters began to whisper when more than an hour passed without word.

Eager for news, journalists found that NASCAR officials had closed the garage to outsiders early. But officials could do nothing about the fence. Peering through, reporters observed Dale Earnhardt Jr.'s crew clustering silently. A woman emerged from a NASCAR hauler in tears.

"I've never seen anything like it," remarked broadcaster Ned Jarrett, Dale Jarrett's father, and himself champion twice in the 1960s.

Back at the media center, a public relations specialist announced that Tony Stewart, who'd taken the worst beating in the nineteen-car wreck, had sustained only minor injuries. He'd be ready to race again the following weekend.

Someone asked about Earnhardt.

The specialist said she had no information.

At about 6:30 P.M., nearly two hours after Earnhardt crashed, the *USA Today* Web site reported that he was dead. Almost immediately, other sites began to report the same news.

Only then did NASCAR president Mike Helton walk into the media center with emergency physician Steve Bohannon. The two men took the podium.

"We've lost Dale Earnhardt," said Helton, his voice choking.

The opening race had barely ended, but already the 2001 Winston Cup season was one of the most extraordinary in the history of automobile racing.

CHAPTER 3
GAMBLING

Dale Earnhardt's death had yet to be announced when Jeff and Kim Burton left Daytona International Speedway the evening of February 18. They were crossing the track when a flatbed tow truck carrying Earnhardt's wasted vehicle passed by. A tarpaulin covered the car.

Jeff and Kim exchanged looks. Kim was ashen.

"Don't assume that means the worst," Jeff told his wife. Like most, he still believed that Earnhardt had only been injured—that the NASCAR story of the week would be The Intimidator rising heroically from his hospital bed to drive in the following week's race, the Dura-Lube 400, at Rockingham, North Carolina.

Burton kept that belief as he flew home to Charlotte. But when his jet landed, he noticed an official from the nearby Lowe's Motor Speedway in the airport lobby; one glance at the official's face, and Burton knew that Earnhardt was dead. He felt as if he'd been punched. Earnhardt wasn't just another racer—he was American auto racing's biggest star, one of the keys in NASCAR's transformation from a redneck diversion to a national sensation.

"A person of that stature you just don't think is going to be killed," Burton said. "It's a mental game that I think racecar drivers play with themselves. When a young guy gets killed, it's 'Well, he wasn't strong,' 'He didn't know enough about this,' and 'I wouldn't have done that.' When it happens to him it's like, holy shit. Now it hits home."

Like his fellow drivers, Burton remained in a degree of shock during the week between Daytona and Rockingham—the week Earnhardt was buried. Bill France Jr. could have canceled the Dura-Lube 400, of course, but he decided not to: He and Earnhardt had been good friends, sharing a love not only of racing but of saltwater fishing in the Bahamas, and he believed that Earnhardt would have wanted the race to proceed. "He'd have been the first one to say that you've got to go ahead with things," France would later say. "No question in my mind about that. Life has to go on." Officials conducted a tribute to The Intimidator before the start of the race, drivers and crews wore Earnhardt hats, and fans held No. 3 flags and raised three fingers. Spectators and another huge national television audience experienced a moment of horror on the first lap when Dale Jr., traveling at some 150 miles per hour, slammed head-on into the wall. It seemed a virtual replay of his father's deadly accident—until Junior, disoriented but not seriously injured, crawled out of his car.

Steve Park, one of Earnhardt's three drivers, won at Rockingham, providing an emotional ending to the first race of the post-Earnhardt era. But Roush's drivers disappointed their fans: Mark Martin finished 20th, Matt Kenseth 28th, and Kurt Busch 36th, after brushing the wall. "Another rookie day," Busch said.

Jeff Burton could offer no such explanation for his even worse performance. He never wrecked alone anymore—but on lap 121, untouched by anyone, he fishtailed and hit the wall going into Turn One. Losing track position to repairs, he rode out the remainder of the Dura-Lube 400 in unfamiliar territory, the end of the pack. Burton finished the race in 37th.

This was the driver picked to be the 2001 Winston Cup champion. Two races into the season, he stood 33rd in the points.

Burton blamed himself for the wreck—not his car, nor track conditions, nor someone on his crew, as another driver might have. But he could not explain exactly what had happened in that fraction of a second when he slipped from control. He suspected that his relative unfamiliarity with a new type of tire NASCAR had introduced this year might have contributed to his wrecking. Daytona still cast a shadow, as well.

"Earnhardt got killed, and I spent a hard week on that," Burton said as he sat in his hauler on Saturday, March 3, the day before the season's third race, the UAW-Daimler Chrysler 400, at Las Vegas Motor Speedway. "It was a real hard week to get focused: to step in and get your head in the game. And I'm always taking pride in being able to do that—anything that was going on in my life, put it behind me when I get to the racetrack. And I don't think I did that last week. I'm not saying that's why we got in the wreck, but I wasn't as effective as I needed to be."

Burton had arrived in Las Vegas yearning for a finish that would soften the memory of his first two races in 2001. "Our year is not over based on Rockingham and Daytona," he said. Yet confidence hardly overwhelmed him that first weekend of March. He had in his head the image of Earnhardt's tarp-draped car; he worried, knowing fate can turn unkind. "I don't like where we are and I'm nervous about going even further," Burton said. "It puts more pressure on us. Every race you have a bad race means you have to have a great one. You never make a bad race up."

Still, if any track was destined to provide a fresh start—for all of the Roush drivers—surely it was Las Vegas. In the three Winston Cup meets that had been run at the track since it opened, Burton had finished second in one race and he had won the other two, in 1999 and 2000. Martin had won the inaugural race, in 1998, and Kenseth had placed 17th in his first and only Cup appearance at Las Vegas, in 2000, his rookie year. The Roush drivers seemed to have divined the secrets of the gently banked, 1.5-mile oval, which sits across a desert road from Nellis Air Force Base, home of the Thunderbirds, the Air Force's aerial demonstration team. And Las Vegas was also Kurt Busch's hometown.

Kurt Busch was the first child of a couple from suburban Chicago who had dated in high school and married soon thereafter. Gaye took a job as a secretary, Tom as an automobile mechanic. In his spare time, Tom built and restored hot rods, custom cars that are displayed but not raced. His only direct exposure to competition had been when his father, a partner in a Ford dealership, had brought him to races at the Milwaukee State Fairgrounds—and once to Daytona International Speedway, in 1959, when Tom was a young boy, for the inaugural Daytona 500.

Weary of Illinois winters and a climate disrespectful of lovingly tended cars, the Busches moved to Las Vegas in 1977, when they were in their twenties. An acquaintance at the dealership where Tom found work sought his help in preparing a 1968 Mercury Cougar for small-time stockcar racing. Tom did not expect to drive it—but when the friend asked if he would, Tom figured: Why not? He ran his first race at a quarter-mile track in Las Vegas in 1978, the year Kurt was born—and he won. Tom had experienced the glory of speed, and he liked its taste.

In the ensuing years, Tom enjoyed success driving cars he'd modified or built with parts from junkyards, dealers, friends, or whoever offered the best deal. He raced for love, not money. In some events, first place earned just twenty-five dollars and a line of agate type in the local paper. Even with Gaye's income from her job in data processing, Tom, a traveling tools salesman now, could afford only the occasional race outside of Nevada. But he won state championships and a measure of Las Vegas renown.

Meanwhile, a growing boy became enchanted.

"I want to race with Dad," Kurt started saying before he was in first grade. He wanted to work on cars—and Tom let him, there in the Busch family garage, where he'd installed a TV so he could watch Winston Cup races on the weekends. When Kurt was six, Tom bought him a used Herbie Love Bug go-cart with a Briggs & Stratton engine, more commonly used to power lawnmowers. Tom considered Kurt too young to compete, but he encouraged him to drive a course they laid out with plastic buckets on the cul-de-sac where they lived. As his father timed him with a stopwatch, Kurt demonstrated fearlessness and precision. Uncommon instinct seemed to guide him—and speed thrilled him.

The year he turned sixteen, Kurt became eligible to compete in a class of racing called Dwarf Cars. Tom himself was racing Dwarfs, which are powered by motorcycle engines and weigh half a ton, less than a third the weight of a Winston Cup car. A racer with deep pockets could spend $25,000 or more on a Dwarf, but a data processor and a peddler of tools didn't have the means, so Tom and Kurt built Kurt's car for $6,400—a strain on the family budget, but a bargain nonetheless. Kurt's first race was on a dirt track. Video camera rolling, Gaye cried as her older son debuted. Kurt started dead last—and finished fifth, behind the winner, Tom. The son's first victory came a few weeks later, on his initial race on asphalt, which is faster than dirt. Tom placed second, but was happy to be beat. It was too late for him to have a professional racing career, but his firstborn had his whole life ahead of him.

Kurt realized his early promise, proving the master of every increasingly competitive class of car that he raced: Nevada Dwarf Car Rookie of the Year in 1994, Nevada Dwarf champion in 1995, Rookie of the Year in 1996 in another league, Legends. After running a limited slate in NASCAR's regional Southwest Tour Series in 1997, Kurt was named top Southwest rookie in 1998. Cars in that division are nearly as large as Winston Cup cars, and the series brought Busch to tracks in Colorado, Arizona, and California.

An honors student who excelled in science and math in high school, Busch attended the University of Arizona for a year, pursuing an interest in pharmacology. He raced on weekends, but weekends failed to satisfy his passion, so he quit college. Racing becomes increasingly expensive the further one advances, and with the Busch family budget still tight and sponsorships for newcomers tenuous, Busch took employment with the Las Vegas Valley Water District fixing broken water mains. He hoped to eventually compete in Winston West, the next step up in NASCAR's regional system; success there might launch him into the national Craftsman Truck Series.

One day in the summer of 1999, an official on the Southwest Tour asked Busch for his résumé. The official didn't say why he wanted it, and Busch didn't ask; he handed over a two-page document that summarized his racing experience but did not mention the fact that he was only twenty. He'd more or less forgotten the encounter when, a month later, at about the time he turned twenty-one, a rumor surfaced that Roush Racing was seeking a driver. Busch assumed that Roush was planning to start a Winston West team.

In truth, Roush wanted a new Craftsman Truck driver—someone to race alongside his last great discovery, Greg Biffle, the Truck Series' Rookie of the Year in 1998. Roush had instructed his people to comb the dirt tracks and the short tracks, the speedways and the fairgrounds, the great racing states and the racing backwaters, for candidates—but anyone could apply to a Gong Show, and hundreds did, some legitimate prospects, others not.

"I currently work for a large paper mill where I drive forklifts," wrote one man. "As funny as this may seem, this is where my real qualification comes in. I drive these forklifts on wet and very slick surfaces, which require that special touch of feathering that throttle. I feel even though this being much smaller than a truck, that this skill would help me tremendously." The allure of speed was certainly wide-reaching.

The forklifter received no invitation to audition—but Kurt Busch did, and he joined three other racers who were summoned in early October. Busch had never set foot in a Craftsman Truck, nor had he visited the speedway in Toledo, Ohio, near the Michigan headquarters of the Roush Truck teams, where the first of two test drives was staged. Busch did not find comfort in his turn behind the wheel, although he did keep pace with his competitors.

I need another chance, Busch thought as he left Toledo. *But I don't have a shot.*

The people who were conducting the audition agreed with Busch's gloomy assessment—all but two. Matt Chambers, crew chief for the driver that the Gong Show winner would replace, favored Busch; he'd seen him in an actual race and had recommended him, before the Gong Show, to Rich Reichenbach, the manager of Roush Racing's Truck fabrication shop and a spotter on race weekends. "You're kidding me," Reichenbach had said. "He looks about fifteen." But Busch's performance in Toledo impressed Reichenbach as well, and he believed the young driver deserved another chance.

Busch did not make the list of four candidates invited for the final test, to be held in Phoenix at the end of the month, but when someone canceled, Reichenbach and Chambers successfully argued to include him. Busch had just claimed the 1999 Southwest Series championship.

Busch tore up the track in Phoenix, his slowest lap two-tenths of a second faster than any of his competitors' best—an extraordinary difference in a game of inches, especially when all the racers drove the same vehicle. Busch returned to Las Vegas confident that Roush would hire him.

In fact, Reichenbach had already made that recommendation. "He's got it," Reichenbach told Jack Roush. "He will show the world."

But three weeks passed, and Busch heard nothing.

One morning just before Thanksgiving, the phone rang. Gaye Busch answered, and the caller introduced himself as Geoff Smith, president of Roush Racing, the man who negotiated the contracts after Jack Roush had blessed a driver. Kurt was sleeping—he'd just come off the graveyard shift.

"How would you like to move to Michigan?" Smith said when Kurt got on the line.

"I don't think I'd have any trouble," said Busch.

Busch soon signed with Roush Racing, but he did not quit the Water Authority; he requested, and received, a year's leave of absence. "Just in case," he told his boss, who'd watched his racing career develop. "You know how this business is."

Busch traveled an uneven path after his stunning Craftsman Truck Series debut in the Daytona 250 in February 2000. Over the next ten races, he finished second twice—and also 13th, 21st, and 23rd.

Then came the catastrophic race of June 17 at Kentucky Speedway.

By now, frustration ate at the young man. He'd won consistently at every level of competition before—but here he was at almost the midpoint of the Truck season, winless. His teammate Greg Biffle, meanwhile, had recorded two wins and seven top-five finishes, and was well on his way to the series title—in just his third year of driving in the Truck Series.

This is my weekend, Busch thought. *I'm going to win.*

But then he broke a motor, as racers also called their engines, and missed qualifying, which consigned him to starting last.

He still intended to win, and twenty-three laps into the race, he'd advanced to third—not with masterful racing, but by knocking hard on the edge. Busch was driving so aggressively that once he slid sideways, a misstep that required consummate skill—and luck—to keep from wrecking.

Returning from a pit stop in ninth place, Busch saw that Biffle had the lead. *He's going to win another one!* Busch thought. *This is my race!*

Busch charged—and, rounding a turn at some 180 miles per hour, he fishtailed. He tried to steer through it, but his front tires dug in, sending him spinning toward the wall.

Busch's body tensed, and motion seemed to slow. The impact with the concrete wall destroyed his racecar, but Busch did not hear a sound.

"It was like in the movies," he said, "when they have a scene and they take the sound and everything out, and they have the actor—whether it be floating through the air and about ready to get crunched by another automobile, or an accident happening, with fire and flames and everything—when they just shut off all the music in a movie."

Busch felt nothing. "No pain, no sound, I'm watching everything." "I didn't know where my hands were. I didn't know where my feet were, or my body was. I didn't feel my knee hit the steering column. You're just in God's will, so to speak."

Mangled, the racecar finally stopped. Flames engulfed it.

Modern racecars are equipped with fuel cells that are designed to survive crashes intact. The technology was developed during an earlier era of stockcar racing, when many drivers (the regrettably nicknamed Fireball Roberts, a former baseball pitcher, among them) met fiery deaths when their gas tanks exploded. But like Geoffrey Bodine at the Daytona 250, Busch wrecked so violently that his fuel cell ruptured. In an environment of red-hot metal and exhaust, gasoline goes up fast.

"I looked to my left, I looked to my right, I guess I'm OK. It felt like an hour went by unbuckling the belt, taking the steering wheel off. I'm not in a rush at all, I'm just doing the motions and I climb out of the truck. Now this is all in slow-mo, me getting out of the truck—but I watch the video and I am violent, throwing everything around, trying to get out."

Somehow, Busch's only injury was a bruised knee. But he was

badly dazed, and during an interview after the crash, he babbled.

"My brain just got scrambled," he said. "I said some words that didn't even match what the interviewer was asking me. I looked like a complete asshole, an idiot. Terrible."

Rather than discourage Busch, the fiery wreck reminded him of the need for patience. Speed had an unshakable grip on the young man.

Busch watched Biffle go on to win the Kentucky race, and when he got back to Michigan, he gathered his team for a series of meetings. Busch had never experienced such a low in his short racing career, but a new attitude emerged from the self-analysis. He vowed: *I'm just going to do my best and not worry about anyone else. I'm going to think everything through before I do it and I'm going to be pleased with any result that I get because I know I'm giving 100 percent. And I'm going to work and work and work until I win race*s.

Busch couldn't have known it at the time, but Jack Roush was increasingly impressed with his newest driver during that first part of the 2000 Truck season. Roush valued Busch's quiet confidence, the respect he paid elders, the gratitude he showed his parents for their sacrifices, the fact that in his press kit he had listed "My Dad, Tom," as his Favorite Person in History. "He's a sweet nice kid," said Roush. "You'd like to adopt him, you know. If you could pick him to be in your family or be one of your heirs that would certainly be less painful than raising your own!" Roush's own son and two daughters, all grown now, had not pursued racing.

But character did not move a man faster than his competitors: uncommon talent and dedication did, and here, too, Roush considered Busch a rare find. The kid had never visited most of the speedways on the Truck circuit, never mind raced them—nor had he ever raced against most of his competitors, some of whom were veterans not only of Truck racing but Winston Cup as well. Mindful of his deficiencies, Busch arrived early at each new track in order to become acquainted with it undisturbed. He walked the entire length, examining the composition of the paving, the angle of the banking, the sharpness of the turns, the grooves left by the racecars, the play of sunlight—which, as a race wore on, changed the track temperature, affecting the grip of the tires and necessitating changes in air pressures and suspension. Away from the track, Busch watched videos, replayed races in his mind, sought the advice of his mentor and his crew chief, and pondered. Like Roush, he forgot nothing.

And that was another quality that impressed the boss. Roush tolerated rookie mistakes; they were an essential part of learning—but he loathed seeing the same mistake twice. Busch never repeated a mistake. He'd crashed at Kentucky, but Roush was certain he wouldn't again, not for the same reason.

Busch followed his Kentucky wreck with a second-place finish in the next race, at Watkins Glen on June 24. The following Wednesday, just days before his first Truck win, in the Sears Diehard 200 in Milwaukee, Roush pulled Busch aside.

"What do you think about driving in Winston Cup?" Roush said.

"Jack," said Busch, "if you're ready, I am."

Fixing broken water mains had brought Busch no headlines, but his hometown anointed him a celebrity when he returned as a Winston Cup driver for the 2001 UAW-Daimler Chrysler 400.

TV and print journalists clamored for him, his parents, and his brother, Kyle—too young to drive legally on the street, but already a formidable racer on the same local tracks Kurt had raced. In their accounts, reporters cast Kurt's ascension to stock-car racing's highest level as a Cinderella story. It was a beguiling way to recount events since July 2000. Busch won the race at Milwaukee, then the thatlook.com 200 at New Hampshire—and then, over the Truck season's remaining nine contests, he won twice more. He also finished second once, and third twice—and he seemed to master qualifying, earning the first starting position, or pole, three times in the season's last four races. Busch ended

2000 in second place in the point standings, behind champion Biffle, and was named the Truck Series' Rookie of the Year.

In a half-kidding way, some sports writers had questioned Roush's state of mind when his plans for Busch had leaked out. Now, in Las Vegas, some were picking Busch for the 2001 Winston Cup Rookie of the Year. Busch himself could hardly believe it. "It's like I'm supposed to be watching a Winston Cup race, not racing in it," he said as he walked to his racecar to drive his qualifying laps for the UAW-Daimler Chrysler 400.

When Teresa Earnhardt reached Las Vegas International Speedway the morning of the race, she found reminders of her late husband virtually everywhere. No. 3 flags flew over infield campsites, and it was impossible to miss the 62-by-83-foot numeral 3 that workers had created from pansies and petunias at one end of the track; according to speedway officials, 33,333 flowers comprised the memorial, which was framed by a sign proclaiming IN MEMORY OF A CHAMPION. If Mrs. Earnhardt had read any of the local papers, she would have found photos and stories galore.

Las Vegas was hardly alone. From the moment Earnhardt's death was first reported, America mourned his passing with an emotional outpouring reminiscent of that accompanying Elvis Presley. Grieving fans remembered Earnhardt with poems, wreaths, candlelight vigils, teary calls to radio talk shows, Internet tributes, and a 353-foot-long "3" that a Florida man tilled into a field for passing pilots to see. As with Elvis, the impact of Earnhardt's death rippled beyond loyal followers. People who before February 18 could not have named a NASCAR driver now earnestly discussed pit-stop strategy, and editors who would have been hard-pressed to distinguish a spring from a shock absorber proclaimed Earnhardt a national treasure. *The New York Times* ran two front-page stories on Earnhardt's death, and *Time* magazine put him on its cover with the headline "Death in the Fast Lane." Predictably, many columnists and broadcasters glorified the stock-car racing icon. Mostly lost was The Intimidator's on-track personality: The fact that he would send a competitor into the wall, endangering life and limb, if that's what it took to win.

But Teresa Earnhardt hadn't crossed the continent to memorialize Dale, nor did she desire publicity for herself. Instead, she had left North Carolina to build support in her fight against a newspaper that sought autopsy photos of her late husband.

The paper was *The Orlando Sentinel,* which circulates in Daytona Beach, home not only to the speedway but also to NASCAR's headquarters. *Sentinel* writers had covered motorsports for more than half a century, and their interest in accidents predated Earnhardt's fatal crash. Concerned by the deaths of Adam Petty and Kenny Irwin Jr. the previous summer, the paper had begun an investigation of driver safety. Published the week before Earnhardt died, the paper's three-part series concluded that NASCAR and the racing industry in general had failed to adequately protect its drivers by not taking such measures as mandating the HANS (head and neck support) device, designed to restrain the violent whipping action of the head during severe crashes. "Adam Petty should be alive today," the paper declared. "So should Kenny Irwin."

Earnhardt's death, so strikingly similar to those of Petty and Irwin, prompted *The Sentinel* to open another investigation. Not trusting NASCAR, which had been less than forthcoming during the earlier probe, the paper intended to hire an independent expert to review the medical records, including a review of photographs of Earnhardt's dissected body.

Reporters jammed the Las Vegas Speedway's media center as Teresa and her stepson Dale Jr. took the podium.

"I am here to tell you that the trauma we have suffered has only grown since that tragic day two weeks ago," Mrs. Earnhardt read from a statement. "In fact, I have not even had time to caringly unpack Dale's suitcases from Daytona, let alone have time to grieve for him. The main reason is we have been caught up in an unexpected whirlwind as a result of efforts to gain access to the autopsy photographs of Dale."

Mrs. Earnhardt noted that a Florida court had issued a preliminary order keeping *The Sentinel* from the photos—but the court had ordered mediation to resolve the widow's dispute with the newspaper. Mediation might result in the photos' release, and now Mrs. Earnhardt wanted the Florida legislature to act, by passing a law banning release of any such photos, except under a handful of instances requiring a judge's permission. The proposed law would make unauthorized release a felony punishable by a $5,000 fine and up to five years in prison. "Even people in the public eye have a right to privacy," Mrs. Earnhardt said. "The right is more important than the desire to exploit a tragic situation—especially when no public good is being served. There is nothing to be gained by the release of these images from Dale's autopsy."

Mrs. Earnhardt urged fans to contact Florida legislators and the state's governor, Jeb Bush, whose brother, the president, had telephoned his condolences to Teresa and her young daughter the night Dale died.

"Finally," Mrs. Earnhardt said, "we encourage you to let *The Orlando Sentinel* know how you feel about this unfortunate situation."

What Teresa neglected to mention was that *The Sentinel* did not intend to publish the photos; the paper wanted its outside expert to view them in order to draw his own conclusions about the cause of Earnhardt's death, nothing more. "We are NOT going to publish the autopsy photos," wrote the paper's editor, Timothy A. Franklin, in a letter published the day Mrs. Earnhardt faced the TV cameras in Las Vegas. "We are NOT going to copy the photos."

The point was lost on Earnhardt's fans. Dale's widow had barely finished speaking when the first of more than 10,000 e-mails began to arrive at *The Sentinel*.

*

As his drivers and crews completed their final preparations for the Las Vegas race, Jack Roush expressed optimism regarding the outcome. He considered Kurt Busch's performances at Daytona and Rockingham valuable lessons that would serve the rookie well when he visited those tracks later in the season, and he discounted his three other Cup drivers' poor finishes the last two weekends.

"It's not even a bump in the road," said Roush. "If we were breaking our engines, if we were having trouble with our setups and we weren't able to keep from wearing our tires out—if we had horrible fuel economy—those would be things that I would really feel bad about. But we're racing just fine. This business ebbs and flows and it's just fine."

But Las Vegas didn't turn out just fine for Roush.

Though Kurt Busch finished 11th, the best run of his young Cup career, and Mark Martin wound up 6th, Matt Kenseth placed 17th, no better than his previous race there—and Jeff Burton came in 39th, ahead of just four other drivers, all of whom had crashed out of the race or blown an engine. Two former champions dominated Las Vegas: Jeff Gordon, the winner, and Dale Jarrett, who placed second.

Burton's day puzzled everyone, no one more than the driver himself.

For the second week in a row, he spun out—by himself. He was on lap 2 when he lost control of his car and smashed into the wall, badly damaging his rear quarter panel, bumper, and frame. Repairs took more than seventy-five laps, and when Burton returned to the race, he bore little resemblance to the driver who'd won more Cup races than anyone at Las Vegas. Heading home, he had dropped to 36th in the point standings. At 33rd, rookie Busch was better.

"I don't know what happened," Burton told reporters. "The car was in the middle of the corner, and it just started coming around. I have no idea what happened because I was even off the gas."

Twice in a row now, Burton had lost his edge.

Earnhardt fans rejoiced the next weekend at the season's fourth race, the Cracker Barrel 500, at Atlanta Motor Speedway. In only his third Winston Cup race, Kevin Harvick, the twenty-five-year-old driver chosen to succeed Earnhardt on the circuit, won by six one-thousandths of a second—roughly a foot—over Jeff Gordon. Harvick had inherited Earnhardt's superior personnel and vehicles, although a white color scheme and a new number, 29, had replaced the black No. 3. "I kept praying for Dale to help us out," said Richard Childress, who owned Earnhardt's cars, now Harvick's, during the victory celebration. "I know he's somewhere, I can see him with that mustache of his just breaking into a big grin."

Originally planning to race the year at the Busch Grand National level, Harvick was now Kurt Busch's chief rival in the contest for Winston Cup Rookie of the Year. With his victory, Harvick pulled ahead of Busch, but Busch nonetheless found reason to be pleased in Atlanta. Although NASCAR officials forced him to start last for missing mandatory drivers' introductions (he had misread his schedule), he finished tenth. "I had hoped for a top-ten finish at Las Vegas last weekend, but we'll take it today," Busch told reporters. "This team has really come together."

The other Roush teams had not.

After starting fourth, Mark Martin lost his engine and finished 41st. Matt Kenseth's engine also blew, his car caught fire, and he finished 37th. And Jeff Burton finished 30th, after having been penalized for an improper pit stop and hobbled by the partial failure of his engine. He now held 38th in the standings, an almost unbelievable 336 points behind leader Jeff Gordon.

Burton and Martin were not the only top drivers who seemed to have fallen under a curse. The defending Winston Cup champion, Bobby Labonte, stood 26th in points, and Ward Burton,

Jeff's brother, ranked 21st after having placed 10th in 2000. The new season's top ten included such unlikely contenders as Daytona winner Michael Waltrip, who'd finished the 2000 season in 41st place, and Bill Elliott, who hadn't won a race in almost a decade.

Only half in jest, given the tragedy of Daytona, some writers sought explanations to the 2001 season in the supernatural.

"Every weekend, I look forward to the Winston Cup race with the level of anticipation one might have towards finding a brand-new *Twilight Zone* episode," wrote a columnist for *The Sporting News*. "To start, there's the Roush team. I expect that one might find Freddie Krueger lurking in the shadows during a visit to the house that Jack built."

But Roush's misfortunes did not elicit good-natured barbs from all. Like others who live under the media eye, Roush played favorites with the press—agreeably availing himself to reporters he liked, shunning and sometimes ridiculing those he didn't. Whether favoring or disdaining, Roush always spoke with a candor that often gave his public relations staff fits. For those outside his good graces, here, finally, was an opportunity for payback.

"Those teams have grown accustomed to blowing raspberries at the rest of the suckers who continue to show up on Sundays," a reporter for the *CNN/Sports Illustrated* Web site wrote after Atlanta. "Jack Roush? The man has finished second or third in owners' points in three of the last five years. So gilded is the name that it was widely believed that Kurt Busch, a 22-year-old kid whom you last saw delivering your Sunday paper, was an automatic contender for the Rookie of the Year award."

If racing indeed involved an element of alchemy, the implication was that Roush had lost his sorcerer's touch.

CHAPTER 4

THE DEEP END OF THE POOL

Jeff Burton returned from Atlanta with his family on his jet, then drove to their home on the shore of Lake Norman, the exclusive community north of Charlotte where bankers, doctors, lawyers, and many of NASCAR's drivers lived.

On the flight, Burton had sensed his wife's puzzlement. *What's going on?* Kim's eyes seemed to say.

Now, at home, Kim told Burton to spend some time in the downstairs den, where he displayed his many trophies. "You haven't forgotten how to drive," she said. "You'll figure it out."

Midnight approached, but Burton couldn't unwind; a cable channel was airing twenty-four hours of *Andy Griffith* reruns, and he watched, alone, as Kim and the children slept. Dawn neared, the reruns rolled on, and Burton fretted.

Next week, he would race at Darlington, South Carolina, on a track so perilous that it was known as The Lady in Black. Burton had enjoyed extraordinary success at Darlington—two wins, three seconds, never worse than fifth over the previous eight races, a record that had prompted some competitors to call it The Jeff Burton Track—but Las Vegas had proved the folly of using the past to predict the future. Burton worried that he might not even run the race, the Carolina Dodge Dealers 400.

The reason was NASCAR's rules of entry, which guarantee the first thirty-six spots in a Cup race to the thirty-six fastest drivers in pre-race qualifying. The last seven places are filled with so-called provisionals—in essence, a way for good drivers to make the race despite an off day in qualifying. Burton had long had the insurance of provisionals, which were awarded according to a convoluted system based on owners' standings. But at 38th in the young season, Burton had precious few provisional points; drivers with more who qualified poorly could bump him home to Charlotte, a humiliating development that would damage his team's morale.

And Burton had his own pride to consider: He treasured the respect of his peers, but the season so far had jeopardized it. "My team and I have put a precedent out there," Burton said. "We've said we're a top five team—we're going to win races, we're going to be a pain in everybody's butt competitive-wise. It's difficult for me to walk in the garage."

Finally drained, Burton briefly slept.

The next morning, a Monday, he visited the No. 6 and No. 99 shop, Mark Martin's and his, where the mood was somber as Roush's people endeavored to determine how three of the finest motors in the world could have failed on the same day. Later in the day, Burton visited a boat dealer. Since he was a little boy, boats had fascinated him. One of his favorite childhood pastimes had been thumbing through the advertisements in the back of boating magazines, fantasizing about the yachts for sale—and now, as an adult, he spent some of his spare time designing yacht interiors with the drafting tools he kept in his den. He even looked ahead to the days when his children were grown and he would feel free to circle the world alone in a sailboat.

"I don't want to sound like a brat," Burton said, "but it's been a lifetime dream of mine to have a yacht and to be able to take my family, my parents, my brothers, my wife's family, and spend time with them. I thought I had myself able to do that—and now I'm realizing that I don't. Sometimes it takes a swift kick in the ass to make you realize that you're not in that position. And the last four races have been a swift kick in my ass."

Expecting a great start to the 2001 season, Burton had finally been negotiating the purchase of a yacht. Kim had relented.

But now, Burton told the dealer, the purchase was off.

Burton grew up the youngest of three brothers in South Boston, Virginia, a small town in tobacco country near the North Carolina border—the kind of place where everyone knew just about everyone and no one locked the doors at night. His father, John Burton, owned a successful construction firm; his mother, Meredith, assumed a leadership role in civic causes and the local United Methodist Church, and was known for her quiet acts of kindness to elderly shut-ins and others in need. Fellow citizens recognized the Burtons as pillars of their community. Few knew that their marriage was doomed.

Jeff was a fair-skinned, slight boy with an impish humor and an evident intelligence—just not of the bookish sort. He despised high school, although he would manage to graduate despite scorning homework and regularly skipping classes to mess around with his friends. "Because my father was successful in business," he said, "all of us Burton boys had a stigma—you know, we were the rich kids in town. I think my teachers probably looked at me as I was lazy, I was rich, that kind of thing."

The oldest Burton boy, Ward, was almost six years Jeff's senior, too old to be a childhood buddy. But Jeff was only two and a half years younger than the middle son, Brian, and they were as close as best friends, and would remain so into their adult years. "Everyone wanted to be Brian Burton," said Jeff. "He was a good athlete, he was a real nice person, he dated the homecoming queen, he had the best parties. He had a red Trans Am with a Hurst shifter in it—so he was cool 'cause of that, too. He just had it all going on. And he took me with him everywhere."

Jeff was riding with Brian in downtown South Boston one summer day when they passed a girl on a bicycle. She was uncommonly pretty—a fact Jeff noted when he called out to her.

Kim Browne was a doctor's daughter. She thought: *This crazy kook—who is that?*

She discovered a short while later, when Jeff telephoned her at home. "I'm gonna meet you," Jeff said. He did, soon after, at a high school football game.

Kim thought Jeff was funny and cute, and she liked that he traveled with South Boston's In Crowd—and was fifteen and a high school freshman, a year older and a grade ahead of her in school. Before long, Kim was in love. That did not please Doctor and Mrs. Browne, for whom Kim was the oldest of their four daughters, for the Burtons enjoyed a reputation as party boys, and Jeff certainly wasn't bound for Harvard. "I don't like this boy," Kim's father said. But Kim wasn't listening.

John Burton never raced professionally, but he savored speed. He drove fast on the highway, and he brought his sons to Winston Cup races at Rockingham and Darlington. The boys had yet to reach grammar school when he put them behind the wheel of a tractor—a lowly form of speed, but for a kid, speed nonetheless. Soon, John had his sons racing go-carts in organized leagues.

Fiercely competitive in golf and tennis, the sports he liked best, John expected his sons to win—and toward that end, he bought the finest carts and equipment, hired a mechanic, and devoted every weekend of the racing season to his new obsession. Ward won state championships, as did Brian and, later, Jeff, who first competed when he was seven. Brian eventually left racing to run the family construction firm and Ward took time off to decide his future, but Jeff stayed with speed, moving from go-carts to stockcars, which he raced at South Boston Speedway, where Richard Petty and Ned Jarrett had competed.

Jeff did not progress without rancor at home. John's need to win notwithstanding, Meredith did not want her sons behind the wheel of a stockcar, which was faster and more dangerous than a go-cart. Meredith had attended a NASCAR race in 1960 at Darlington where two mechanics and an inspector died when two cars collided and plowed upside-down into the pits—and she still carried in her head the image of a body flying through the air. "I'm not going to let you do that," Meredith said. But John and Jeff prevailed, and the teenager, soon to be an adult, kept racing.

Meanwhile, Jeff's girlfriend, Kim, had enrolled as a premedical student at North Carolina State University, but on the eve of her sophomore year she decided against medicine. She knew firsthand the personal sacrifices a good physician must make, and if she attended medical school and then completed an internship and residency while Jeff raced, she and the man she loved would rarely see each other. "We've always been best friends, and I think if you have that plus the other attraction you've got it made," Kim said. So she earned a degree in math and science and became a teacher. If Burton's career stalled, she reasoned, they would need the income.

Bankrolled in part by a $250,000 investment from his father, Burton started racing full-time in NASCAR's Busch Grand National division in 1989. But even a quarter of a million dollars, a sum Kurt Busch's parents could never have imagined, bought only a limited racing inventory: two cars and three engines, less than half what a top Busch Series team carried through a season. Burton finished the year 13th, and failed to win a pole or a race.

The next year, Burton entered into partnership with Sam Ard, a former Grand National champion, and won his first race, at Martinsville, Virginia—but 1990 otherwise proved discouraging. Equipment broke, bills mounted, and tempers flared inside the twenty-three-year-old driver's team. Burton ended the 1990 season in 15th place, with less than $87,000 in winnings. "Physically and mentally, that year just killed me," he said. "I learned more that year about myself and about how things can go wrong and how you handle things than any other year."

Kim helped sustain Burton during that time, but despite a steady relationship that had now lasted a decade, her boyfriend balked at marriage. Jeff had seen his fiercely competitive father grow apart from his mother, whose foremost lesson to her children was not to win but to act charitably to all—and it was at an impressionable stage in his life, when he was in high school, that the Burtons finally divorced. Worried that a legal commitment would somehow damage his relationship with his girlfriend, Jeff kept the diamond he bought Kim a secret for a year before proposing marriage. They wed on February 1, 1992, before heading to Daytona, where Jeff was racing in the NAPA Auto Parts 300, the Busch Series counterpart to the Daytona 500.

Driving for new sponsors, Burton would persist in Busch Grand National competition for three more seasons. He won three more races and placed as high as ninth in the point standings, but his future remained speculative; as in few other sports, success in racing depends on several factors, money primary among them, that are only indirectly related to talent, ambition, and work. Burton didn't know how long he could continue to drive, but he figured he could always find employment building racecars, and so he learned that trade, too. Kim's parents had come to admire their now son-in-law's spirit, but they assumed it was only a matter of time before reality set in.

Instead, Burton got a chance at the big time: His Busch Series performances had caught the attention of the Winston Cup owners Stavola Brothers, and they signed him for the 1994 Cup season. Burton failed to win that year—but his 24th-place finish was sufficient to capture the Rookie of the Year title over his brother Ward, who had finally settled on a career in racing, and John

Andretti, nephew of the legendary racer Mario Andretti. But 1995 would return Jeff Burton to disappointment. He would finish 32nd in the standings, and the Stavolas, who ran a New Jersey asphalt company, would be nearing the end of their tenure as car owners.

Burton already was negotiating to race the 1996 season for another owner, former Ford executive Michael Kranefuss, when Ward called him with word about an opening at Roush Racing. Jack Roush had asked Ward to fill it, but Ward intended to stay with his current owner. "Are you interested?" Ward asked Jeff. "Well, God, yes!" Jeff said. Ward contacted Geoff Smith, who called Jeff Burton with the details. An offer to drive soon followed.

Jeff Burton was actually Roush's third choice to join his expanding Winston Cup operation—his first choice, Kyle Petty, had also declined. Roush considered Jeff something of a diamond in the rough, and to help develop his potential, he hired as crew chief the wise old Buddy Parrott, who in more than two decades of Cup racing had enjoyed success with such drivers as Rusty Wallace and Richard Petty. Burton's only personnel request was to bring on Frank Stoddard, who was then the crew chief for a driver in one of NASCAR's regional series. Stoddard had almost no Cup experience, but he had worked briefly on Burton's Busch Series crew in 1990, so impressing Burton that the driver wanted him as his crew chief someday.

Burton won no races his first year with Roush, but he won three in 1997, when he placed fourth in the point standings. Four years later, it came as little surprise that he began the season as the Winston Cup front-runner. He had contended for the title late into 2000, when he won four times—including the fall meet in New Hampshire in which he led every lap, a feat last accomplished in a Cup race almost a quarter of a century before. Burton drove some of the best cars in all of racing—and he had some of the best mechanics, tire changers, and other personnel, headed by Stoddard, who had demonstrated himself worthy to succeed Parrott as crew chief.

But it was Burton's mind as much as his driving that distinguished him in the world of automobile racing.

In an era when many drivers forsook candor for clichés when talking to the press, Burton spoke forthrightly, whether on matters of safety, NASCAR rules, or his own performances, good and bad. Unlike many of his peers, who defined themselves strictly by their calling and who planned to race as long as age allowed, Burton viewed himself as a work in progress—a man whose upbringing had left him with conflicting values, and a fancy for grappling with life's complexities. "When I look at my mom," he said, "the thing I think about is 'Do unto others as you'd have done unto you.' That's what she taught us—that's how she lives her life. So from my father, I got this burning desire to compete, and from my mother I got this need for people to respect me. And so that's my makeup—I've got two different things that I've been taught growing up. I'm trying to merge them together."

Burton already played a key role in designing racecar chassis, and someday he expected to manage the competitive operations side of Roush Racing, an expectation that Jack Roush shared. Sometime after that, he hoped to win election to the U.S. Senate, focusing on education, health care, and family issues. Burton had already chaired a $1 million fundraising campaign for Duke Children's Hospital, where Kim served on the hospital board. "I enjoy being outspoken," the driver said. "I enjoy talking about a subject that I believe in. I should be financially able to do whatever it is I want to do later in life. I have no ulterior motive—I'm really interested to see if you could get into government with no ulterior motive and make a difference."

In the meantime, racing dominated the Burtons' lives. Kim favored designer clothes and diamond rings, and she was well-versed in the social graces—but on race weekends, she claimed a seat next to Frank Stoddard on top of the No. 99 pit cart. Wearing a headset and monitoring a computer, she logged lap times and chronicled radio traffic, later adding her insights to the post-race review. At home, racing often was the topic of conversation.

So, of course, were the children: Kimberle Paige, five, and Harrison Brian, born in October 2000. Named for Jeff's brother, baby Harrison had arrived at a momentous time: Uncle Brian and his wife were expecting their first children, twins, only a few months later. But the twins arrived prematurely, and with doctors unable to save them, one died on Christmas Eve and the other on Christmas Day. Jeff stayed with his brother on that Christmas, accompanying him from the hospital to the funeral home, where two tiny caskets were being prepared.

The death of his brother's children gave Jeff another of life's complexities to ponder.

"I do want to be a good father, I do want to be a responsible citizen, and I do want to do all these things—but I also want to be a racecar driver," he said. "Sometimes they don't all mix together. And I've struggled more with that in the last year than I ever have."

Although they had never discussed it, the thought crossed Jack Roush's mind that Burton's life circumstances combined with Earnhardt's death might be among the factors affecting his 2001 season. For a racecar driver, Jeff seemed to spend an inordinate amount of time thinking.

Darlington proved daunting for Jack Roush. To everyone's relief, Jeff Burton made the race—only to finish 18th after a questionable penalty for a tire that got loose during a pit stop. Matt Kenseth came in 19th, and Mark Martin placed 21st. Racing for his first time at the perilous speedway, Kurt Busch repeatedly scraped the wall and wound up 30th. "I had a rookie day at Darlington," he said. "I hit everything out there."

Further peril loomed the next weekend, the last in March, when Cup racing moved to Tennessee's Bristol Motor Speedway for the Food City 500.

Many racers considered Bristol the nastiest track on the Cup circuit—nastier even than The Lady in Black, with 16-degree straightaways and turns banked at 36 degrees, so steep that track workers could get winded just walking to the top. Racecar drivers reached obscene speeds at Bristol, up to Steve Park's record of 126.370 miles per hour, a virtually inconceivable velocity given that the speedway was just double the length of an ordinary high school running track. Bristol billed itself as The World's Fastest Half Mile, and Darrell Waltrip likened it to a giant cereal bowl; others compared it to the Coliseum, with cars instead of gladiators, and 146,000 spectators watching from stands that reached almost to the sky. With forty-three cars aiming to circle the unforgiving concrete 500 times, mayhem was inevitable; many drivers never finished the race, and even the victors rarely left Bristol with their vehicles intact. It had been this way from the first race, forty years earlier, when only nineteen of forty-two cars were still around at the end.

But the speedway's hazards did not preoccupy Roush when he arrived at Bristol on Friday morning in his Citation jet, which he piloted when he wasn't flying his P-51 Mustang fighter plane. Nor did motor failure burden him: He and his technicians had successfully addressed the causes of Atlanta's three malfunctions. Pistons were the culprits in Martin's and Kenseth's cases, and Roush had approved modifications to improve durability. A broken valve spring had hobbled Burton. "I had 7,000 of them and we've used half of them over a six-month period of time and there were no failures—3,500 with no problem," said Roush. "There's nothing you can do about that. You endure that and go on."

And Roush did not dwell on his teams' press coverage, some of which had progressed from Freddie Krueger allusions to suggestions of skullduggery and treason inside the Roush camp. According to one writer, three engines failing had so infuriated Martin, Kenseth, and Burton that they now wanted to lease motors from an outside builder. Another writer implied that Roush and Martin, together for thirteen years, were at each other's throats. Still another suspected that Burton was plotting to leave Roush for Richard Childress. None of the stories was true, but they made good copy and lit up the chat rooms.

"I kind of put my head in my work and try to keep my mind on my game and don't get caught up in all the emotions from the things that are written," said Roush. "If you wind up letting yourself get carried away with all of the euphoria that flows from the real happy times—when maybe people are saying things that are maybe more positive than would be justified—then that's bad. And if you let yourself get your heart broke for all the things that are unfair or inaccurate, that's also a problem. I try to stay out of that." He usually did, albeit feistily. "I've been racing longer than many people that are writing the stories today—and I'll be racing when most of the people that are writing the stories today are doing other things," Roush said. "They can only have my ass for a little while and they'll be gone!"

Thirty-one of thirty-six points races remained in this strange season, still sufficient time for superb racers, who had stumbled early, to prevail.

"We're going to have a great year," said Roush. "This bad luck that we've had—the wrecks and breaking things and missing some setups won't continue. We will have great pit stops, we will have good durability throughout the year, and we'll steadily climb our way back in points."

What irked Roush coming into Bristol was NASCAR itself, which had recently levied penalties against two of his teams. One had temporarily cost Kurt Busch his crew chief. The other had hurt Jeff Burton the previous week at Darlington.

Roush accepted sanctions that he deemed warranted—but he became infuriated at those he deemed wrong, especially if he believed stupidity or vindictiveness had motivated the officials who levied them. Roush still could not forgive NASCAR for the 1990 season, when he fielded a single Cup car, Mark Martin's. All season long, Martin, then an upstart in Cup competition, battled

Dale Earnhardt for the points lead. Entering the season's last weekend, Martin was ahead by six points, a negligible advantage under a system that awards winners of a single race up to 185 points. Earnhardt beat Martin in the season finale, taking the Cup championship with a 26-point margin—a loss that Roush would have accepted, but for a penalty that had cost Martin 46 points earlier in the year. In levying the penalty (and a $40,000 fine), NASCAR officials had claimed that a carburetor spacer on Martin's car was too long. Roush insisted that the part had passed inspection several times before—and in any event, it had provided Martin no competitive advantage, a fact that NASCAR conceded. But in the end, NASCAR rejected Roush's appeal, and Martin subsequently lost the title. A decade later, Roush still could not discuss the 1990 season without anger in his voice.

Nor could he unemotionally recount a more recent penalty that had cost him the 1999 Craftsman Truck Series title.

Once again, NASCAR had gone after Roush for a part it alleged was illegal: an intake manifold on Greg Biffle's car. Roush claimed that the part had passed inspection, but an inspector denied that, and NASCAR fined Biffle $47,000 and penalized him 128 points. Biffle went on to lose the title by 8 points. "An inspector lied," insisted Roush, who demanded that NASCAR officials undergo polygraph tests (they refused), his own employees already having been subjected to them (they passed) as part of Roush's campaign to prove his innocence. Although he lacked evidence, Roush believed that NASCAR had imposed the penalty near the season's end in order to slow Biffle's charge to the title, thus setting a race with the two drivers who were behind him—a race that increased fan interest in the relatively new Craftsman Truck Series.

"They took two championships from us," Roush said as he sat in Martin's hauler that March weekend in Bristol. "This is not as big a deal in that sense—but it smacks of the same thing."

He was referring to the penalty an official had levied against Jeff Burton at Darlington. The official ruled that during a pit stop a loose tire had rolled into the open, which is a violation of the rules; forced to give up position, Burton, who had been running fifth, lost any chance to win. After interviewing Burton's crew and reviewing a videotape taken from the camera mounted on Burton's pit cart, Roush concluded that the official had acted wrongly. Armed with the videotape and accompanied by Stoddard, he flew to Daytona Beach to present his case—"Perry-Mason style," he called it—to NASCAR president Mike Helton. Helton could not change the outcome of the Darlington race, but he did apologize to Roush. And the inspector was never to be glimpsed near a Roush driver again.

The penalty against Kurt Busch's team came after a NASCAR inspector found outdated seat belts in one of Burton's racecars. (Because materials can degrade during extended storage, NASCAR required all belts to have been manufactured within the last five years.) NASCAR fined the No. 97 team $5,000 and suspended crew chief Matt Chambers for two races, starting with Bristol. That the belts were too old seemed uncontestable: They were labeled with the date of manufacture. Roush could not determine whether the belt manufacturer had shipped old inventory in a new box, or a Roush parts manager had erred, and he chose not to appeal the sanction—but the implication that he put his drivers at unnecessary risk piqued him.

"We've been safety advocates in every way," he said, citing several features his engineers had devised, then made available to anyone in motorsports. Among them were roof flaps that helped keep racecars stable at high speeds, and an ingenious device developed after the deaths of Adam Petty and Kenny Irwin that instantly shuts down an engine when its throttle sticks and a driver cannot rein in his car with only his brakes.

Roush believed that NASCAR had penalized Kurt Busch's team to deflect growing criticism in the wake of Earnhardt's death. "I see the action they've taken against me as a cheap shot in order to try to relieve the pressure that they've got," Roush said. "They're trying to hide from lawyers, they're trying to hide from people who would come in and who would subject them to scrutiny and legislation and other things. And they're just going to get it based on the way they're dealing with things."

Roush may have been right: The pressure on NASCAR was indeed great, but even before Earnhardt's death, NASCAR's commitment to driver safety had been openly questioned.

Three NASCAR racers had died in accidents in 2000: Petty, Irwin, and also Craftsman Truck driver Tony Roper, who crashed on Friday the 13th of October. Yet despite reporters' inquiries and the concerns of many racers, most outspokenly Jeff Burton, NASCAR disclosed scant details of its response to the tragedies. What little was known raised an alarm. Months after Petty and Irwin had gone to their graves, NASCAR had not requested copies of the autopsy reports, according to the New Hampshire state medical examiner. No videotapes existed of either crash, police had arrived too late to conduct a credible investigation, and no outsiders had examined the wrecked cars. Irwin's owner promptly destroyed his, and the Pettys buried Adam's.

"We know what the cause of death was from the death certificates," Helton told a reporter—basilar skull fractures, which destroyed the brain. Preventing such injuries might be possible, but not without proper study and NASCAR's unwavering resolve. Neither was forthcoming in 2000. What NASCAR did, Bill France Jr. made sure everyone still understood, was NASCAR's business.

Predictably, NASCAR at first declined to disclose anything about its investigation of Earnhardt's death. Then, five days after the Daytona 500, Helton dropped a bombshell. At a news conference on the eve of the Rockingham race, he announced that Earnhardt's seat belt had "separated." Helton did not speculate as to whether emergency workers had broken it trying to free Earnhardt from his car or whether it had failed during the accident, but Steve Bohannon, the doctor who had treated Earnhardt at the scene, said that he favored the failure scenario—to the best of anyone's knowledge, the first such case in more than a half century of NASCAR racing. Reporters requesting copies of the written autopsy report found that the coroner had concluded that Earnhardt died of "blunt force injuries" producing a basilar skull fracture like those that killed Petty and Irwin. "If his restraint system—his belts—had held, he would have had a much better chance of survival," Bohannon said, but he discounted the possibility that Earnhardt would have lived had he been wearing a HANS or similar head restraint. "I'm not convinced the HANS device would have made a difference in this case," Bohannon declared.

Beyond that, NASCAR officials said almost nothing in the weeks following Earnhardt's death. In such an atmosphere, rumors spread, racers' worries multiplied, and ill will inevitably flourished throughout NASCAR and beyond. Many reporters wondered how NASCAR could be so tight-lipped after losing its biggest star. Was it trapped in the mentality of stockcar racing's early days, when men transporting hooch sometimes lost their lives on twisting mountain roads? Did France Jr., who ruled with an iron fist, fear government regulation, such as that governing another high-risk sport, boxing? Did he fear the formation of a drivers' union? The sports that he sought to emulate—football, baseball, and basketball—all had players' unions, but NASCAR, with its southern roots, had always squashed any notion of that.

Or did France fear lawsuits—if not by Teresa Earnhardt or the Pettys, then by drivers as a class, or some later victim's family? NASCAR's rules made a driver's well-being the responsibility of the driver, owner, and track owner, not NASCAR. But whether those rules could withstand a vigorous legal challenge was another matter.

Despite his power and wealth, France was a down-to-earth man—a man who found some of his greatest pleasure in a simple passion, the ocean, which he loved to fish from his yacht. He could be gracious, and a long but ultimately successful battle with cancer had shown him a humbling side of life. But France was no advocate of full disclosure, not to the media, at least—some members of the media, he believed, twisted truths. "With the Internet now," France would later remark, "people will write anything they want, and somebody will pick something up and go with it. They don't check anything out, you know? Crazy world out there with the media, I don't mind telling you that."

And so, as March neared an end, outsiders could only guess what was transpiring behind closed doors in Daytona Beach.

In the outside world, the criticism continued to mount, precipitating a public relations disaster of such magnitude that it warranted exploration in national publications including the *Chicago Tribune, USA Today*, and even the media watchdog journal *Brill's Content*, which had never mentioned NASCAR before. "NASCAR is an organization in crisis, and it is a crisis brought on by its own success," wrote Jim McLaurin, who covered NASCAR for *The State*, South Carolina's largest newspaper. "Long story short, it was a minor-league sport that stepped up to the major leagues, but is having a hard time shaking its minor-league mentality."

Yet despite the bad press, NASCAR kept the support of many Dale Earnhardt fans. They knew that their hero had been no candy-ass sissy—he understood the risk when he started his engine, just as they understood the risk when they pressed their sunburned faces against chain-link fencing to experience the sensation of automobiles rocketing by at speeds they would never drive. Spectators died at auto races, too—more than 80 one bloody day in 1955, when Pierre Levegh crashed into the crowd at France's 24 Hours of Le Mans. More recently, three fans perished and eight sustained injury during a race at Lowe's Motor Speedway in Charlotte in 1999. This wasn't tiddlywinks, a point France made in one of his rare interviews, with *The Washington Post*.

In the weeks since Teresa Earnhardt spoke in Las Vegas and

the Florida legislature moved to ban the release of autopsy photos without a judge's order, Earnhardt's fans had cast the media as stockcar racing's vile enemy. In their view, the press cared only about profit, and imagining some newspaper publishing photographs of their hero's dissected internal organs enraged them. A ghoulish element undeniably attended the matter. Knowing that the Florida legislature was about to pass the law that Teresa Earnhardt wanted, the operator of a Florida Web site obtained and posted the autopsy photos of the two drivers killed in 1994 at Daytona: Rodney Orr and Neil Bonnett, Earnhardt's friend. The photos were shocking in their grisly detail. "I can't sleep at night," said Orr's father, Beacher Orr, required to view the photos for a court proceeding. "I lay down and I see him on the table there naked. That's what I see."

Not surprisingly, Earnhardt fans directed most of their wrath at *The Orlando Sentinel,* NASCAR's nemesis now. The fact that the paper intended only to examine, not publish, Earnhardt's autopsy photos mattered not.

"Of all the lowlives in the world, this paper has to rank near the bottom of the food chain—somewhere around plankton or pond scum," wrote one NASCAR fan on his Web site. "'We demand to see the autopsy photos! We want our expert to check the photos to make sure how he died.' Hey jerks! I've never seen the photos and I can tell you exactly what killed him. He hit a concrete wall doing 180 MPH. And I don't need his photos to sell newspapers to figure that out! You want to make sure there was no conspiracy? Who do you think you're kidding? The bottom line is publicity and selling newspapers. And if Teresa and the family have to get hurt to sell your newspapers? Well damn 'em! You give scum a bad name."

Those who shared the newspaper's distrust of NASCAR comprised a smaller group. "I have attended the Daytona 500 every year for some ten years," a Miami resident wrote. "But this last one I must decide was my last. That is, until there is a paradigm shift in NASCAR's attention to safety. That would have to include soft walls at all tracks, collapsible steering columns and steering wheels, mandatory head restraints like the Hutchens or HANS and full coverage helmets, engine cut-offs to prevent stuck throttles, a safety committee including representation by the drivers it should protect, an emergency rescue team that travels with the series."

The Miami resident was not the only one who believed such steps merited NASCAR's consideration, but months would pass before the public learned whether NASCAR had done anything.

As the Food City 500 weekend opened, the Roush drivers had reason to hope that the race would start the climb that their boss predicted. During qualifying, Mark Martin won the pole, with a breathtaking lap that was a mere eight thousandths of a second slower than the Bristol Motor Speedway record.

A slight man with close-cut graying hair, piercing blue eyes, and a warm smile, Martin was close to giddy as he took the microphone at the Bristol media center for the customary interview session accorded pole winners. Like most veteran drivers, speed alone no longer served as Martin's elixir; experience had taught him that winning at speed, whether in qualifying or in races, delivered a far more potent high. And Martin had not won a pole since February 2000, or a race since last April. By his own admission, his craving had grown intense.

"I think this is the first time I've been to the media center this year, so it's good to be here!" Martin said.

As the racer talked on, unprodded, the reporters listened raptly. Most of them liked the forty-two-year-old Martin—and so did legions of NASCAR fans, even some who cheered on other drivers. His thirty-two wins ranked him 17th on the all-time list, and his $25.3 million in Cup winnings placed him fourth on the all-time money list, behind only Dale Earnhardt, Jeff Gordon, and

Dale Jarrett. Martin's blue-and-white No. 6 car, sponsored by Pfizer to promote its latest wonder drug, Viagra, was one of the enduring images on the Winston Cup circuit. If Burton didn't take the 2001 title, some in January had predicted, Martin would.

But racing success alone did not ensure popularity in NASCAR. Jeff Gordon, a three-time champion, routinely received boos along with applause, especially in the south, where Dale Earnhardt's fans deplored the driver's California roots and appearances as one of *People* magazine's "Sexiest Men and Most Beautiful People." It was Mark Martin's personality and life story that endeared him as no other driver to the stockcar community.

Son of a hard-drinking Arkansan who loved all kinds of speed and who eventually died while piloting an airplane, Martin had traveled the long road to the pinnacle. A racer before he was old enough for a license, Martin toiled for years on tracks throughout the nation's heartland. He had survived bankruptcy and suffered many injuries, which had so battered him that he could barely walk anymore without pain. The result at middle age was an uncommon mix of pride and humility—and a man, like Burton, who refused to be scripted.

"I'm not a yes man," Martin said, "but I'm not a crybaby or a blabbermouth either. I'll give my opinion whether people like it or not—but I try not to give an emotional opinion and I try not to do a lot of complaining. And I've never complained much about losing races or being treated unfairly on the racetrack by somebody. I'm not much on all that. I'm a straight-up guy."

That Friday in Bristol, after talking enthusiastically for several minutes on topics of his choosing, Martin took questions. Reporters asked the usual—about his qualifying run, about the weekend's competition. Then a reporter asked about his nine-year-old son, Matt, who had been racing a small class of cars called Quarter Midgets for two years. Martin had helped build a track for Matt and his young competitors—and this summer, he and his son would be featured on 15 million boxes of Life and

Cap'n Crunch cereal. Matt already had his own Web site, mattmartin.net, which featured the slogan "SPEED . . . it runs in the family."

"Matt did really good Wednesday night," Martin said. "He won his heat race in a spectacular pass after he took the white flag. I didn't even know he had a chance to win. I thought he was gonna get second and all of a sudden he darted inside of the kid and won the race. It was pretty awesome. Then he finished second in the feature and ran a great race. The *ABC World News* was there covering it. He's had kinds of inquiries for shows. Like I told him, 'I've never been on *ABC World News*!'"

Martin spoke as exuberantly about his son as about winning the pole for Sunday's race. "Oh, man, it's so cool!" he said. "I'm having more fun this year than I've had since I was a kid."

Across the infield, Kurt Busch looked like a kid—but he was not enjoying himself that weekend. His car hadn't cornered well during qualifying, and he'd been forced to use a precious provisional to make the race. Busch found no consolation in the fact that another newcomer, the twenty-five-year-old Jason Leffler, didn't make the race at all; Kevin Harvick, his chief competitor for Rookie of the Year now, had turned in a blistering qualifying lap, and would start third on Sunday.

Bristol was another of the speedways where Busch had never raced, but he knew its forbidding reputation, and late on Saturday morning, before the final practice, he continued to seek insights into what the Food City 500 held. Buddy Parrott, now Roush's performance development manager, joined Busch and his car chief Mark Price (second to the crew chief in the team hierarchy) in the No. 97 hauler. A critical member of the team was absent: Crew chief Chambers was serving his two-week suspension.

Parrott compared racing at Bristol to a folk tale in which a tiger goes around and around, faster and faster, until it turns to butter. "You won't even have time to think," he said.

"This is all foreign to me," said Busch. "I'm not used to this shit."

"This is where everybody wants to be, man," said Price. "You wouldn't be here if you weren't the best. Keep your head up, dude!"

Busch had visited Bristol earlier in the year to test the car that Roush's specialists had built to race there, and he had returned home from that session satisfied with its handling and speed. "It hurts to spend all that time and then come up with a provisional," Busch said. "Everybody tells me that these cars take time to learn—I'm not agreeing with that. I've jumped in everything from a Legend car to a Craftsman Truck and picked up on it within seven races."

But here he was—missing Chambers, stuck with a slow car, and starting fourth from last on a track so snug that it required pit boxes on both sides to accommodate all of the cars. No amount of practice could ever prepare a rookie for Bristol's frantic, frequent pit stops, which transformed the speedway into a vortex. "When the green flag drops," Busch said, "it will all be new to me. What's going to happen? Am I going to get run over? Are people going to leave me alone? Am I going to be able to pass?"

Growing up, Busch admired Mark Martin, and to race alongside a childhood hero was perhaps the greatest honor of his young life. Busch was likewise grateful that Martin, who took an interest in new drivers, had made a point of advising him, as had Burton and Kenseth. But the older drivers' graciousness had also reminded Busch of his novice status in Winston Cup racing. "I talk with them every now and then but I feel as if I'm like a five-year-old talking to a sixteen-year-old," he said.

Even the news that Roush Racing was soon to announce a major sponsor of the still virgin-white No. 97 team failed to cheer Busch at the moment.

"I remember I made a mistake when I was a kid," he said. "I was learning how to swim—I was four or five—I had done my laps in the shallow end to prove that I could go in the deep end. I got the approval of the lifeguard that I was OK to go in the deep end. I jumped in—and I expected my feet to hit the bottom, like they did in the shallow end. They didn't; I went straight down. And I had to figure out how to get back up. Usually I could use my feet to push myself up from the bottom of the pool to get back above the surface. It caught me by surprise. I can't remember how I got up, but I ended up getting up by myself."

Busch smiled for the first time that morning.

"Soon we'll be springing off the high dive, though, right?"

On the morning of the Food City 500, Roush retained his confidence in all his drivers—even Jeff Burton, who at 36th in the standings was the most disappointing of the four. Roush had only casually wondered if Burton's cerebral inclinations might have contributed to his poor performances; a more likely explanation, he still believed, was the new tires that Goodyear was providing to Winston Cup racers. Harder and more durable than those used in 2000, the tires were an answer to increasing speeds resulting from improvements in engine horsepower and aerodynamic performance. A nonprofessional driver might not have noticed the change, but the best racers develop an almost extrasensory connection to the rubber beneath them that allows them to go faster, and the connection can be a delicate one. Burton wasn't the only driver having difficulty reestablishing the feel; last year's champion Bobby Labonte, among others, continued to struggle.

Like Roush, Burton was in good spirits the Sunday of the Food City 500. He awoke early and traveled through the cold day to the CITGO hospitality tent, where a crowd waited expectantly. They didn't care where Burton stood in the points—he was a Winston Cup driver, a man who knew speed at 200 miles per hour.

"We're starting 32nd today, which is obviously not where we want to start—but the good thing about starting in the back is that we have a lot of experience at that!" Burton said, to laughter.

Someone asked Burton about the effect of the day's weather, which was unseasonably cool. "Will you be able to keep warm in there today?" the fan said.

"It won't be a problem keeping warm in there. Will you be able to keep warm—that's the question. Drink some of that motor oil right there—CITGO's good for a lot of stuff!" The crowd roared. "Don't try that at home," Burton added. "I've got to put a disclaimer on that."

Burton answered more questions, and then a fan asked about the race a month later at Alabama's Talladega Superspeedway, a track virtually identical to Daytona—only faster. Even before Earnhardt's death, Talladega had spooked racers, and now many of them wanted NASCAR to change the engine and aerodynamic rules so that racecars did not travel in such large, tight packs, an invitation to the sort of accident that had ruined nineteen vehicles at the Daytona 500. But despite the spotlight that Earnhardt's death had put on safety, NASCAR wasn't budging—the rules created a type of racing that thrilled spectators, more than a few of whom yearned for mangled metal and the heart-stopping suspense of waiting to see if the driver would climb out of his wrecked car or the Jaws of Life would be summoned. The rules governing races at Daytona and Talladega sold tickets and earned high TV ratings, which brought profit to all, including those most at risk, the drivers.

"We're not in favor of going to Talladega and running in a forty-three-car pack," Burton said. "I can't tell you any better than this: The twenty-eighth-place car at Daytona got landed on top of by the car that was running fifth. Something wrong with that. We don't need to have that many cars running in one pack. NASCAR seems to want to put on a great show—I don't think you have to have twenty-car wrecks to put on a great show. I think we can have good racing without big wrecks. They seem to do it that way. It's their ballgame—if we don't like it, we don't have to go. But we're going to be there. And that's the way it works."

In closing, Burton predicted better days for the No. 99 car. "We've got a great race team, we've got the same driver, same crew chief, same crew members, the same cars that have won a lot of races," he said. "I've never been 35th in points in my career—I've also never been more excited about my race team. I'm pumped up and believe that we have a better team than we've ever had—I really believe that in my heart. We're just going through a time right now where we're being tested."

In the last three decades, only five Winston Cup champions had failed to win by the season's sixth race. Asked if he still believed he had a shot at the title, Burton said: "You know, strangely enough, I think we do."

The Oscar Meyer Weinermobile circled the track, an Air Force drill team marched, Miss Food City paraded across the stage, an official introduced the forty-three drivers, the 146,000 spectators remembered Earnhardt with a moment of silence followed by three cannon blasts, a Church of Christ minister recited the invocation, Billy Ray Cyrus sang the National Anthem, and, at 1:05 P.M. on Sunday, March 25, drivers started their engines for the Food City 500.

Mark Martin led for the first two laps, until Kevin Harvick passed him. Just four laps further in, the race's first wreck damaged two cars and sent Kurt Busch spinning—but Busch regained control, and continued on. Barely a dozen laps later, another wreck caught Jeff Burton, who sustained minor damage to the rear end of his car and fell to 41st. The race was only 5 percent complete, and already Bristol was living up to its notorious reputation.

After the third wreck, drivers avoided contact for almost fifty laps. Then, coming down the backstretch on the seventy-ninth lap, Busch spun into the wall. He was unhurt, but the impact ripped apart the front of his car. Busch unstrapped himself and sought the seclusion of his hauler as his crew began repairs. No one knew if they could finish in time to rejoin the race.

The green flag flew, and racing resumed. Over the next nearly 200 laps, Martin stayed near the front of the field. Kenseth, who had started 24th, survived a brush and drove methodically toward the front, reaching fifth by lap 149; he was in good race form this weekend, having won the Cheez-It 250 the day before, a race in the Busch Grand National Series, in which he and Burton occasionally still competed. Burton climbed, too, to 23rd place a third of the way through the race, a position that kept him in contention.

Then, on lap 247, Burton's right-front tire blew.

Burton bounced off the wall—and Martin, close behind, could not avoid smashing into him. Burton's car was ruined for the day, and Martin's was damaged.

"We're done," Burton radioed.

"Glad you're OK, baby," Stoddard radioed back. Burton felt sore, but he was not seriously injured.

Before returning to his hauler, Burton apologized to Martin—in all the years of Roush Racing, two of Roush's Cup teammates had never wrecked each other. Back in his hauler, Burton discussed tires with Roush and showed his boss a scratch on his helmet, apparently from his impact with the wall.

"You're a crush dummy this year!" Roush said. The two men laughed. There was no sense in recriminations.

Martin's crew managed to repair his car, but when it returned, minus a front bumper seventy-five laps later, Martin had lost any chance of winning. He had started the weekend with promise—and he would go home with a 34th-place finish, which dropped him to 27th in the points, a level of mediocrity he'd not experienced in more than a decade. But like Roush, he did not take Burton to task. "I just wasn't in the right spot today," he said.

Roush, meanwhile, had consoled Kurt Busch—and advised him to return to Charlotte and study the notes about car setups that the Burton and Martin teams had compiled for races they'd won in previous years. Roush wanted his rookie to better utilize his finest racing asset, his brain.

It took more than half the race, but by lap 374, Busch's crew had fixed his car. No. 97 reentered the race.

Six laps later, a line of cars ahead of him crashed, and he had no place to go but into the heart of the mess. The flagman waved the yellow caution flag, and an official dispatched a tow truck to haul Busch's beaten car away. As the truck left the track, with Busch riding inside for all in the national TV audience to see, Roush knew that the No. 97 team was heading into a black hole. He knew he would have to make immediate changes.

Uninjured but humiliated, Busch stepped off the tow truck, swept past Melissa into his hauler, packed a duffle bag with his clothes, and walked alone toward the exit gate. Unlike the larger tracks, Bristol features no access tunnel, and everyone inside the infield remains trapped until a race ends. Busch wanted to be the first out when this one did.

As he walked, the scoreboard proclaimed the new race leader. It was No. 29, Kevin Harvick.

Though Harvick was a more experienced racer than Busch, he had started the 2001 season in the Busch Series, expecting to run only the seven Cup races allowed to still qualify for Rookie of the Year in 2002. Then Earnhardt died. Fate had claimed one man, smiled on another, and given a third a formidable new rival.

Each amply gifted in ability, Busch and Harvick had different racing styles. Like his three Cup teammates, Busch avoided tangling on the track, while Harvick competed like the man whose cars he now drove. "We just have to go out and do what we have to do—and if that means moving somebody out of the way, then that's what we have to do," said Harvick. "I've been aggressive since I started racing when I was five years old." Busch and Harvick differed in their off-track demeanor, as well. Busch spoke modestly of his achievements and graciously of his competitors; Harvick crowed about his success and disparaged those with less success. In the Favorite Quote section of his Web site, Harvick quoted himself, on the hazards of racing near the end of the field:

"You run with the crap, you wreck with the crap." An article posted on the site summarized the Harvick camp's opinion of their driver: "Fans love every minute he spends on the track. His fierce competitive driving style, refusal to lose, and impressive stats make them proud to display his merchandise. He's a legend in the making."

Many outsiders contributed to the hype. Even as Busch waited for the race to end so that he could leave, a radio announcer whose broadcast was carried live on Bristol's loudspeakers noted Harvick's race lead and predicted a runaway victory in the Rookie of the Year contest. Harvick currently led Busch in rookie points, 57 to 43. Four other newcomers trailed the two leaders.

"They ought to start engraving the trophy," the announcer said.

A few laps later, Harvick's tire went down, and with it his chance of winning. Third at the start of the Food City 500, he finished 24th. His legend, if he were to have one, would be a little longer in the making.

Eighteen racers, nearly half the field, failed to complete all of the Food City 500's laps, and almost no car escaped damage. As the crews loaded the battered remains onto the haulers, a surprise winner was celebrating: Elliott Sadler, who'd started 38th—in his backup car, after he'd crashed his preferred vehicle during Friday's practice.

Sadler, twenty-five, had never won in his seventy-five Cup races—and his team owner, Wood Brothers Racing, which had competed for more than half a century with such luminaries as A. J. Foyt and David Pearson, had not won a points race since 1993. Jack Roush joined Sadler and Eddie and Len Wood, sons of one of the founding Wood brothers, in Victory Lane—and during a press conference, Sadler and the Woods thanked him. Fearing that the historic Woods might go out of business during the 1990s, Roush had entered into a partnership in which Roush

Racing provided the Wood Brothers their cars, engines, and marketing and administrative support.

During the press conference, a reporter asked Eddie Wood if he'd been tempted to give up during their long winless streak. "Never," he said. "Even on your darkest, worst day, you never think of stopping racing. This is what you do. This is what you eat, drink, and believe in. We don't care about anything but racing and that's why it's so special."

Except for Sadler, Bristol had proved another dismal weekend for Jack Roush. Mark Martin had placed 34th, Jeff Burton 40th, and Kurt Busch next to last. Only Matt Kenseth, who finished 14th and now led all Roush drivers in the standings at 25th, might have found some small satisfaction.

Characteristically, though, Kenseth was harsh on himself. "Our Winston Cup car has been pretty dismal," he said.

Kenseth was the most laconic of the Roush racers—a reserved twenty-nine-year-old whose wry humor he mostly kept from outsiders. Handsome and blond, Kenseth derived no great pleasure from the celebrity of being a top NASCAR racer, although he fulfilled his public responsibilities without complaint during signings, interviews, and appearances for his primary sponsor, the DeWALT Industrial Tool Company, a division of Black & Decker. Kenseth's idea of a perfect evening was staying home with his wife, Katie, a lively and pretty young woman from his hometown whom he had married in the off-season. They lived near Burton on Lake Norman, but Kenseth's idea of a great place to hang out was the log cabin he and Katie were building in the woods near Canada. There, he didn't have to fret about the strangers who inevitably approached him for autographs and pictures whenever he went out in public—nor about making small talk, which was not his cup of tea, with some VIP.

On the track, Kenseth was methodical, intense, and unflappable. He arrived full-time in Winston Cup racing in 2000, after narrowly losing the Busch Grand National championship to Dale

Earnhardt Jr. the previous year. Many had assumed that Junior, then 25, who drove the No. 8 Budweiser car and made no secret of his appreciation for his sponsor's product, was all but guaranteed to be the 2000 Cup Rookie of the Year—an assumption that seemed sound when he won a Cup points race on May 6 of that year, and then The Winston, NASCAR's nonpoints all-star event, the following race weekend. But Kenseth, whose sponsor sold saws, won the next points race, Memorial Day weekend's Coca-Cola 600, NASCAR's longest event. As the 2000 season continued to unfold, Junior's partying made headlines and a film crew followed him for an MTV documentary. Kenseth quietly raced to an impressive 14th place in the overall standings, two spots above Junior—a performance that earned him the rookie title.

Jack Roush started the 2001 season expecting Kenseth to wind up inside the top ten, which would secure him a speaking role at NASCAR's annual banquet, at New York's Waldorf-Astoria Hotel. Plenty of time still remained to meet those expectations, but Kenseth was frustrated. Last year at this time, he'd already posted tenth- and sixth-place finishes—but his 14th-place showing at Bristol was his best of the 2001 season.

"You always think that you made your stuff better over the winter," Kenseth said, "and you should run better the next year. It just doesn't always turn out like that. We just need to keep working."

Like his Roush teammates, Kenseth also needed a bit of alchemy.

CHAPTER 5

A NEED FOR SPEED

On Saturday morning, March 24, the day before the Food City 500, account manager Lori Halbeisen knocked on the door of Mark Martin's motor coach, parked with those of the other drivers in a secure area adjacent to the track. Fans pressed against the fence, hoping to be acknowledged by their idols.

Halbeisen escorted Martin to a van, and a guard waved it through the gate. Martin sat in back, talking by cell phone to his wife, who was back with their son in Florida. Arlene and Matt traveled infrequently with Martin now; a season with thirty-six points races stretched on interminably, and a million-dollar motor coach, no matter how luxurious, served as a poor substitute for home. Arlene reported that Matt had overturned his tiny car the previous night in a Quarter Midget race, but he was unhurt. Martin laughed on hearing that Matt had earned the traditional "flip trophy" for his mishap—like his father, the son ordinarily finessed his races.

The van delivered Martin to a tent occupied by representatives of Pfizer Inc., the $30-billion-a-year worldwide pharmaceutical firm that was the primary sponsor of Martin's No. 6 Viagra car.

Later in the day, Pfizer professionals would conduct free health screenings for race fans in this tent. A film crew was using it this morning to tape Martin, star of a health-improvement video that Pfizer was making.

Martin left the van, greeted the excited crowd that invariably materialized wherever he went, and walked into the tent, where a blonde woman dressed in black greeted him. Hired by Pfizer to conduct the interview, producer Lori Lee Arnold towered over Martin, whose official biography listed him as five-foot-six-inches tall and weighing 130 pounds. Martin took his seat, the filmmakers ran their checks, and Arnold began asking him questions.

Without a script, Martin first expounded on the aversion many men hold for regular health checkups: "There's a little part inside that says: 'I feel fine, everything's OK, I don't want to find anything.'" Then he urged men, particularly those with wives and dependent children, to overcome their doctor fears. "Those kids need a father in their lives," Martin said.

Asked about his own prescription for health, Martin said that he lifted weights five times a week, completed a cardiovascular workout almost as often, slept about seven hours a night, tried not to worry about things beyond his control, and ate a diet low in fat and rich with fruits, vegetables, and lean meats. "I haven't had a scrambled egg or whole milk or a real potato chip for over ten years," he said. "It takes a long time to get away from Twinkies, cookies, and all those kinds of things—but today, I love what I eat." One result of Martin's regimen was 7 percent body fat, well below average for a middle-aged man.

Arnold asked Martin to name the health issues that concerned him most. The driver, who'd suffered multiple broken bones and survived numerous horrific wrecks in his nearly thirty years of racing, and who lived now with frequent back and knee pain, did not mention speed. He mentioned cancer—prostate cancer in particular.

"Those are the things that scare me," he said. "I've learned how important it is to get checkups regularly, especially if you're over thirty-five years old." The chance to promote healthy living, Martin said, had motivated him to enter into a relationship with Pfizer. He neglected to add that one exceedingly unhealthy habit, heavy drinking, had once nearly destroyed his dreams.

By any measure, Mark Martin's father, Julian, was no ordinary man. Intelligent and hard-working, he had built a successful trucking company in Batesville, Arkansas—but he was also possessed of a volatile temper and he was unusually immature. Julian drank excessively, partied enthusiastically, and enjoyed the company of women, including Mark's mother, Jackie, whom he married and divorced—twice. "He was crazy," said Mark. "My dad had some demons chasing him."

Raised in rural Arkansas, where a life worth anything in the middle of the twentieth century required wheels, Julian was driving by the age of ten. He never competed professionally, but speed intoxicated him, whether tearing up country roads alone or drag-racing against his friends well into adulthood. Inevitably, speed caused accidents, most brutally in 1971, when he crashed his motorcycle into a concrete post; more than a dozen operations later, Julian was left with a permanently disabled right knee, right ankle, and right hand. "I was extremely wild and reckless and I didn't ever feel rules were made to be followed," Julian told a biographer. "I think a thrill is worth just about any risk and the bigger the risk, the bigger the thrill."

Fathers like Julian desire fast sons, and Mark was just five when Julian stood him in his lap and gave him the wheel of a moving car; soon, with the father operating the pedals, the son was driving at seventy miles per hour and more. "The bigger he got, the faster I'd take him through the turns," Julian said. "A lot of times, he'd beg for mercy. He'd want me to slow down." But Julian didn't, and the son developed control and his own compulsion to go fast—and soon enough, to seek the greater rewards of winning at speed.

Julian took his boy to NASCAR races at Daytona and Talladega, and regularly to the local short tracks. In 1973, a year after divorcing Mark's mother for the first time, Julian bought a share in a stockcar that raced on a nearby quarter-mile dirt oval known as Locust Grove. Fourteen-year-old Mark helped out in the pits, and one afternoon he drove the car in practice. But practice laps only partly satisfied Mark; he wanted to compete, and he pestered his father to let him.

That winter, Mark and Julian salvaged a junked 1955 Chevrolet from the weeds near Julian's garage. Often working past midnight, they gutted the old hulk, built a roll cage, and installed a driver's seat in the car's center, where Julian, always a study in contradictions, believed his son would be safest. Painted bright orange, Mark Martin's first racecar debuted on April 12, 1974, at Locust Grove, where the competitors were mostly adults. Martin was just fifteen—only five feet tall and weighing one hundred pounds. He placed third and sixth in his first two races that day, and won fifty-six dollars; a week later, he scored his first victory. More followed, and the high school freshman's reputation grew. "Mark Martin of Batesville really showed some of the older boys a few things about driving a racecar Saturday night," a track promoter wrote during Martin's first season. "Mark, who looked like he might have to have a booster chair in the car seat, sure knew what it was all about." When the season ended that September, Martin had claimed the six-cylinder division state championship. The youngest champion ever, he had experienced speed's most potent high.

Racing had preoccupied the father and son at season's start, and now it consumed them. They built a better car for 1975, and Martin began competing on a larger circuit of tracks, enjoying success wherever he went. In 1977, the year he turned eighteen, Martin moved up to the American Speed Association, which staged races on tracks throughout the Midwest. Martin skipped his high school graduation in order to race, the first of several of life's milestones he sacrificed to his sport—and at season's end, he was named the ASA's Rookie of the Year. A succession of ASA championships followed, but Martin yearned for NASCAR competition—and not at the regional level. In 1981, driving a car he'd help build, Martin made five Winston Cup starts, recording a top five and two poles, and earning $13,950. At twenty-two years old, Martin believed he had arrived.

But racing is a tempestuous affair, and 1982 began a long period of heartbreak for Mark Martin.

Running his first full Cup schedule that year, Martin finished 14th in the standings and lost the Rookie of the Year contest, in which he'd been favored, to Geoffrey Bodine. His eight top-ten finishes demonstrated his potential at stockcar racing's highest level, but adversity overshadowed his successes: Equipment broke, a highway accident badly damaged his hauler, bills went unpaid, and not even the near million dollars that a desperate Julian Martin had borrowed at almost 30 percent interest could keep the collectors at bay. The 1983 Cup season was still young when, at 10 A.M. on Saturday, April 2, an auctioneer in Charlotte raised the gavel on the sale of every car, part, machine, and tool that Mark Martin Racing owned. In 1983, Martin drove in only half the Cup races, for three different owners, but none of them offered long-term promise. Nor did anyone else.

Martin had encountered misfortune before. He'd lost big races, and he'd suffered injuries, most seriously in July 1980 when a competitor in Wisconsin slammed into the driver's side of his car, breaking his left foot and ankle. Doctors placed his leg in a cast and sent him home to Arkansas with orders not to race again that season, but Martin, who was contending for his third straight ASA title, refused to indulge in a long recuperation. A month after the accident, his cast freshly removed, he returned to Wisconsin—and drove, using a hand-operated clutch, in a race made more treacherous still by rain, wind, and tornado warnings. At times during the race, Martin's leg throbbed so painfully that he radioed to his crew that he couldn't go on. "You have to do it," Julian said—and Mark did. He won the race, and, later in the year, the ASA championship.

Broken bones had healed, new contests had always beckoned; a young man who'd passed on his high school graduation in order to race had always been able to get back into his car. But as 1983 ended, Martin had no car, no owner, no sponsors, and seemingly no future in racing.

Martin's father drank, and now the son did, too.

It was at this time that Martin's sister, Glenda, mentioned her friend Arlene Everett, whom she thought Mark might want to meet. Mark was intrigued—but not Arlene, who declined the first several times that Glenda offered to arrange an introduction. A college graduate and the mother of four young daughters, Arlene was coming off her second divorce and she wasn't much interested in another man. Moreover, Glenda's brother was five years younger than she.

But Arlene finally relented, and in December 1983 she met Mark Martin at a dinner at Julian's house. The twenty-four-year-old driver surprised her—he talked easily but without conceit, and he seemed honest and generous. Unlike her two ex-husbands, Martin struck Arlene as the real deal: *He's not a fake,* she thought, *he doesn't put on.* And he didn't fit the redneck image she had of racers.

Still, Arlene was not seeking romantic involvement. Mark returned to his new home in Wisconsin after the Christmas holidays and he continued to telephone her—and she found herself talking to him for hours. She was eager to see him when he visited Arkansas again, and she accompanied him to the Daytona 500 the following February. Her first race turned out to be more enjoyable than she'd expected, and the enormous popularity of stockcar racing astounded her. But for Mark, it was another humiliating career moment: He wasn't competing in the race, and he couldn't even mingle with the drivers and owners before the green flag flew. He didn't have a garage pass.

Before meeting Arlene, Martin had been living the bachelor life—"running hard," he called it—but he had tired of that. He wanted a degree of stability, and he was instantly attracted to Arlene: She was pretty and slim, and he saw in her many of the same personality traits that she saw in him. *She's the right person for a serious relationship rather than a big party*, Martin thought. And her four young children didn't faze him, either. They married on October 27, 1984.

Without a Winston Cup slot, Martin had returned to ASA competition, but he won only a single race in 1984. He drew support from his new wife—but not sympathy. "She has not babied me," said Martin. "That was a time that I had to stand up—I had to do that myself. But I did have someone who loved me behind me."

Driving for a new owner in 1985, Martin won four ASA races, and he took his fourth ASA championship in 1986. His racing confidence restored, Martin returned full-time to NASCAR competition in 1987, driving a Ford in the Busch Grand National Series. His first win, in May, made NASCAR history, because it was the first time a Ford had won since the Busch series began, in 1982. He went on to take two more races and six poles before finishing the 1987 season in eighth. Martin was hoping to drive in Winston Cup competition the next year and he found his opportunity through owner Jack Roush, who had his sights set on NASCAR after dominating other racing circuits.

Roush in 1987 was screening drivers for his inaugural Winston Cup team—in essence, he was conducting an early version of his Gong Show. Martin's mastery of a Ford particularly impressed the owner, whose engineering firm did significant business with the automaker. And Roush appreciated Martin's attitude. Unlike some others he had interviewed, Martin asked only questions about engines, cars, tires, personnel, and testing—not the driver's salary. Roush also appreciated Martin's size. A small man himself, he believed that stature influences the boy that becomes the man. And small boys, experience had taught him, often become intensely competitive men like him.

Martin had heard about Roush since he was a child, but nothing on the dirt tracks and Saturday night ovals where Martin had learned to race had prepared him for meeting the owner, who'd once taught college physics. "The smart people that I had been around in the past were smart based on their experience at the track," Martin said. "Jack Roush could talk to you about things in words that I'd never heard—and things that totally locked me up because I hadn't been in that world. That's what struck me: 'Wow, this guy's over my head.'" But the men proved more similar in many regards than not, the born driver complementing the brilliant engineer, and Roush hired Martin for the 1988 Cup year.

But once again, Martin failed to realize his potential. He finished 1988 in 15th place, worse than his troubled 1982 Cup season, and won just $223,630, a fraction of the $1.5 million that the champion, Bill Elliott, took home. And he was still drinking, becoming so inebriated on some nights that he remembered nothing the next day. Martin never drank before driving a racecar, but challenging for a title required his full concentration on every day between races, when work at the shop and on the test track was greatly demanding.

Roush was concerned, although hardly shocked, for he knew that Martin drank when he signed him, and he had written a clause into his contract allowing him to terminate the driver in the event that his drinking proved detrimental. Roush wanted a championship, not a debacle—and especially as a newcomer to the sport, he needed smooth relations with NASCAR and the sponsor of Martin's No. 6 car, which happened, ironically, to be the Stroh Brewery Company.

Roush issued an ultimatum to his driver. "Mark," he said, "I know you've been drinking, and you know that I can't put up with it. I've either got to make a change—or you've got to communicate with me in some way that would cause me to believe, in the face of what you've been doing, that you're not going to drink anymore."

Martin, who had reasons of his own to stop drinking, pledged sobriety—from then on, speed would be his only addiction. He had started the year abandoning a diet heavy with cheeseburgers and French fries for one emphasizing nutritional foods, and now he ended it by taking his last drink and committing to an intensive daily workout regimen. A man of obsessions, Martin now indulged only those that would help him win races.

Years later, Martin reflected on alcohol: "You know, I watched my father and I said, 'I'll never do that—I'll never be like that,' when I was a kid. And one day I looked at myself and said: 'You know what? You're like that.'"

Although he never spoke of it in such terms, overcoming alcohol ranked among the great triumphs of Mark Martin's life (as it did for Julian, who eventually quit drinking, too). "I live in a warped sense of reality because of racing—everything in my life has pretty much been judged off of my performance and success on a race track," Mark said. "But I think that's very accurate in saying that was a huge triumph because lots and lots and lots of people don't close that chapter. And it tears their lives apart, it tears their families apart, it kills their dreams. It wasn't going to ruin mine."

Martin won his first Cup race in 1989, his second year with Roush, and finished third in the standings. And but for the controversial penalty that Roush would never forgive, he would have beaten Dale Earnhardt for the championship in 1990. Over the next decade, Martin finished second in the point standings twice more, and placed in the top six every year but 2000, when he was eighth. Building on Martin's success, Roush expanded from one team to the largest operation in NASCAR. By 2001, his partnership with Martin had endured for thirteen seasons, an extraordinary example of mutual loyalty in a sport where allegiances shift so swiftly that the part of each year when drivers, owners, and sponsors are jockeying for change is known as Silly Season. Roush and Martin had failed to win a title—but that was their only unrealized aspiration.

"Today I would say we're like blood brothers—because we've been there, we've wrestled it down, we know each other, we know each to the core, to the depths of our heart," said Martin. "Our hearts are very, very similar, and some of who I am today— some small part of who I am today—is from the experience that I've had with him over the past thirteen years."

When Martin's longtime sponsor Valvoline failed to renew its commitment past the 2000 season, Pfizer needed scant persuasion to back the No. 6 Ford Taurus. Martin's fitness and his longevity in a punishing sport positioned him as an ideal spokesperson for the overall "healthy living" campaign around which Pfizer marketed Viagra—and his popularity and success in NASCAR ensured high visibility in Viagra's core market, middle-aged men.

Martin, however, needed persuasion to partner with Pfizer. He feared that his fans would assume that an endorsement of Viagra implied that he used the product (he didn't), and he worried about the reactions of children—how could Mom or Dad explain that strange new word in big blue letters on their hero's car? But Geoff Smith persuaded Martin that Pfizer's free track-side screenings and overall health pitch outweighed the negatives, including the jokes, which soon enough appeared on Martin's roushracing.com bulletin board. "Did you hear about the first death from an overdose of Viagra?" went one. "A man took twelve pills and his wife died."

Dirty jokes troubled Martin less than a child's curiosity. "I can't say that it hasn't hurt me to have mothers ask me what they're supposed to tell their children," he said. "My answer is: You have to give an age-appropriate answer. I told my nine-year-old son that it was a medicine for men with a health problem. And if they're three years old, they get a different story. And if they're sixteen, they get another."

In the end, Martin remained conflicted, but he found satisfaction in the message that he delivered through television advertising, trackside screenings, and the Pfizer video that he taped that March morning in the heart of NASCAR country. The message was that kids need healthy dads.

"Valvoline is popular—but it ain't important, not like a kid having a father," Martin said. "That's how I've accepted it and that's how I've handled the pain and disappointment that I've had to suffer—through the triumph and the importance of the good things that we've been able to do with it."

Jack Roush was fielding just Mark Martin's team in NASCAR when he named Geoff Smith to head Roush Racing. Smith had been Roush's business lawyer for most of the 1980s, but his entrepreneurial ambition spurred him to sell his Michigan law practice. Success on the track would remain Roush's purview, but Smith would direct marketing, licensing, merchandising, and sponsorships. An erudite man by nature, Smith was one of a handful of managers who sought to reshape the business side of a one-time redneck sport.

Smith spoke the language of corporate America, and he would organize Roush Racing like a prosperous independent firm. He hired people with college degrees, rewarding their long hours and weekend duties with competitive salaries, bonuses, and company cars. Image mattered: Smith's people wore business attire, and his headquarters featured polished woods, a glass-walled conference room, and framed photographs of many of Jack Roush's hundreds of wins during a lifetime of racing. Except for the photos and the displays of diecast toy cars and other collectibles that Smith's group produced, a visitor to Roush Racing's offices might not have guessed the purpose of the venture. It could have been the offices of an investment bank.

Smith knew how Silly Season could wreak havoc with financing, so he pursued long-term, stable sponsorships with corporations run by executives like him. Experience had taught him the importance of being valued, and so he offered sponsors more than candy-colored decals for the millions of dollars they paid each year to back a Roush car. Smith staged Roush sponsor summits, which were strategic planning sessions scheduled around golf, cocktails, dinners, and twilight cruises. He devoted a section of the slickly designed roushracing.com Web site to sponsors. And never underestimating the return that a few minutes' contact with a driver could bring, Smith made sure the VIPs received the coveted garage and pit passes. In this world, an encounter with a Mark Martin—or a Jeff Burton, Matt Kenseth, or Kurt Busch—was akin to meeting Shaquille O'Neill. More than one executive regressed into a wide-eyed little boy when shaking the hand of a celebrity driver.

Star quality enveloped Jack Roush himself, whose prominence in automobile racing extended back to the 1960s, when he and fellow Ford Motor Company employees competed with a drag-racing team they called The Fastbacks. Recognizing the cachet in his boss's name, Smith determined to establish it as a brand—a cause in which Roush's distinctive fedora became the logo. One result was J.R.'s Garage, a retail sales business that reached customers online, at trackside trailers, and in stores.

By June 2000, a decade after it opened with a single staff member, Smith's division had grown to fifty employees, excluding the racing teams. Roush Racing's revenues had increased from $5 million to more than $100 million and were still rising. Smith's responsibilities included not only marketing and sponsorships, but also administration of the racing teams and drivers' contracts. And in June 2000, the contracts of two drivers, the underperforming Chad Little and Kevin Lepage, were much on Smith's mind.

Jack Roush was inclined to give Lepage the rest of the 2000 season to see if he could turn things around—but he had already decided to replace Little with Kurt Busch, and that had created a potentially delicate situation with Little's primary sponsor, Deere & Company, the $13-billion-a-year Illinois-based manufacturer of John Deere tractors and other agricultural and industrial equipment. Deere executives liked Little: He was a personable family man who almost certainly was the only Cup competitor ever to earn a law degree before racing full-time, and he was also a hit at Deere functions and on race mornings working the crowd inside the hospitality tent.

But Roush and Smith managed to convince the Deere executives that Little no longer served Deere's purpose: Never winning, and rarely running near the front, the driver gave the company less media exposure than a multimillion-dollar investment warranted. Kurt Busch, however, was no easy sell—after all, he was a kid who less than a year before had been living with his parents. So Roush and Smith emphasized Busch's talent and potential— the "blue sky" they called it. "If it were my money," Roush told the Deere executives, "I'd put it on Kurt Busch."

In the end, Deere agreed. Smith began drafting a new sponsor contract, and after Roush informed Little that he was being let go, Smith began negotiating a settlement with the driver. Gone were the days when a driver and an owner shook hands and went racing. By June 2000, a driver contract numbered many pages and covered every detail of salary, prize money distribution, licensing royalties, public conduct, sponsorship obligations, and termination, among a myriad of other subjects.

By the end of June, Deere and Roush Racing had agreed on a document binding Deere to Busch for the 2001, 2002, and 2003 seasons. Once Little had settled with Roush Racing, the document would be signed.

But summer progressed without Little settling. Meanwhile, unknown to outsiders, the new chairman and chief executive office of Deere, Robert W. Lane, had decided he had to act drastically to shore up the company's stock, which had dropped from nearly $50 a share in May to barely $30 in August—and which Bear Stearns and Morgan Stanley Dean Witter had downgraded. Lane was cutting tens of millions of dollars in costs, and one of them was the NASCAR sponsorship.

In late August, a Deere executive telephoned Smith with the news.

"This is when I got my lesson on how the price of corn affects my ability to get a Winston Cup sponsor," said Smith. "They said basically that when commodity prices are low because there's been a long-term, worldwide glut—production success—the farmers can't make any profit, and when they don't make profit from their growth crops, they don't buy (machines)."

Deere executives were honorable, however, and they accepted Smith's argument that backing out now jeopardized chances of quickly finding another sponsor for Busch and the No. 97 car, since by late summer, most corporations have already drafted their budgets for the next fiscal year and a $10 or $12 million outlay can hardly be paid out of petty cash. So Deere confidentially agreed to fund the car through 2001, or until a sponsor was secured. Smith, meanwhile, finally reached a settlement with Little, who spent Silly Season seeking a new Cup owner. (None wanted him, and he would begin 2001 in the Busch Grand National Series.)

Given the luxury of having funding for Busch's car through 2001, Smith felt no pressure seeking Deere's successor; he could afford to reject candidates who might argue that Busch's inexperience should command a substantial sponsorship discount. No new sponsor had surfaced when 2001 began, but Smith was not concerned. He had time on his side—and a clever form of advertising, an attention-getting white fire suit and white car. "There's an empathy that's created when there's an unsponsored car from the media," he said. "The poor rookie and the poor team that didn't have the money, you know." White also symbolized Busch's potential. "It was a blank canvas," said Smith. "People didn't know Kurt as a person at all and his image would be largely developed through this next two, three years' worth of sponsorship activity and marketing and PR activity. He carried no baggage from another sponsor." He was not, for example, the Coors driver switching to M&Ms.

In January, Smith received word that a Cup sponsorship interested Joseph Galli Jr., the new president and CEO of Newell Rubbermaid Inc., a $7 billion consumer products giant that counted Rubbermaid, Little Tikes, Graco, and Sharpie pens among its brands. Galli had previously worked for Black & Decker, the parent company of DeWALT, the primary sponsor of Matt Kenseth's car, so he knew the benefits of investing in NASCAR. Where specifically to invest was another matter. Besides Roush, Galli's lieutenants explored opportunities with owners Richard Childress, Rick Hendrick, and Joe Gibbs. Then, the week before the Daytona 500, Smith invited Newell Rubbermaid executives to be his guests in Florida. There, in the privacy of Jack Roush's hospitality tent, Smith brought the executives together with Jack and his Cup drivers, crew chiefs, and engineers, all of whom spoke enthusiastically of the white-uniformed driver's ability and promise—the blue sky. Although Busch went on to wreck in the Daytona 500, the fact that he ran with Earnhardt for much of the race impressed them. So did Busch's personality.

Before February was out, Galli had decided to bet on the kid.

Roush left Bristol Motor Speedway that last Sunday in March convinced he had to replace Matt Chambers as the crew chief for Kurt Busch. The issue was not NASCAR's suspension but rather Chambers's lack of experience in Winston Cup racing. In deciding the previous year to promote Chambers from the Craftsman Truck Series, Roush of course knew that pairing a rookie Cup crew chief with a rookie Cup driver could invite trouble—but Chambers's success in Truck racing, the bond he and Busch shared, and the chance for him to prove himself persuaded Roush to give him the job. Roush believed in opportunity.

But he did not believe in endless opportunity.

Watching the Food City 500 disaster unfold, Roush had concluded that Chambers's inexperience had been a factor in Busch driving cars with inferior setups (the adjustments of suspension, sway bar, weight distribution, tire pressure, and the like)—and that inferior setups had contributed to Busch crashing, since a rookie frustrated with his car's handling is prone to overreact. "The rationale for his wrecking the cars," said Roush, "would be when his prospects were so far diminished from his expectations that he just had to grit his teeth and set his jaw and make his knuckles white and drive off into oblivion—that's what drivers do a lot, out of frustration."

Concerned also about team chemistry, an intangible element that profoundly affects on-track performance, Roush also intended to fire a crew member who, he'd been told, had been politicking for Chambers's job. Before making his moves, Roush slept on it—two nights—and then, on his regular Tuesday trip from Michigan to North Carolina, he confirmed his decision with Harry McMullen, general manager of the No. 97 team, and Robbie Reiser, Matt Kenseth's crew chief and a sort of mentor to Chambers. Then he drove north to the track in Martinsville, Virginia, where Busch's team was testing cars.

Busch agreed with Roush's decision to fire the crew member, but he pleaded for another chance for his chief, who had helped him to such success in his Rookie-of-the-Year Truck season. Roush did not relent. He offered Chambers a demotion to car chief, one step below crew chief, but Chambers wasn't interested. He then offered Chambers a job back in Michigan with the Truck program—but Chambers had relocated to North Carolina and he didn't want that, either. So he left Roush Racing, to become crew chief for another Cup rookie, Jason Leffler, who drove the No. 01 Cingular Wireless car, which had been Kenny Irwin Jr.'s before he died.

Always an expeditious man, Roush had gone to Martinsville with the man he'd picked to be Chambers's replacement: Ben Leslie, the car chief for Matt Kenseth, who shared a shop with Busch. A man of few words, the twenty-eight-year-old Leslie had served as a crew chief before (for former Roush racer Johnny Benson), and his wife, Shelley, coordinated the Roush teams' travel. Busch had once yelled at Shelley when he was dissatisfied with a travel arrangement she had made for him, thereby earning Leslie's disfavor; Busch, in return, had avoided Leslie, considering him "a hard ass and a guy who didn't want to talk to anybody." Now Roush had married them.

The new team debuted the next weekend, at Texas Motor Speedway near Fort Worth, host of the Harrah's 500 race. Leslie had changed the setup of Busch's car—and Busch noticed the difference on his first practice lap.

It feels right, he thought, *this car's fast.* Leslie, it seemed, knew his stuff.

Meanwhile, after weeks of final negotiations, Busch's new sponsorship was ready to be announced. On the morning of the Harrah's 500, Sunday, April 1, Roush, Smith, Busch, Leslie, and Newell Rubbermaid executives gathered at the Texas Motor Speedway media center with word that for the next three years, Busch would drive the No. 97 Sharpie Rubbermaid Ford Taurus; for now, at least, Galli had decided to emphasize his housewares and pen brands, with smaller decals on Busch's car representing other Newell Rubbermaid brands. NASCAR drivers needed no introduction to Sharpies—many of them already carried the pens to sign their autographs in permanent ink.

Roush and Newell Rubbermaid were still refining the car's red, black, and blue color scheme, and the final version would not be unveiled until the following week. Nor were the new uniforms yet available. Still, Busch expressed relief to be shedding his white—clever marketing device that it was, it had made him feel like an orphan in an arena of color and hype. "To have Sharpie Rubbermaid and a pretty car—I'm done with this white-out stuff," he told a reporter.

In his faster car, Busch had practiced and qualified well, and he started his first race with his new sponsor in 16th place. He was running strong when, on the fifth lap, Michael Waltrip lost control of his car—immediately in front of him. In that instant decision afforded a driver at full throttle, Busch had one option if he was to have any chance of avoiding a wreck: Veer left, into an empty section of infield. He cut the wheel, and his car spun sideways at nearly 200 miles per hour.

Grass and dirt flew, but somehow Busch kept his car from overturning. On it went, twirling through the infield—now hurtling toward his own pit stall, where the Newell Rubbermaid contingent watched, horrified, as their blue-sky investment seemed poised to send them to heaven.

With feet to spare, Busch pulled it out; his car undamaged, he stood on the gas and sped back into the race. He was in last place now.

But by driving smartly, executing flawless pit stops, and taking advantage of the Leslie's improved setup, Busch climbed back into contention. Eventually, he was running in the top ten—and he challenged for the lead during the final minutes, even passing Jeff Gordon on the next-to-last lap. Busch finished fourth, the best performance of his Cup career, and he rose four positions in the points standings, to 30th. He also gained on Kevin Harvick, who finished seventh, in the Rookie of the Year contest.

"It was good to get back up front again—to be familiar with what was going on," Busch said. "The race up there at the front reminded me of the times when I had to use my brain to actually think like a racer. . . . There's give and take and I felt the respect of the top five racecar drivers for that day. It was just the warm, fuzzy feeling you get when you're proud that something was accomplished."

Leslie told a reporter: "Kurt, he's a helluva wheelman."

But the rest of the Roush team lagged. Jack Roush had come to Dallas as the most successful owner in Texas Motor Speedway's four years of operation, with six wins in NASCAR's top three divisions—but Mark Martin finished 9th in the Harrah's 500, Jeff Burton 19th, and Matt Kenseth 20th. All three climbed in the standings, but the highest, Martin, still stood at only 22nd. At 35th, Burton ranked behind Busch—and he was a depressing 521 points behind Dale Jarrett, the standings leader and winner of the Harrah's 500. Something was still amiss at Roush Racing—and elsewhere in NASCAR. While Jarrett led in the points and Gordon stood second, the rest of the top ten included such unlikely contenders as Bobby Hamilton, who at this stage the year before was ranked 30th, and Bristol winner Elliott Sadler, 29th through seven races in 2000. Former Roush driver Lepage, who had found a new owner, finished the Harrah's 500 in 11th place—but Bobby Labonte came in next to last after his engine blew, and he dropped six places in the point standings, to 25th.

Inside Roush Racing, some drivers and crew members were beginning to criticize their engines. No one had forgotten the three failures in Atlanta, and NASCAR testing after the Harrah's 500 disclosed that Mark Martin's motor was producing some fifty horsepower less than Jarrett's, built by Robert Yates, one of Jack Roush's longtime rivals. Busch's engine lagged by thirty horsepower, which might have been sufficient for him to win.

Unlike those in Formula One racing, where state-of-the-art technology was demanded, the basic design of a Winston Cup engine had changed little since the 1950s, when NASCAR founder Bill France Sr. had decided on his winning format. Like a production automobile from the Elvis era, a modern Winston Cup engine featured eight cylinders arranged in a "V"; a displacement of about 355 cubic inches; a carburetor, not fuel injection; and a decades-old ignition system that was distributor-based, not electronic. NASCAR strictly enforced the fundamentals of this old-fashioned design—but it permitted experimentation in certain other components of an engine (intake manifolds, for example), and it was in these areas that the best engine-builders, working in secrecy, coaxed superior power out of their V-8 motors. During Roush's thirteen years in NASCAR racing, the average output of a Cup engine had increased from less than 650 to nearly 800 horse-power, some four to five times greater than that of a car that the everyday person drove. The intense competition at NASCAR's highest level was behind this never-ending spiral.

Jack Roush was furious after Texas. That week, he gathered his engine specialists to express his displeasure. "If we don't fix this," he said, "I'll go to one of the other shops that sell engines or lease engines and I'll put you guys out of business."

Most doubted Roush actually would, but no one was foolish enough to test their belief: Like an artist with a painting, Roush put part of his soul into his engines, and he demanded that his employees do the same. The motor-builders got very busy.

At Martinsville, the site of the next race, the Virginia 500, held on Sunday, April 8, durability more than power or fuel economy was the demand on motors. The constant braking and sudden acceleration at the half-mile oval punished engines (and brakes), and the track's small size concentrated the heat from the sun and the exhaust. Engines at Martinsville were prone to overheating and failure, but the ones that Roush's builders had prepared for the race would prove their worth.

Though brake failure cost Busch a chance of winning the Virginia 500, his engine ran well and he finished ahead of Harvick. Mark Martin, whose last win had been at the spring 2000 race at Martinsville, ran near the front and even captured the lead before hitting the wall and crashing out just past the halfway point of the race. Kenseth scored his best finish of the year, sixth, and he now led all Roush racers in the points standings, at 17th—not where he wanted to be in his sophomore year, but respectable.

But it was Jeff Burton who delivered the most welcome news to Roush. After qualifying near the front of the pack, a rare occurrence for him, he went on to place third in the Virginia 500, which Jarrett won. "We're gonna get down now, this is what the 99 can do," Burton told reporters after the race. "Here's the start of our season." Burton did not tell reporters about the good luck charm a crew member had given him, and which he now carried inside the cockpit of his car. It was the baculum of a raccoon, a slim bone that supports the penis, which some Appalachian hill people hold capable of working magic.

Teresa Earnhardt didn't travel to Martinsville, but a representative conveying a plea from her did. Acting with unusual speed after the widow's public plea at Las Vegas, the Florida legislature had just passed a law banning the release of autopsy photos without a judge's order, and Governor Jeb Bush had immediately signed it, with Teresa standing at his side. But a Web site and three newspapers, including *The Orlando Sentinel,* had challenged the new law's constitutionality—and once again, Mrs. Earnhardt hoped to sway public sentiment.

"As grateful as we are to the Florida legislature and Governor Bush for their sensible approach to protecting an individual's right to privacy, I want to let the NASCAR community and the people of Florida know just how much pain this is causing my family," Mrs. Earnhardt said in her statement. "Each day we are faced with new threats that these photos will wind up on the Internet. We just want it to end. No one should be subjected to the kind of harassment and torment to which we are by the media."

The two weeks between Martinsville and the next race, at Talladega, brought further developments. Before the new Florida law had passed, the court-ordered mediator had permitted the medical expert hired by *The Sentinel* to examine the photos—behind the closed doors of the coroner's office. On April 9, Dr. Barry S. Myers, a crash-injury specialist at Duke University who held a medical degree and a doctorate in biomedical engineering, released the findings of his investigation.

Myers downplayed NASCAR's suggestion that seat belt failure had contributed to Earnhardt's death, instead concluding that the violent whipping motion of the driver's head had fractured the base of his skull, shearing blood vessels and damaging the brain stem, which controls breathing and other essential bodily functions. Myers did not maintain that a HANS or similar device would have saved Earnhardt, but he did note that head restraints can prevent basilar skull fractures.

On the day that Myers's report was released, NASCAR issued its first formal statement about its own investigation. Calling safety its "top priority," NASCAR said: "The accident-reconstruction review is being conducted by a team of experts from around the country with the cooperation of NASCAR officials, including an internationally-respected occupant-safety restraint analysis and research corporation; independent experts in crash investigation and data analysis from a nationally recognized automobile crash analysis and research facility; and medical/biomechanical engineering specialists. The review is well underway and will be comprised of numerous steps, including but not limited to crash model development and testing; crash model simulation; sled and real crash tests; impact barrier testing; data analysis and cross check; and biomechanical/medical analysis."

The statement read as if it had been written by someone who believed big words were the close ally of clever obfuscation. A NASCAR official recited it during a conference call to reporters, then took no questions.

Inevitably, a fresh round came to mind: Who were these independent experts and internationally respected firms? Under the new law, would they be denied access to the autopsy photos? Their conclusions, NASCAR said, would not be available before August—Why so long, when Myers had required only a few weeks for his study? Would NASCAR's report be released to the public? And did Petty, Irwin, and Roper matter—or had they been forgotten, the lessons of their accidents buried with them, their deaths in vain?

If NASCAR officials hoped their statement would defuse their crisis, covered now by the national press, they were disappointed. "If there is such a doubt about NASCAR today," wrote a columnist for the *St. Petersburg Times,* "president Mike Helton and his officers need to realize they have invited it. The more you refuse to say anything, the more people think something is there." And this was a subdued voice. In his weekly list of "12 Random Items from the World of NASCAR," longtime motorsports writer Monte Dutton listed reasons NASCAR's investigation would take months. "Long line of NASCAR officials at polygraph test station," was one. "Fan claims guy sitting next to him looked just like Lee Harvey Oswald," was another.

Among the most stinging criticism was that from a source NASCAR could not dismiss as the disgruntled press: Darrell Waltrip. "NASCAR talks about it but they haven't gone nearly far enough to make it safer for drivers," the three-time Cup champion told a writer for Nashville's *The Tennessean.* "If they had really gotten serious about this and taken steps to make it safer, Dale would be alive today."

The Easter holiday passed, the dreaded Talladega approached, and NASCAR's public relations disaster deepened.

*

When he decided to build the world's fastest stockcar speedway, NASCAR founder William H. G. France chose a location in rural Alabama on the road from Birmingham to Atlanta. Legend held that part of the site had once been an old Indian burial ground, but superstition didn't deter France. His marketing instincts told him that two major cities with a broad expanse of old Confederate turf in between would pack a NASCAR racetrack. Extreme speed would establish the track's reputation internationally.

Talladega closely resembled the lightning-fast Daytona International Speedway—but with more steeply banked turns (33 degrees, versus 31 for Daytona) and slightly greater length (2.66 miles, longest of any Cup track), it allowed greater speed. Talladega Superspeedway quickly fulfilled France's ambitions. Within a year of its opening in 1969, Buddy Baker became the first driver in history to break the 200-mile-per-hour barrier on a closed course. Five years later, Mark Donohue, a Brown University graduate who enjoyed success in NASCAR, Indianapolis, Trans-Am, and other racing (and who died, in 1975, while practicing for a Formula One event in Austria), set a world closed-course record (in a 12-cylinder Porsche, not a stockcar) of 221.160 miles per hour at Talladega.

In 1987, Bill Elliott established the world stockcar speed record when he circled Talladega at 212.809 mph during qualifying competition for that year's Winston 500—a record that still stands. Fans marveled at Elliott, the one-time Cup champion who was nicknamed "Awesome Bill from Dawsonville," Georgia, but the 1987 race itself demonstrated the danger of such speed. On the twenty-second lap, a tire on Bobby Allison's car blew. As his son, Davey, the race's eventual winner, watched in his rearview mirror, Allison's car spun backward and lifted into the air, clearing the wall before the catch fencing along the main grandstand pulled it back to earth. Allison was not seriously hurt, nor were any spectators, but the crash convinced France's successor, his son Bill Jr., that it was only a matter of time before injury or death—and lawsuits—resulted from races that were run at speeds faster than small airplanes could fly.

Bill France Jr. could not easily or cheaply rebuild the track, so instead he slowed the cars raced at Talladega by reducing horse-power (with so-called restrictor plates that reduce the flow of air to the engine) and by increasing drag (with roof- and rear-mounted spoilers, and other aerodynamic changes). Spectators would be safer, but not necessarily drivers: With less power to pull away from competitors, cars tended to bunch up, and the aerodynamic phenomenon known as draft further compressed the field.

The track that allegedly stood on an Indian burial ground scared many drivers, and Jeff Burton was one of them. "I don't get nervous for very many races," he said, just before Easter. "I do get nervous before Talladega. I think all the drivers do."

Like any automobile racer, Burton had reached an accommo-dation with the risks of his profession. An ingenious man who remembered the misery of a broken back, he'd modified his seat and cockpit to increase his chances of walking away from a wreck, and he'd recently invested $100,000 of his own money to test a seat that might benefit him and his colleagues. He wore a Hutchens head restraint system (it was similar to the HANS), and, like Mark Martin, he stayed physically fit. Since the deaths of Petty and Irwin, he'd pressured NASCAR, publicly and behind the scenes, to improve safety. Nearly two months later, the death of Dale Earnhardt, who'd ridiculed him as a "candy ass" for his safety preoccupation, infuriated Burton.

"A lot of attention has been paid on this thing since Earnhardt got killed," Burton said, "but the real problem—what to me con-firmed that we have a problem with basal skull fractures was when Kenny got killed and when Adam got killed. Everybody wanted to say that was a fluke—that's bullshit. There's no flukes. You don't in a fluke have a basal skull fracture. That's how people try to rationalize it: 'Well, that was just a fluke.' NASCAR is doing that today. They'll say everything went wrong that could have gone wrong for Earnhardt to die. They're full of shit.

"We have a problem and they don't want to own up to it, they don't want to help fix the problem. They're spending a lot of money and a lot of time figuring what happened to Earnhardt. Well, they didn't spend a dime figuring what happened to Adam Petty. It's a bunch of shit. What they need to do instead of figuring out what happened to Earnhardt—what they need to do is figure out how to prevent a basal skull fracture, 'cause that's what's killing them."

Beyond advocacy, Burton philosophized; he understood that life entails choices, and that he chose to race. "I spend a tremendous amount of time thinking about how to make it safer," he said. "I don't spend much time thinking about what's the consequences of it not being safe. Maybe I don't want to know. Maybe I'm just better off ignoring it."

That was a bit of dark humor: He didn't ignore it, of course. "I'm not afraid of dying," Burton said. "I'm afraid of leaving my family without a father, without a husband. That's the only thing that bothers me about if something were to happen to me: my children having to deal with that, my wife having to deal with that, my parents, my brothers."

Burton couldn't specify exactly when, but he foresaw the day when he would decide racing's risks outweighed its benefits, and when that day came, he would quit; he would not follow the path set by drivers like Earnhardt, who drove as they neared or passed fifty.

"I think that at some point you start understanding that it's not just about going fast and winning a race—there's other things in life that are more important. That starts weighing on you—not weighing on you, but you start to understand there is a danger in what we do the older you get. That's why I won't do it [overly] long. 'Cause I know that when I'm forty years old I won't be as effective as I am at thirty-three."

Concerned that Burton's impassioned public safety advocacy might affect his performance—and, perversely, increase the very risk that he sought to reduce—Jack Roush asked Burton before

Talladega to consider toning down his statements to the media. So did Bill France Jr. Burton agreed. "I've kind of made a new rule to myself," he said before heading south. "I'm not going to talk about Earnhardt or safety issues or any of those things at the racetrack. It gets me off kilter." Away from the track, however, Burton intended to maintain his high profile on issues affecting drivers' lives.

But reporters had safety in mind at Talladega, and the issue dominated press conferences and interviews with other drivers before the race.

"This is one place the good Lord didn't give us enough eyes," said Dale Jarrett, the points leader.

"It is going to be packs and packs of cars on top of each other—a madhouse," said Bill Elliott. "You hope and pray nothing happens during the race. You take forty-three cars, put them together for 500 miles and somebody has a flat tire, a blown engine, whatever, it can cause a problem. You can't run that long for that many laps without somebody making a mistake. You just hope you're not part of that mistake."

Earnhardt himself had won ten Cup races at Talladega, including one the previous fall, when he staged a run from eighteenth to first on the final five laps—a dramatic comeback that his fans still stirringly recounted. Asked if returning to Talladega without The Intimidator concerned him, Elliott said yes. "I think we all are," he said. "I think it brings reality out what happened to the last four drivers over the last year."

But profit remained another reality, and Bill France Jr. was reluctant to tamper with success. Every week of the 2001 season had brought record TV audiences to the Fox broadcasts, and International Speedway Corp., the public arm of the France family empire and owner of Talladega Superspeedway, had closed out the previous year's books with revenues of $440 million, up from $299 million in 1999. A share of ISC stock now traded in the mid-$40s, up about $10 from the previous autumn. When managed properly, speed sold, something that drivers, regardless of their safety concerns, also understood.

"There is really nothing you can do about it," said Tony Stewart when asked about the possibility of a big wreck at Talladega. "You do the best you can and we do it to put on a good show for these fans. None of us are going to let those people down."

Kurt Busch arrived in Alabama refreshed from his Easter break, which he had spent back in Las Vegas with his family and Melissa, who was about to graduate from high school—and who would soon move east to live with her racer boyfriend. Busch was optimistic about his chances at the track that proclaimed itself "Big and Bold" in its advertisements. He had never driven at Talladega, not even in a pre-race test, and at more than two-and-a-half miles, the track was too long to walk—so he hitched a slow ride in a pace car to make acquaintance with its bumps, banking, surface, and turns. Busch was continuing his education in advanced NASCAR racing.

The rookie's first drive on Talladega, during practice, reminded him of his earliest racing, when speed in and of itself could still thrill. "It's a kick in the ass the first few laps," Busch said. "It just feels like I could put aside any troubles or any happiness or any thoughts whatsoever and just enjoy the moment. It's me and the race track, pure silence. It's like a roller coaster the first time."

Busch's car for the Talladega 500 was brand new, and Leslie had put it in fine race trim. Busch qualified only in 27th place—but he was the fastest of anyone, 192.5 miles per hour, in one of the weekend's three practices, and that thrilled him, too. "Talladega—this is the biggest, the baddest, the meanest!" he said. "I'm a twenty-two-year-old living a dream." But Busch was not reckless. Racing's dangers had profoundly impressed him several years earlier, when his father broke his neck in a racecar. "That's when I put every safety device I could find in my car that I was comfortable with," he said. Before Daytona, he'd ordered a HANS device.

On race morning, smoke from campfires hung low over the Talladega infield, where thousands of bleary-eyed men and women, some accompanied by children, were crawling forth from their tents, campers, and RVs. Talladega traditionally drew the most brazen crowds in Cup racing, prompting authorities to operate a jail on the premises throughout a race weekend. Within days of the Talladega 500, pictures of naked women swilling beer with potbellied, ponytailed men would appear on the Internet; in the background of many of the shots, Confederate and Dale Earnhardt flags flew. Such was the fruit of the Frances' labor.

Worlds away, Jeff Burton awoke in his motor coach at about 5:30 A.M., and by 8 A.M. he was holding court in his hauler. Like a high school kid about to take the stage on Talent Night, he hummed with nervous energy.

Studious for a moment, Burton discussed the always provocative issue of whether racecar drivers are athletes. Not like basketball players, he told a public relations specialist hired by CITGO who was preparing an article on his health habits, but could an NBA star keep his wits for four straight hours in the confinement of a stockcar, where the temperature could surpass 140 degrees? As he spoke, Burton was cutting up Styrofoam coffee cups, which he would place inside the heels of the heat shields he wore over his race shoes. Stockcar exhaust pipes run directly beneath a driver, and even with double protection blistering often results— a fact Burton demonstrated by taking off his socks to reveal calluses on both of his feet. Even the carbon monoxide accumulating from so many engines could be a hazard. At Martinsville, where exhaust tends to build up, racers had conducted post-race interviews while receiving intravenous fluids and oxygen.

But Burton did not remain serious for long; energy brings out the comedian in him. Wielding one of the golf clubs that his crew chief, Frank Stoddard, had received for his thirty-third birthday two days earlier, Burton jokingly threatened account manager Becky Hanson, who managed the never-ending media, appearance, and sponsor demands from which Burton hoped someday to periodically escape on his own yacht. He joshed the CITGO public relations specialist, telling her that steroids constituted part of his diet, and that his small stature (five-foot-seven, 150 pounds) meant that he was "genetically challenged." Peering through the hauler window at a large-breasted woman who was standing near Jack Roush, Burton noted that it would require effort to keep his own eyes from straying were he talking to her. But he joked about what Roush might say if introduced to the woman: "Let's talk airplanes."

The morning passed. Burton left his hauler to check on his car and visit driver John Andretti, one of his best friends, returning by 11 A.M. for the No. 99 team meeting. Stoddard began with instructions on how to escape the track after the race ended, when a traffic jam lasting into the night would clog roads.

"Sometimes this is our biggest strategy here!" whispered engine specialist Mike Messick.

Stoddard moved on to matters more directly related to racing: With as many as thirty or more cars coming in at once for tires and fuel, he warned that pit stops could be unusually chaotic. But Stoddard had faith in his team, which numbered seventeen men on race days. "Pit stops have been pretty good all year," he said. "We'll have to continue that today."

Chris Farrell, Burton's spotter, voiced his concern about a section of track that was difficult to see from the distance, but the driver put him at ease. "Like I said," Burton declared, "I drive the car. If I go in there and cause a wreck, it's my fault."

The meeting ended. "All right guys," Stoddard said, "let's get it done today. Be safe."

At the regular drivers' meeting that followed, Mike Helton urged unusual concentration and courtesy on the track today; he wanted the drivers to be safe, and it went without saying that another disaster could have dire consequences for NASCAR. Saturday had brought a reminder of Talladega's danger: In the Subway 300, a Busch Grand National Series race, fears of the big wreck had materialized on lap 87, when fifteen cars crashed. The drivers escaped injury—but only by means of a miracle, many believed.

Kim Burton was among those with that belief, and as she escorted her husband to his racecar, she expressed anger at NASCAR for refusing to modify the restrictor-plate and aerodynamic rules for the Talladega 500. Like Jeff, safety had long been on her mind—more so as marriage and motherhood had changed her perception of racing's risks. She said: "When you're young, you think: 'Well, if you live right—if you have your priorities in perspective and all of that is good—then nothing bad is going to happen to you.' But that's not always true. Things can happen to good people—bad things."

The death of Dale Earnhardt, who liked to tease her about boats, deflated a rationalization many like her had embraced. "He supposedly was the best," said Kim. "He supposedly had the best equipment."

Kim contrasted racers to professional basketball players, who enjoy cycles of success and failure—but whose lives or minds are rarely at risk. "They only have the competitive ups and downs," she said, "they don't have the worry. They're not going to have their whole life taken from them. They might have their career taken from them if they break their leg in the wrong place—but they won't have their mental capacity taken away."

Kim maintained equanimity by reminding herself that racing was her husband's passion, and that his success had brought her family many of the good things in life. "I want him to do what he wants to do," Kim said. "This makes him happy and he's able to provide for our family what we need. You only live once, and going to work has to be enjoyable. I can't imagine going to work seven days a week, eight hours a day, and not liking it.

"So that's one way. The other way is I never let myself go too

Jack Roush, with his brother and friends, on the go-cart he built when he was a boy in Ohio.

Car owner Jack Roush today, wearing his signature fedora.

Kurt Busch at the start of his rookie Winston Cup season. Lacking a primary sponsor, he wore a white firesuit.

Mark Martin, Jack Roush's original Cup driver, and one of the most successful NASCAR racers ever.

Jeff Burton, picked by many as the favorite to win the Winston Cup title in 2001.

Matt Kenseth, who beat Dale Earnhardt Jr. to become the 2000 Cup Rookie of the Year.

Dale Earnhardt, the fearless driver known as The Intimidator, and Jeff Burton run side-by-side at Daytona in the opening race of the 2001 season.

Caught in the big wreck of the Daytona 500, Jeff Burton sits in his car as his crew makes repairs.

Dale Earnhardt died in this crash on the last turn of the last lap of the 2001 Daytona 500.

A year after Earnhardt's death, a statue of The Intimidator was unveiled outside Daytona International Speedway.

Jack Roush with Kurt Busch's white No. 97 car at the UAW–DaimlerChrysler 400, Busch's first Cup race in his hometown of Las Vegas, March 4, 2001.

Kevin Harvick, Dale Earnhardt's successor, was Kurt Busch's chief rival for Rookie of the Year.

Mark Martin gets ready to race at the Food City 500 at Bristol Motor Speedway on March 25, 2001.

Jeff Gordon won six races and his fourth Winston Cup championship in 2001.

Kim Burton, Jeff's wife. They began dating when he was in high school in their hometown of South Boston, Virginia.

Kurt Busch and girlfriend Melissa Schaper, in their motor coach in the summer of 2001.

far up or too far down. Because if you do, you could drive your-self crazy."

As he strapped himself into his car, Kurt Busch was mindful of his only other Cup race on a superspeedway. He hoped to redeem himself from his 41st-place finish in the Daytona 500—and so did Bruce Hayes, his spotter.

"All right pardner, couple of deep breaths, make sure your belts are tight, and let's go do it," Hayes said over the radio as the drivers started their engines.

"Thanks for a good car, guys," said Busch. "We're going to take care of it."

Busch advanced through the field swiftly, reaching fifth place about a third of the way into the race. "I'm riding around with the top down," he radioed. "Feelin' good!"

"Nice and smooth," Hayes said on the next lap, when Busch had reached fourth. "It's all single-file behind you. Just nice and smooth."

Three laps later, Busch was in second.

The next lap, 79, he took first.

"Clear all around," said Hayes. "How's she feel?"

It felt terribly exciting. For the first time in his Winston Cup career, Busch was leading, the decal-covered cars of his every competitor visible only in his rearview mirror, the road ahead promising pure speed. "What a sensational feeling to have all of the colors behind me!" Busch later reflected. "It was as if the world had changed to black and white. All that I could see was the asphalt and the concrete wall."

A few laps later, Busch lost the lead but stayed near the front of the pack. With just twenty laps to go, he was running in sec-ond place, followed by Mark Martin in fourth and Jeff Burton in fifth. Sitting on her husband's pit cart, Kim Burton chewed a pen. But so far, no one had wrecked.

"You're doing great, Kurt," radioed Leslie. "Stay lined up and we'll burn some laps off."

"Just hold a pretty wheel," said Hayes.

With four laps remaining, Busch was running second. Watching from atop Martin's cart, Jack Roush thought his rookie could win.

But suddenly, the No. 55 car of Bobby Hamilton was closing in.

"He's coming!" said Hayes. "That 55's coming! Outside. Outside! Still there. Still there!"

Busch tried to hold off Hamilton, who was twice his age. The cars roared past pit road to begin the final lap. The flagman signaled a clear track.

"White flag—white flag, my brother!" said Hayes. "Nice and easy. Fifty-five is charging, 8 on the outside. Two-wide. Watch that 10 car."

Hamilton beat Busch to the checkered flag—and Tony Stewart stole second place away. But Busch finished third, the best showing of his Cup career and better than any other rookie this day. He now stood only two points behind Kevin Harvick in the Rookie of the Year contest.

"Wonderful job, guys," Busch radioed to his crew.

Busch parked on pit road, and reporters pounced on him. Sipping an orange Gatorade, he stood by his car, thanking his crew and his new sponsor and coolly discussing the race on live radio and TV. "It went as fast as you put a quarter in a slot machine in Vegas," he said.

And though no one had expected an accident-free race, the Talladega 500 amazingly had ended without a single wreck. For only the second time in superspeedway history, the caution flag never flew.

The 175,000 spectators and the biggest television audience for any sports event that weekend got what NASCAR had gambled its drivers' lives on: excitement, with thirty-seven lead changes spread among twenty-six different racers, and drama, with the first-place starter (Stacy Compton) finishing dead last, and the last-place starter (Mike Wallace) placing ninth. Martin and Burton joined Busch in the top ten, and Kenseth finished nineteenth; with three-quarters of the season remaining, all four Roush drivers were now within 150 points of the top ten in the standings. Their universe was still skewed, but less so today.

As the race's top-finishing rookie, Busch, accompanied by Jack Roush, joined Hamilton and Stewart on the media center stage. "He did a great job," Stewart said of Busch. "For a rookie, he drove like a veteran who's been here a long time."

"You seem pretty happy," a reporter said to Busch.

"Very happy with everything and the way the team has come together with Ben Leslie as the new crew chief and just all the testing that we've done," Busch replied. "It was just a great weekend that Jack put together."

Roush recounted a conversation the year before with his friend Benny Parsons, another former Cup champion who would be broadcasting races in the second half of the season, when Fox would pass its duties to NBC/Turner.

"We talked about what we might do," Roush said, "and we both agreed that Kurt coming in directly from one year in the Truck Series into the Winston Cup Series was probably the craziest thing we could do this year—but we felt the need for speed."

CHAPTER 6
FLOATING IT IN

Racing continued the following weekend, with the NAPA Auto Parts 500 at California Speedway, a two-mile-long oval track some fifty miles east of Los Angeles. Owned, like Talladega, by International Speedway Corporation, the track had brought NASCAR directly into another prime market when it opened in the summer of 1997. Sellout crowds of almost 100,000 spectators since had confirmed the wisdom of the Frances' $120 million investment.

For the second week in a row, Kurt Busch finished higher than his Roush Racing teammates—and how he managed to accomplish that made headlines.

Starting 32nd, Busch got a flat tire during his warmup laps. He returned to pit road for a new one—and while he was in, his crew topped off his gas, which they thought might give him an advantage later in the race. "I was like, 'Man, it would be cool to top off and we can go 55 laps where everybody's gotta come in at 52 or whatever,'" Busch said. What the rookie and his young crew didn't know was that he had violated a NASCAR rule. An official penalized Busch by holding him at pit road for a race lap—and then sending him to the end of the field. In essence, Busch was starting the NAPA Auto Parts 501: one lap behind all the others, and dead last. But California Speedway's long frontstretch and longer backstretch suited Busch, and unlike most of the tracks he was visiting this year, he had competed there before, in the last Craftsman Truck race of his career, the 2000 season-ending Motorola 200, which he won.

Driving near the edge, Busch made up his lost lap, only to suffer another mishap: A wheel started to loosen, and he had to return to pit road, which put him down another lap. But he soon regained it, and with less than a fifth of the race to go, he had climbed to 16th place. During the remaining laps, he advanced three more positions, finishing 13th. "What an amazing turn of events," wrote one reporter. "How can this be possible—from a rookie no less?" Busch had beaten Kevin Harvick, who finished 25th, and now led in the Rookie of the Year contest—by a single point, 106 to 105.

"It was a lucky and wonderful day in sunny California," Busch said.

But not for the other Roush racers in the NAPA Auto Parts 500, which Rusty Wallace won: Matt Kenseth finished 17th, Jeff Burton 31st, and Mark Martin 40th, after accidentally smashing into Jeff's brother Ward, who was hospitalized two days for a concussion. When Jack Roush arrived in North Carolina on the Tuesday after the race, the drivers' and crew chiefs' frustration was evident. Roush had something resembling a mutiny on hand.

Horsepower deficiencies had preoccupied the Roush teams earlier in the season—but now they were criticizing the handling of the cars, especially on turns, where better grip allows faster speed. Many factors influenced grip, including the manufacture of tires, which Goodyear controlled under NASCAR supervision, and tire air pressure and suspension, the purview of drivers and their chiefs. Another factor was aerodynamics: how the car body was shaped and attached to the chassis, and the size and position of the rear spoiler, roof rails, and front air dam. Engineers played the dominant role in aerodynamics, in which excellence required a delicate symphony. Engineers were the ones with the college degrees, the computers, and the knowledge of wind tunnels.

Long in the forefront of certain other forms of automobile racing—Formula One, for example—engineers had come belatedly to NASCAR, with its roots in junkyards and garages. Indispensable now in most owners' view, engineers still sometimes elicited resentment from the men who drove and maintained stockcars. After all, what did guys who carried their pens in pocket protectors know about racin'?

On that Tuesday in North Carolina, Roush found that his engineers were under attack. He gathered everyone—the engineers, the drivers, the crew chiefs, Harry McMullen, Buddy Parrott, and Geoff Smith—and for almost three hours he encouraged the heart of Roush Racing to have it out.

"Any bitch or any complaint that anybody had about anybody else, I made sure it surfaced," Roush said. "And when they slowed down, I slapped one of 'em and shoved him back into the fight. They just fought until everybody was bloody." Roush chuckled at a favorite old memory—he'd learned the technique from his father, who had settled a peashooter dispute between Jack and his brother by forcing them to shoot at each other.

At one point in the meeting, Kurt Busch contended that his interest in learning how Jeff Burton's team tuned Burton's cars was irritating Frank Stoddard. That opened the door to airing of another beef: that some at Roush Racing believed Busch's rapid rise to the top had left him unappreciative of the longer road the others had traveled. Busch tried to convince everyone of the gratitude he felt for his rare opportunity—and of his respect for their greater wisdom and experience—but his supplication fell on deaf ears that Tuesday. "I felt like a monkey's ass after the meeting," said Busch. "But you have to take a hit to learn."

As Roush had expected, the meeting ended with agreement

on the need for better communication and goodwill. "They didn't want to fight anymore when they were done," he said. "They wanted to live together and love together!"

The session also resulted in something more concrete: a new aerodynamic initiative. Roush's engineers had designed their fleet of cars before the season began with Goodyear's new tires in mind—but the drivers had now made the case from their on-track experiences that they needed modifications to shift the balance in the ratio of downforce generated on the front of the car versus the downforce on the rear. New computer analyses and wind tunnel testing would commence immediately, but weeks would pass before the reshaped cars began to appear at the track.

Had he lived, Dale Earnhardt would have turned fifty on April 29, the day of the NAPA Auto Parts 500. Fans of the late driver noted that unattained milestone—as did *The Orlando Sentinel.* One story the newspaper published that day sentimentally depicted still-grieving fans of the driver.

Another implied that NASCAR had lied about the circumstances of Earnhardt's death.

The story centered on emergency medical technician Tommy Propst's account of efforts to save Earnhardt. Speaking publicly for the first time on the issue, Propst told the newspaper that he and a partner were among the first to reach Earnhardt's wrecked car, and that the suspect seat belt "was in one piece at the time," not "separated," as Mike Helton had claimed. Propst further insisted that he had seen no one cut the belt—and he said that more than two months after the Daytona 500, no NASCAR official nor any of its anonymous accident investigators had sought to interview him. Propst's account wasn't the only part of *The Sentinel's* story that lengthened the shadow over NASCAR: Another EMT who had tended to Earnhardt cryptically told the paper, "I know the truth, and I'm not allowed to talk."

Helton and Bill France Jr. both happened to be at California Speedway the day before *The Sentinel* ran its story. Asked by one of the newspaper's reporters to comment on the account that was about to be published, Helton declined. France, however, had something to say. "I'm not going to talk to you about any of that stuff," he said. "So just mosey on back to the media center, because we've got a lot more to do than mess with that goddamn shit."

Privately, France was disturbed what he believed were inaccuracies and false assumptions in some of the reporting in the aftermath of Earnhardt's death. "I thought some of the articles were unfair, they weren't correct, they were taken out of context," France would later remark. "I've learned this: The bigger you get, the more the media comes after you and tries to second-guess and micromanage everything that happens. Not just in motorsports but all over."

But to some of NASCAR's critics, the EMT episode sounded like a cover-up. "Conspiracy isn't too strong a term," declared a writer on one racing Web site. "It's pretty obvious that someone is lying, not merely mistaken, and the implications are chilling." More restrained voices continued to wonder when France and Helton would finally begin to manage their public relations crisis, which now threatened not only NASCAR's credibility but its financial underpinnings. Publicly silent for the most part, car owners were privately expressing the fear that continued bad press could endanger corporate sponsorships.

The answer came less than a week after *The Sentinel's* story. On Friday, May 4, when the Cup circuit was in Richmond, Virginia, for the Pontiac Excitement 400, Helton summoned owners and drivers to a closed-door meeting unlike any he had called before. Helton apprised his audience of the status of NASCAR's investigation, and he maintained that Propst, while well-intentioned, was mistaken in what he had seen during those frantic moments when workers sought to save Earnhardt: The driver's belt had broken during the accident, Helton said, and NASCAR's investigators would prove it. Helton assured racers of NASCAR's commitment to honesty and to safety, and he urged them to speak publicly on the matter if they were so inclined.

Helton himself subsequently released a statement to the press, and then agreed to an interview with *The Atlanta Journal-Constitution*, which portrayed him in a sympathetic feature as still grieving the loss of "one of his greatest friends." But it was owners and drivers who made the more persuasive case that NASCAR had done something more than bungle since February 18. NASCAR now intended to publicly release the results of its investigation in August, and Helton's unprecedented meeting prompted Mark Martin, Jeff Burton, and Dale Earnhardt's son Junior, among others, to commend NASCAR.

Burton characterized the week's seat belt controversy as a waste of time; what he'd learned, combined with his knowledge of laboratory testing, convinced him that Earnhardt's belt had broken during the accident. "The hell with 'he said, she said, I saw, she saw,'" Burton remarked. "Let's figure out how to prevent major head trauma."

NASCAR, Burton now believed, finally was determined to move in that direction. "There's no question that pressure from the drivers and some car owners—and continued pressure from the media—has changed NASCAR's opinion about doing things," he said. "I'm so happy with them I can't stand it. And two months ago, I wanted to shoot 'em."

Mark Martin won the pole at Richmond, and went on to finish the Pontiac Excitement 400 in 13th place, which advanced him two positions in the point standings, to 21st. Jeff Burton placed 14th in the race and moved up to 25th. Kurt Busch finished 18th—one spot behind Kevin Harvick (who regained the lead in the Rookie of the Year contest), but good enough to climb to 20th in the overall standings. Matt Kenseth finished the race at eighth. He now held

11th in the standings, immediately behind Dale Earnhardt Jr., his rival for rookie honors during the preceding year.

Unlike his teammates, Kenseth, who amazingly had never suffered a racing injury, declined to involve himself in the safety controversy. "I try as hard as I can to stay away from all that," he said. "They have people hired to take care of all that stuff. Whatever rules NASCAR makes for us and wants us to do, we'll live by."

The older of two children, Kenseth was raised in rural Cambridge, Wisconsin, a small town some twenty miles east of Madison whose main street featured a bank, a barber shop, a feed mill, a dime store, and two automobile dealerships. His father, Roy, worked in a furniture factory and later opened a furniture store, which he subsequently sold to build a motel, a laundromat, and a video-rental store. His mother, Nicola, initially stayed home with Matt and his sister, Kelley, but as they grew older, she took a job as a receptionist.

Two things fascinated Kenseth as a young boy: fast things and things with engines, even a simple one-cylinder Briggs & Stratton. "I loved mowing the lawn," he said. "I'd go to my Grampa's and get the lawnmower and drive it down and mow our lawn and stuff. One day, me and my dad went out and he bought me an old riding lawnmower with no mower deck or anything on it. I had that thing painted up and I'd drive it around town—I'd drive everywhere. As I became more familiar with it, I figured out different things about speeding it up: fixing the governor, changing gears on it to get it to go faster, stuff like that. It was pretty cool—I had the only riding lawnmower you could do wheelies with!"

Roy drove Corvettes, and he liked to speed around town with his son riding beside him. Roy's three brothers raced stockcars on Saturday nights at the local short tracks, and Matt often attended—and sometimes got to sit in the cars. "That was like the coolest thing ever," he said. When Matt was thirteen, Roy decided to join his brothers in racing, so he bought an old Camaro and set up shop in his garage. He didn't own any racing tools or equipment, so he bought those, too, and with his brothers' help he learned how to set up a racecar. Matt was his shop assistant and a member of his tiny pit crew. Seeing his father's thrill in winning races, Matt knew he had to race.

In 1988, the year Kenseth turned sixteen, Roy bought his son a stockcar that had won a local championship several years before. The $1,800 car lacked an engine, so Roy gave Matt the one from his Camaro—and Matt scrounged a clutch and other parts from junkyards to put the car in racing trim. Matt debuted that summer at a quarter-mile asphalt oval near Columbus, Wisconsin. He didn't win his first race or his second—but he won his third, beating older teens and adults, including the previous year's local champion. "I was pretty surprised," said Kenseth, "and my dad was so excited." Roy was not alone. A reporter for *Midwest Racing News* compared Matt to another racer who had left his mark locally. "The last true phenomenon to hit Wisconsin was a skinny kid with a squeaky voice from Arkansas," he wrote. "Today, Mark Martin sits in a NASCAR Winston Cup car."

Kenseth played basketball his freshman year, but no high school sport after that. Nor did he fit into any clique. Speed consumed him, although he never expected to make a living at it. "I thought I'd have to work all week and then maybe race Saturday night at the local tracks," he said.

Kenseth advanced on the local circuits, winning championships and breaking records, including some held by Martin. He got his first taste of NASCAR competition in 1996, driving in a Busch Grand National race at Lowe's Motor Speedway, a longer and faster track than any on which he had raced. He started 37th and finished 31st, winning $5,745, an inauspicious debut—but experiencing almost 200 miles per hour of speed for the first time thrilled him, and he craved more.

One day in 1997, when he was racing for the American Speed Association, where Martin had claimed four titles, Kenseth received a telephone call from a onetime driver named Robbie Reiser. A fellow Wisconsinite, Reiser had raced against Kenseth but he had since given up the wheel to become an owner of a Busch Series car driven by Tim Bender, a former snowmobiling champion. An injury at Bristol Motor Speedway had sidelined Bender, and Reiser, seeking a replacement, wanted to hire his old competitor. Kenseth signed on.

He started third in his first race with Reiser, at Nashville—and finished 11th. The next weekend brought him to Talladega, where Mark Martin also happened to be racing. Martin introduced himself, complimenting the younger driver for his success on the Midwest tracks where Martin himself had excelled. Martin was impressed not only by Kenseth's driving, but also with his intimate understanding of racecar construction and setups. Kenseth was flattered, but considered the encounter no more than a pleasant exchange between two men who shared a compulsion to race.

A week later, Martin telephoned Kenseth. Martin had shown no idle interest—he wanted to further Kenseth's career, and, remembering his own big break, he had recommended that Jack Roush hire the young driver. Roush had no immediate openings in Winston Cup racing, but he liked what he saw in Kenseth and so did Geoff Smith, who signed him to a long-term contract and helped negotiate a deal with Lycos to sponsor Kenseth's Busch Grand National car. Kenseth continued in the Busch Series for two more years, advancing to full-time Winston Cup racing in the 2000 season.

Kenseth's sophomore year was not turning out as he had imagined over the winter; his Rookie-of-the-Year glow had faded, and almost a year had passed since visiting Victory Lane, the longest dry spell of his NASCAR career. Like all Cup drivers, Kenseth made plenty of money, and he spent many of his waking hours at extreme speed, but there was a growing void in his life.

"Winning is the only real great thrill for me now," Kenseth said.

*

Mother's Day, the second of only three holidays during the long Cup season, followed the Pontiac Excitement 400. Then it was on to Lowe's Motor Speedway for two weekends of racing featuring The Winston and the Coca-Cola 600. Jack Roush used the Thursday between the two events for the grand opening of his J.R.'s Garage retail store and museum, in a suburb of Charlotte.

Roush cut a ribbon, delivered a speech, and signed autographs—on tee shirts and photographs primarily, but also on a used racing tire that a fan rolled in. Then Mark Martin, accompanied by Arlene and Matt, arrived. Martin regularly gave autographs on the fly at speedways, but only infrequently anymore at scheduled signings. The line of several hundred fans awaiting him had started to form the previous evening, when, as the sun was setting, Ann and Eddie Bean pitched a tent on the sidewalk outside the store, and quietly began their 13 1/2-hour overnight vigil.

Not all of Martin's fans were as benign as the Beans. Martin was frequently invited to strangers' weddings, and one fan wrote letters for months begging the driver to be his best man (Martin declined). Martin appealed also to women, and one who was middle-aged and married called Roush Racing several times every week to wish the driver good luck—and she wrote long letters professing her love for the man she considered the handsomest in the world. Other Roush drivers could share similar stories.

But Ann and Eddie Bean, a North Carolina couple, belonged to the great majority of fans: They idolized Martin while keeping a polite distance. Eddie, a mechanic, had maintained his loyalty since the driver began racing for Jack Roush in 1988; his wife, a florist, had been a fan for about five years. The Beans appreciated Martin's racing talent, and his on- and off-track personality: "He just goes and gets the job done," said Eddie. Said Ann: "If he has a bad race, he doesn't whine or boo-hoo it: 'Someone did this, someone did that.' He's just Mark."

The Beans could not state precisely how much money they

had spent over the years on Mark Martin merchandise, but they could recite a rough inventory of their collection, which filled one room of their house and spilled over into another. Eddie said that he owned about a hundred and ten large die-cast cars, which come in differing colors and level of detail—and which Roush Racing sells for up to $115 apiece. "That's not counting the little one–64th cars," he said. "I've probably got two hundred of those, plus about forty shirts and two jackets." Ann mentioned unopened cereal boxes, mugs, shot glasses, shoestrings, cigarette lighters, and a leather checkbook cover, which she carried in her purse. "My Doberman wore a Mark Martin dog collar until she outgrew it," she said.

Much of the Beans' collection consisted of items with the name of Valvoline, the previous sponsor of the No. 6 car, but the couple had moved effortlessly with Martin to Pfizer. "People gave me a hard time when he changed," said Ann. "They said: 'Are you going to wear Viagra?' I said, 'Hell, yes, that's his sponsor!'"

The speed with which Martin's fans embraced Viagra-labeled products had surprised Geoff Smith and his staff, who had been prepared for the worst. Before the season started, sales personnel had been trained in handling the off-color jokes (don't laugh, steer the encounter toward Pfizer's overall health pitch), and Roush licensing manager Jamie Rodway had approved production of Mark Martin merchandise in three subcategories: with the Pfizer name only, with a No. 6 only, and with the Viagra name. To get an early read on demand, Rodway spent hours in the Martin souvenir trailer at the Daytona 500. "A lot of jokes were made," he said, "and a lot of people were asking for Viagra." Rather than turn consumers off, continued strong sales in that subcategory proved the Viagra name created a compelling if quirky cachet. "Everyone wants Viagra now," Rodway said. "It's one of the hottest things going." The only closed market was children; under Food and Drug Administration regulations governing adult pharmaceuticals, the Viagra name could not appear on products specifically aimed at women or youngsters—toy cars, for example, which were smaller and cheaper than the $115 die-cast models.

The Viagra experience also demonstrated the selling power of a successful driver's name, regardless of his sponsor. According to an internal NASCAR study, so-called true-believer fans spent $791 a year on apparel, collectibles, and other merchandise; and less ardent fans were no skinflints, with an average annual expenditure of $522. For a driver like Martin—and a company like Roush Racing, which shared in the royalties—this translated to millions of dollars in income over the course of a career.

But continuing success was critical: The old adage "win on Sunday, sell on Monday" still held, with the exception of Dale Earnhardt, whose death created such a demand for No. 3 products that the licensing head of Dale Earnhardt Inc. proclaimed him "our Elvis"—and eBay, the online auction house, reported that Earnhardt memorabilia topped all items searched for in the month of March. Mark Martin had won so many races over so many years that his legacy helped sustain him in 2001, but prolonged frustration on the track would eventually affect sales of his merchandise, Viagra's cachet notwithstanding, and that in turn would impact Roush Racing's bottom line.

Jeff Burton, who had won fewer races than Martin, understood such math: As he'd struggled this year, he had watched his sales flatten.

But it was racing, not selling, that preoccupied Burton as the Coca-Cola 600 drew near. His cars still didn't handle to his satisfaction, and he and Stoddard still couldn't find a solution.

"When you are on top of the game," said Burton, "and the thing doesn't do what it's supposed to be doing, you know why; you can put your finger on it very quickly. And when you don't have that, you end up doing a lot of guessing. We're just a little confused right now. We aren't as in tune to the car—to what the car needs to feel like on these tires."

As the season had progressed, some competitors had sought to boost Burton's spirits: Rusty Wallace, Dale Jarrett, and his friend John Andretti among them. None of his opponents had openly ridiculed him, but Burton suspected some were snickering behind his back. "Part of competition is driving your competition into the ground," Burton said. "I know that there's some people out there that find this humorous—or find this gratifying." Asked how he coped, Burton laughed and said: "You seek solace where you can!"

But more than humor sustained him. Burton was a fan of many sports, and he knew that sometimes competition goes in cycles, for reasons that defy explanation—or immediate correction. "I've watched golfers that couldn't win for a long time," he said. "I've watched basketball teams, football teams, that just go through periods where you get on the wrong side of things." Burton needed to look no further than professional baseball that May of 2001 for an example. After leading his team with a 3.50 ERA and 194 strikeouts in the 2000 season, St. Louis Cardinals pitcher Rick Ankiel had seemingly lost his ability to even get the ball over the plate by the 2000 playoffs, when he threw nine wild pitches in four innings. The pitcher's 2001 spring training had proved equally embarrassing, and he began the 2001 season with a 7.13 ERA and 25 walks in 24 innings. The Cardinals demoted Ankiel on May 11 to the club's Triple-A team in Memphis—where he walked 17 men and threw 12 wild pitches in only 4 1/3 innings. What made Ankiel's situation most disturbing was that the young pitcher was physically healthy. The problem was his head, a part of the body that obeyed different rules than muscles or bones.

The situation, of course, was hardly so dire for Burton—at least, not yet. While he, Stoddard, and the rest of the crew labored to fix the No. 99 car, Burton took satisfaction in everyone's morale. So far, team chemistry had not dissolved in the disappointment. "I'm real proud of my team for not freaking out," the driver said. "And I've handled this better than I ever imagined I would. Now, maybe I'm just not handling it—so I think I am. But I am telling you—and this isn't any bullshit, this is the truth—I haven't lost sleep. I haven't gone home and yelled at my wife. Frank and I haven't got at each other's throats."

With nearly a third of the season gone by, Burton had virtually no chance of winning the Winston Cup championship: He was in 25th place, 524 points behind leader Jarrett, a deficit that would all but require divine intervention to overcome. His dream of buying a yacht seemed a long way off.

Burton knew he'd let Jack Roush down, too, even though Roush had not told him so. "Jack doesn't call me and say, 'You dumb son of a bitch, what's wrong?'" said Burton. "He's letting us fix this. That means a lot to me."

Nonetheless, Roush was not blasé. He puzzled over how a driver who had been dominant for four straight years could wind up where Burton was today. And in his search for answers, he had enlisted the help of Frank Stoddard.

Stoddard was not only Burton's crew chief—he was also the driver's confidant and friend. The two men golfed together, wagered on the same college basketball games, and shared the same sometimes sophomoric sense of humor. Stoddard's wife, Heidi, managed the public relations for Jeff's brother Ward, who drove the No. 22 Caterpillar car, and she was friends with Kim Burton. Every race weekend, the Stoddards and the Burtons parked their motor coaches in close proximity to each other.

A native of North Haverhill, a small community in New Hampshire's White Mountains, Stoddard fell victim to speed the summer he was ten years old, when he worked on a nearby farm. The farmer owned a quarter-mile dirt track across the Connecticut River in Vermont, and his adult son raced a stockcar. The son let Stoddard change the car's oil and turn the occasional wrench, and Stoddard's mother and his father, who owned an insurance agency, gave permission for their young boy to join the crew in the pits. As he became a teenager and then a young adult, Stoddard worked for a succession of drivers, including as crew chief for Dana Patten, a racer of local note who sought to break into Busch Grand National competition. In 1990, Stoddard headed south with Patten. "We were certainly some hillbillies from New Hampshire coming down there with our open trailer and stuff and trying to compete!" said Stoddard. "But that's how you learn."

Patten finished just once in the top ten of a race, and his dream of becoming Grand National Rookie of the Year expired when his owner's money ran out two-thirds of the way through the 1990 season. Stoddard was left jobless—but only momentarily. He had met Jeff Burton during Patten's abbreviated run, and Burton arranged for Stoddard to be hired as one of his mechanics for the remainder of the season. Stoddard returned north when the season ended, but he left a lasting impression, and over the ensuing years Burton tried unsuccessfully to get him back. Stoddard relented when Burton joined Roush Racing. "I guess I got to the point where I felt like Jeff was going to stop calling if I didn't go ahead and take one of those deals," said Stoddard. "And the names of Jack Roush and Buddy Parrott were icons to me."

As the 2001 Coca-Cola 600 approached, Roush told Stoddard to sound Burton out.

"You're the guy that's in Burton's head," Roush said. "Bring back to me your take on what you think you need to do to help your driver." Roush reminded Stoddard that the No. 99 car's performance wasn't Burton's responsibility alone: As crew chief, Stoddard was accountable, too. Having seen Chad Little and Kevin Lepage leave Roush Racing in the last year, Stoddard certainly understood the boss's low tolerance for sustained mediocrity.

Conceivably, Roush said to Stoddard, all the No. 99 team needed was extra time on Goodyear's new tires. Bobby Labonte, the defending Winston Cup champion, had also struggled, but now seemed to have found the key: Over the last three points races, Labonte had recorded a fifth-place finish and a tenth, which had advanced him from 21st to 13th in the Cup standings.

If Burton's only problem was a slower adjustment, Roush reasoned, he would benefit by spending some days between Cup races on a track. "Burn up a bunch of tires," Roush instructed Stoddard, "and see if you can get the feel that will put him back in the position of being able to make the judgments he needs to."

Beyond tires, Roush wanted Stoddard's take on Burton's frame of mind.

"Dale Earnhardt was killed and it was clear that it was an accident that should have been survivable," said Roush. "And Jeff got himself all immersed in a controversy with NASCAR in the middle of the firestorm of the safety issues of what NASCAR might do and what they weren't doing and what the drivers could do and how they would go forward. Instead of focusing on making his car better every week, he had his head in other places."

Roush also wondered if the birth of Burton's son had affected Burton's racing. Roush had watched as Martin's involvement with his son had increasingly captured that driver's attention; once a daily visitor to the No. 6 shop, Martin now spent more time during the week at home in Florida, where Matt raced his Quarter Midget cars. "I can't do anything with Mark," said Roush. "Mark is going to do whatever Mark wants to do until he quits." Burton, however, was almost a decade younger than Martin, and Roush envisioned him as the cornerstone of his racing operation when Martin retired.

"Get in there and piss Burton off if you need to," Roush advised Stoddard. "Challenge him, argue with him—do something to try to really unearth any issue or any problem that's not on the surface."

If Stoddard thought that it was warranted, Roush would even recommend that Burton see a sports psychologist.

Drenched by rain showers in the days leading up to the race, Lowe's Motor Speedway had turned hot and dry on the afternoon of May 27, the Sunday of Memorial Day weekend. The green flag for the Coca-Cola 600 would fly at 5:45 P.M., and the forecast promised an ideal evening for the 600 miles of racing on the 1.5-mile oval.

As Jeff and Kim Burton rode a helicopter from their home to the track, Jack Roush was parking his car in the crowded infield. Roush often parked outside a speedway to allow a quick escape after the race, but he had a hunch that one of his drivers would win tonight, and if one did, the celebration would continue longer than traffic would impede. No name came with Roush's hunch, but Lowe's had smiled on all four of his men before: Martin had won three Cup races there, and Kenseth and Burton had both won once. And after starting 42nd at Lowe's the previous autumn in one of the seven Cup races before his full rookie year, Kurt Busch had finished an impressive 13th.

Burton spoke at the Coca-Cola hospitality tent after his helicopter touched down, then went to his hauler, where Roush, who had delivered a box of Krispy Kreme doughnuts to each of his four crews, joined him. Burton's television was tuned to the Indianapolis 500, in progress some 430 miles away. Engines built by Roush powered three of the cars in that race, including one owned by A. J. Foyt.

Once the premier automobile race in America, the Indy 500 in recent years had suffered from declining interest, and its television ratings had plummeted while NASCAR's had soared. But this year's Indy 500 had recaptured the public's fancy. Female drivers remained uncommon anywhere in motorsports, but one woman, the twenty-year-old Sarah Fisher, had demonstrated unusual ability in Indy cars, which have open cockpits and sleek bodies that resemble Formula 1 machines—and she had started this year's Indy 500 in 13th place, ahead of such open-wheel luminaries as Al Unser Jr. One of the male drivers who was getting attention was Tony Stewart, who intended to race the Indy 500 and then fly south for the Coca-Cola 600 that same evening.

Others had tried this, but only one person had ever completed such a marathon: Stewart himself in 1999, his rookie year in Winston Cup.

Roush and Burton respected what Stewart was attempting. Not only did racing 1,100 miles in one day require extraordinary stamina, but Stewart and several of his racing associates each intended to donate $100 for every lap he completed to a center for sick children founded by Paul Newman with Kyle and Pattie Petty, in memory of their son Adam. But not everyone shared Burton's and Roush's appreciation. A blunt and sometimes sarcastic man, Stewart rarely held his tongue, and among his occasional targets were fans—many of whom now complained that what they called a stunt would endanger his competitors in the Coca-Cola 600, since surely Stewart would be too exhausted to drive safely. "Superman's last race was February 18," an Ohio fan wrote to a motorsports publication, referring to Dale Earnhardt. But Stewart had prepared for his feat with a special diet and training, and his only concern was that rain or accidents in Indianapolis would ruin his schedule, which left not a minute to spare.

Rain did stop the Indy 500, but only momentarily. As Roush and Burton watched, Stewart went on to finish the race in sixth place. He rushed from his car to a helicopter, which brought him to a waiting jet.

The afternoon was waning.

Roush left Burton's hauler to call on General Michael E. Ryan, Chief of Staff of the Air Force, an associate sponsor of Elliott Sadler's No. 21 car; Ryan wanted to meet the man with the P-51 Mustang and offer him a ride in a modern counterpart, an F-15 fighter jet. Burton received a visitor of his own: Edsel Ford II, a great-grandson of Henry Ford and a longtime racing fan and admirer of Roush—and now of Burton. Burton explained his tire woes to Edsel, and his frustration in reclaiming his edge.

"The new tire doesn't talk to me like the old one did," Burton said. "This hasn't been our year."

After his conversation with Ford, Burton dressed in his fire suit and went to the frontstretch, where performers had just presented a tribute to Dale Earnhardt, winner of five Cup races at Lowe's, his home track. A helicopter swooped down onto the infield and Tony Stewart stepped out, and Burton joined those congratulating him as the drivers were about to be introduced. Had he missed the introductions, Stewart would have been forced to start last, not 12th, where he had qualified.

Mark Martin had qualified the best of the Roush racers and was starting in tenth, far ahead of Kenseth and Busch, who required provisionals to make the race. Burton was in the middle of the field, in 18th. He had no hunch about where he would finish, but he and Stoddard had pursued a strategy that they hoped would result in a strong run. Deciding that last week's nonpoints all-star race, The Winston, was inconsequential to them this year, the No. 99 team had spent most of their energy preparing the car Burton would run in the Coca-Cola 600. It was not one of Roush Racing's new cars, but a three-year-old vehicle that Burton had raced to victory at Las Vegas and New Hampshire, and which they now hauled around as their backup car. New tires notwithstanding, Burton hoped it would return him to the edge.

Burton kissed Kim and strapped himself into his car, and the race began. A new face was starting first: twenty-three-year-old Ryan Newman, who had beaten Jeff Gordon by five one-hundredths of a second during qualifying to win the pole. This was only the third Winston Cup race for Newman, a senior at Purdue University's School of Interdisciplinary Engineering who planned to compete full-time on the circuit in 2002 for owner Roger Penske.

The racers had completed just two laps when Stewart seemed to confirm his critics' pessimistic prediction: Accelerating off Turn Two, he spun out. Stewart managed to stay off the wall, but his car was damaged, and over the next twenty laps he had to return five times to his pit box for repairs, which sent him to the back of the field. Newman also quickly encountered trouble: On lap 11, he lost control and slammed into the wall. His car was too badly damaged to return: as the first to drop out of the race he was consigned to a last-place finish.

Knowing how long the evening would be, Burton drove crisply but not aggressively during the early part of the race. By radio, Stoddard reminded him that they had configured the No. 99 car to run best later on, when the sun was setting, the track was cooling, and tire grip was changing. If he held his own at the beginning, the driver and the crew chief reasoned, Burton should be in position to challenge for the lead when it counted.

Rusty Wallace led on lap 80, a fifth of the way to the checkered flag, and all of the Roush racers had advanced: Martin to eighth, Kenseth to 19th, Busch to 27th. Burton was running in tenth. "You're doing a hell of a job," Stoddard said. Burton had achieved the desired rhythm.

It was almost 7 P.M. now, and dusk approached.

Burton's team had won the 2000 World Pit Crew Championship, a contest judged on precision and speed—and they were delivering prizeworthy service now, with pit stops that were faster than most other drivers'. Into lap 160, two-fifths of the way through the race, Burton remained in the top ten—as high as fourth, at one point. Burton's men smiled: Watching their pit stall television, they could see the No. 99 car on the live broadcast.

"They're showing the car," Stoddard radioed to Burton. "I ain't seen that in a long time, baby."

Burton's men weren't the only ones smiling. At home in Tulsa, Oklahoma, W. A. DeVore, the senior vice president of marketing for CITGO, was savoring Burton's run. DeVore had been instrumental in getting his company's name on Burton's car—but so far this year, his multimillion-dollar investment had failed to deliver as expected. Like other corporations, CITGO measured the worth of a sponsorship in part on the benefits that employees and customers derived from being able to call a driver theirs—the star value. Of greater importance, however, was the driver's mentions in the media, which CITGO tracked through an outside market-research firm; the data collected could be used to calculate if CITGO had gotten its money's worth, or would have been better off buying more traditional advertising. "We look at sponsorship like we would any other investment," said DeVore, "and that is what kind of return do we get. When you're running up front, you're winning, and you have a well-known driver—that just adds value. Winning is what it's all about."

DeVore did not consider the first third of the season a total loss: Not just Burton but all of Roush Racing was faltering, and that was major news in NASCAR. "Because of Roush Racing and Jeff Burton," said DeVore, "the value was still there because the media focus was on them for not winning." Nonetheless, a win would be welcome in the executive suite at CITGO's Tulsa headquarters—and it would give DeVore a break from the talk around the water cooler on Monday mornings. "Can't you pick a driver?" colleagues now joked.

Back in Charlotte, as the halfway point neared and the lights came on, the track temperature had fallen by more than twenty degrees from the 114 degrees at the race's start—a change that increased speed. All of the Roush drivers were now running in the top ten—with Burton in fourth.

"Your shit has been hauling ass on the long run," Stoddard radioed. "We're in great shape here. We're sitting in the catbird seat now."

Laughing, Burton replied: "I appreciate you trying to make me feel better!"

A few laps later, coming off a pit stop, Burton took first place.

"Take care of it, baby," Stoddard said. "Your lap times look real nice—just float it in."

Stoddard wasn't being poetic. He referred to an issue that he and Burton had discussed before the race: the driver's tendency to extend his straight runs, which sent him too deeply into the speedway's corners, pushing him up the banking and slowing him down. He lost only a fraction of a second a lap that way, but over the course of 400 laps, saving those fractions could add up to a win. Afraid that the rhythm of such a long race would lull him into forgetting to ease into the corners—to float it in—the driver had asked his crew chief for periodic reminders.

"Nice and smooth," Stoddard kept on. "Float it in for me."

Burton did, maintaining his lead for almost 70 laps. But further back, Bobby Labonte was on the move.

Labonte had started 24th, but like Burton in his No. 99 CITGO Ford, he was pleased with his No. 18 Interstate Batteries Pontiac. Labonte's momentum concerned Stoddard: Labonte wanted his first win of the year as badly as Burton wanted his, and the computer showed that he was the only driver near the front of the pack who was gaining on Burton's No. 99.

"Eighteen car took over second," Stoddard informed Burton on lap 225. Burton could see Labonte in his rearview mirror, two seconds behind.

Nine laps later, Labonte had narrowed the gap to barely a second.

"You've started to break even with the 18," Stoddard said. "Just do your deal." But rounding Turns Three and Four thirteen laps further on, Labonte pressed past Burton on the outside. "Just ride with the 18," Stoddard advised. "Just keep floating it in. Just keep doing your deal."

A three-car wreck minutes later drew a caution flag—and gave Burton the chance to return to his pit for fuel and fresh tires, inflated to a slightly higher pressure that he and Stoddard hoped would improve the handling. Burton lacked an appetite for food, but knowing that nourishment would help sustain him he asked a crew member during the stop to hand him a high-protein snack bar. But Burton couldn't fit the bar under his helmet shield, and it dropped onto the floor. There went supper.

Burton came off his stop with the lead, but Labonte soon snatched it back. And a second threat loomed: Dale Jarrett was closing in on Burton's rear bumper. A bad crash during qualifying had forced Jarrett to use a provisional and start 37th, in his backup car—and his charge to the front was all the more remarkable in light of the injury he had suffered in that crash. Jarrett tore a rib muscle; unable to take an analgesic without endangering himself and others, he was racing in unmitigated pain.

As the race entered its final hundred laps, Labonte increased his lead over Burton to almost eight seconds, a formidable advantage, but Stoddard remained reassuring: "Remember we started a little bit loose on the last run and then it came to you," he said. "It's going to come to you again."

Stoddard proved a prophet: Burton slowly cut into Labonte's lead. But he lost ground on the next pit stop, and was in sixth place on lap 335.

Then, as often happens in racing, one driver's bad luck became another driver's lucky break. Battling Jerry Nadeau to keep the lead, Labonte spun out. The caution flag flew, and when green-flag racing resumed three laps later, Burton once again was in front.

By now, some 500 miles in—more than the distance from New York to Detroit—NASCAR's longest race was taking its toll.

Ryan Newman was long gone—and Robert Pressley, Bobby Hamilton Jr., Kenny Wallace, and rookies Casey Atwood and Andy Houston, all victims of accidents or engine failure, had joined him. Jeff Gordon limped on after a collision on pit road and a penalty; Johnny Benson had survived running out of gas, but he, too, was out of contention. So was Mike Skinner, who had lost the second and third gears of his transmission.

*

Burton was in the zone, a place where the best racers thrive. The feeling was not what an amateur might have expected.

The novice racer achieving high speed for the first few times typically experiences the human body's instinctive response to danger—the same response that the everyday person may find when driving unusually fast, or riding a roller coaster. The body enters what is know as the fight-or-flight mode, which Hans Selye, the Austrian-born Canadian doctor who first studied it, called the General Adaptation Syndrome. Having judged a situation to be threatening, the brain initiates a complex reaction involving stimulation of the adrenal glands, which release the hormone adrenaline (also known as epinephrine). The heart pumps faster and stronger, the lungs draw in more air through deeper breathing, more blood is shunted to the muscles, energy-sustaining blood sugar quickly rises, the pupils dilate, the hairs stand on end, the palms sweat, and tissue-clotting time throughout the body declines. All of this is an ancient physiological response to help a person swiftly escape danger—or stay and defeat it.

Adrenaline hooks many young drivers, but as they advance toward a professional career, the rush fades; though useful when battling saber-toothed tigers, it is counterproductive when attempting to control almost two tons of metal moving at nearly a third the speed of sound. Burton and the other drivers in the Coca-Cola 600 had indeed undergone physiological changes since strapping themselves in, but they did not result from the release of adrenaline. Rather, their bodies, trained by their minds and by their many hours behind the wheel, had entered what the sports doctors called a state of arousal—the zone. Pulse and respiration had increased along with perspiration, responses to the G forces that drivers experience rounding turns, to the heat of the cockpit, and to the exertion of steering—lessened since the advent of power steering in stockcars, but a factor nonetheless. Drivers in the zone find their ability to concentrate markedly improved, their thinking clearer, their already-fast reflexes faster, and their already-sharp eyesight even sharper. Some begin to achieve a feeling of invincibility.

But drivers in the zone can only achieve maximum performance—can reach the edge—when their vehicle is also in optimal condition, which is where design, construction, setup, and tires come into play. But the desire to reach the zone isn't what motivates a professional racecar driver. It's the winning.

Some drivers, including Burton, claim to rarely or never experience sheer euphoria when they win, only great pleasure; what they crave most from racing is the opportunity to beat others. "I don't do this 'cause I like going in circles," said Burton. "I don't do it because I love the smell of rubber and I love shifting gears. That's not what it's about for me. What it's about for me is: Let's go see if we can do it better than everyone else."

But other drivers speak of the nearly indescribable bliss they feel when they have raced exceptionally well and won—and research in this scantly studied field suggests it results in part from the release of endorphins, whose qualities are remarkably similar to those of morphine, and whose effects other athletes also experience in what is called the runner's high. Produced in the pituitary gland, endorphins are a response to stressful, sustained exertion, such as that endured in driving a long automobile race or competing in a marathon. But losing after such exertion is hardly blissful, and so something else, as yet imprecisely quantified, apparently is involved.

Whatever the exact mechanism, the exhilaration of winning at speed becomes a powerful addiction for racecar drivers, compelling them even through bankruptcy, injury, and sustained defeat—and often well into middle age or beyond, when virtually all other athletes have said goodbye to their sport. "It feels so good it's unbelievable," sixty-one-year-old drag racer Eddie Hill told a Texas newspaper. "It's extremely habit-forming, and incurable. You can cure people of all kinds of addictions, but you can't cure anybody of this."

Said Mark Martin, "I don't know what it is, and I don't care what it is. It just feels good, and it lasts for quite a while, like all evening and into the next morning—until you go out, and somebody's quicker than you are. When I'm the fastest, it's fun for me; if I've got a chance to be the fastest, I'll walk in snow barefooted for one hundred miles."

As the race wound down and No. 99 maintained the lead, Jack Roush departed Mark Martin's pit stall for Jeff Burton's. Roush couldn't remember the last time he had been so tense. Rarely one to express his feelings, he had kept his disappointment in Burton to himself—but inside, he hurt. As early as Atlanta, when Burton finished 30th and dropped to 38th in the standings, Roush had realized that a title in 2001 was probably out of the question. "Instead of looking at his car as being a car that was expected to win a championship, or to be certainly in contention for a championship," said Roush, his hopes had dwindled to wondering if Burton would ever win again. "That's a terrible swing in emotion and expectation," said Roush. "Just grief, almost."

Now, with victory in sight, Roush almost couldn't bear to watch his driver, for anything could still happen—a tire could blow, a valve spring fail, a competitor wreck and knock out an innocent racer. "The thought of being able to turn his year around," Roush said, "and get that kind of good news going back to the sponsor, and good news for his fans, and good news for him and for everybody that worked for the program—I just couldn't stand it! I wanted to be fishing—anyplace else but right there."

But Roush did watch, as Stoddard continued to talk Burton home.

"Get in your comfort level," the crew chief said. "Just float it in. Let it come to you. Let it do what it needs to do. Don't push it."

With fewer than twenty laps left, Burton came up on lapped traffic—cars directly ahead that were a lap or more down. Lapped traffic always presented a headache: threading through it was hazardous, and it often slowed the leader, which could allow cars behind to gain. Some lapped drivers would move aside—another day, they would expect the favor to be returned—but others, perhaps bearing a grudge, or just being ornery, would be deliberately obstructive. Stoddard instructed spotter Chris Farrell to see if he could negotiate with the spotters for the lapped drivers blocking Burton's way. A quick series of radio discussions ensued, and a deal was struck. The lapped cars moved aside, and Burton roared on through.

Burton's pit stall was becoming crowded with reporters and cameramen, many of whom were focused on Kim Burton, who was next to Stoddard atop the pit cart. A tear rolled down Kim's face, and she alternated between watching the race and burying her face in her hands. A win tonight would be worth a quarter of a million dollars, but money wasn't Kim's foremost concern: her husband visiting Victory Lane for the first time since last year was. She knew he hadn't forgotten how to win, but she knew how important it was to him to demonstrate it to the world.

The field shifted again. Proving his doubters wrong—"idiots," he would later call them—Tony Stewart had recovered from his early spinout and now he took third. Kevin Harvick claimed second. Lap after lap, Stoddard counted off Burton's advantage over Harvick: 3.99, 4.40, 3.98 seconds. After almost four-and-a-half hours of racing, Burton remained in the zone.

"Your lap times look awesome," said Stoddard. "Just float it in."

Four laps from the checkered flag, Stoddard began to worry about running out of gas. His calculations indicated Burton would be able to finish with about three-tenths of a gallon remaining, but gas math was always dicey, as Johnny Benson had been reminded tonight. "Easy on your gas pedal just to be sure," Stoddard told Burton.

Kim Burton was openly crying now, and the pit stall was so packed it was difficult to move. The checkered flag flew, with Burton crossing the finish line 3.19 seconds ahead of Harvick, a commanding margin.

"I can't believe it!" Stoddard shouted. "We won the Coca-Cola 600 for the second time! I love you! We got the confidence back tonight!"

Burton's crew exploded in high-fives and hugs—then dashed across the speedway to the grandstand fences, which they scaled like crazed apes. As Burton drove his car to the section of track that served as Victory Lane, Jack Roush was overjoyed: Winning put the feeling of something good in an owner's veins, too. "It's not the cure," he said as he headed to the celebration, "but it certainly gives hope that we'll be able to come back!"

Burton parked his car and sprayed a bottle of Coke everywhere as he climbed out and jumped onto the roof. With confetti showering down and fireworks lighting up the sky, he made his way through the throng to the stage, where Kim embraced him, and he received his trophy and congratulations from Roush, Miss Winston, and Lug Nut, the speedway's goofy mascot. Reporters interviewed Burton live on radio and TV, and then he posed with his wife, his owner, and his crew for still photographs. Finally, he posed alone wearing a succession of hats bearing the names of CITGO, Ford, Goodyear, and dozens of other corporations. This was payday for them, too.

The ceremony lasted more than an hour. Escorted by police, Burton and his entourage left the stage and traveled through the stands, where drunk and weary spectators lingered amid a mess of chicken bones and beer cans, to the press box high above the speedway. Reporters were primarily interested in Burton, but

Roush Racing had made a good night of it all around: Mark Martin had finished fourth, Busch 12th, and Kenseth 18th. The headlines this week would be flattering, the talk in the chat rooms kindly.

Burton praised the dedication of his crew through the season so far, then predicted that despite tonight's win, further difficulties likely loomed. "This doesn't mean everything is great and everything is lovely," he said. "We've got to keep fighting and keep working." Still, Burton allowed himself a moment of glory. Asked to describe his feelings as he had crossed the start/finish line, he said: "I don't want to sound facetious or cocky or anything else, but it felt normal. Winning is what Roush Racing is all about."

Handed the microphone, Jack Roush first praised his motors: Counting Elliott Sadler's, all five of them had excelled. "We ran 3,000 miles on our engines here tonight and none of them had a problem," said Roush. Then he talked about the season. "We just haven't had things go our way this year," he said. "The bright spot almost to this point has been how well Kurt Busch, with one year in the Truck program, has done acclimating himself to our program and to Winston Cup."

The reporters wrapped up their questions. Burton went onto the roof over the luxury suites for another live TV interview, then visited some of the speedway's private clubs, where members had watched the race over lobster and champagne. It was past midnight when Burton got back to his hauler.

Burton's elation had faded as the feeling in his veins had subsided. Next weekend, he would race at Dover Downs International Speedway in Delaware, where a blown tire last fall had ended his championship run against Labonte and Dale Earnhardt. Beyond Dover, two dozen more races awaited in a season that continued to confound.

"We never take a lot of time to enjoy these things, and maybe we should," said Burton as he and Stoddard changed into their street clothes. "I'm just more worried about what we do next week and the week after."

Racing had its great rewards, but the torments followed quickly.

CHAPTER 7

FATHERS AND SONS

Charles Roush returned from battleship duty in the Second World War to his hometown of Manchester, Ohio, a farming community some sixty miles southeast of Cincinnati. His wife, Georgetta, and their two young children, Jack and Frank, welcomed him back.

A millwright in an airplane engine factory before the war, Charles left the service determined to be his own boss. Using savings and a modest inheritance, he bought an ice and coal delivery business, which came with a fleet of old trucks requiring constant maintenance. Charles was gifted with his hands: Fresh from the day's deliveries, his trucks would roll into his garage, where, often working alone, he would tear down and rebuild the engines, often in less than three hours. He encouraged his older son, Jack, born in 1942, to be at his side. Everything about engines fascinated the boy, even the smell of the grease and the sound of the steam escaping the still-hot radiators, sensations reminiscent of old-fashioned blacksmithing.

Like his father, Jack was mechanically inclined, and his parents encouraged his interest. He received an Erector Set the

Christmas he was four, and a short while later a relative gave him the first of many clocks that he took apart and put back together. Jack was about seven when he got his first engine: a thumb-size, one-cylinder motor that powered his model airplane. Little engines led to a fascination in bigger engines, and before the boy was ten, he had figured out how to repair broken lawnmower motors. And this was when Jack Roush first connected power to speed.

His bicycle now failing to satisfy, Jack determined to build a go-cart. But oil-fired furnaces and electric refrigerators by now were killing the home coal and ice trades, and Charles, who had decided to try his luck in another business, wholesale food, could not afford to buy a new one for his son. So Jack cannibalized his red wagon, attaching its wheels and axles to boards he nailed together into a frame; an uncle donated a used lawnmower engine, and Charles advised him on building a transmission from pulleys and rope. Roush raced the thing around his neighborhood on the banks of the Ohio River—and it satisfied, for a while at least, his need for speed. "I swear it would do twenty miles an hour in a straight line," Roush recalled. "That go-cart was wonderful."

Charles Roush failed in the wholesale food business, and in the early 1950s he moved his family from downtown Manchester to an outlying family farm, where agriculture supported them. Charles and Georgetta instilled in their sons the importance of work: Jack and Frank had paper routes and sold greeting cards at Christmas, and they helped their father on the farm. Later, when he was a young teenager, Jack took a job at the local Chevrolet dealership, where he painted and fixed wrecks—and also got to work on engines. But he was not yet old enough to drive.

Strong-willed and disciplined like her husband, Georgetta intended her boys to be someone special. She dressed them well, encouraged perfection, and insisted they get an education. In high school, Jack excelled at science, math, and music, playing the cornet and the baritone horn in the band. But he did not excel at athletics. He failed to make the basketball team, and he didn't bother to try out for baseball or track and field, his school's other major sports. "I was unskilled, I was probably uncoordinated, and I was smaller than average," Roush said. But Jack nonetheless was compelled to compete. "I wanted to run a foot race or catch the biggest fish or climb the ladder the fastest," he said. Winning satisfied, albeit momentarily—and losing hurt, which only pushed him harder, just as it pushed Charles harder when his businesses failed.

Jack's first car was a 1950 Rambler that his father bought and allowed him to drive when he turned sixteen, in 1958, but it had unspectacular power and a knock from a bad rod. Jack traded it for a '51 Ford powered by a V-8 engine that he fine-tuned. His first impulse was to race, and he got his chance one spring evening.

Jack was on his way to meet a girl—he was wearing his finest pink shirt, leather jacket, and penny loafers—when he rounded a corner and there was Jim Bob Jenkins, who worked with him at the Chevrolet dealership. Jenkins was a year older, and he drove a '41 Ford that he'd souped up with a truck engine.

"So I'm going up the road and not going fast," said Roush, "and I come around kind of a bend—and there he is, going 30, 40 miles per hour. And the road is a road you'd be very comfortable on at 50 miles per hour: a wide secondary road that winded up out of the Ohio River valley to the top of the ridge there. I pulled out to pass him—and he sped up. So I slowed down to get back behind him—and he slowed down. He wanted to race me bad. So then I got after it, he got after it, and the race was on."

They were rounding a turn and Jack was trying to squeeze by when the cars made contact, sending Jack toward the bottom of a ravine. "I'm going 80, 85 miles an hour—I don't think I'd been going 90 by then, but at least 85—and so the car's spinning in the air and I'm just hanging on like a squirrel in a cage. And I said,

'This car is going to hit on its roof!' So I put both hands as hard as I could on the roof and forced myself into the seat." The car hit the ravine bottom and rolled along the creek bed, flattening the top, tearing off a door, and sending glass and battery acid flying. Jack lost his penny loafers in the smoking wreck, and he never made it to his date.

"But I didn't have a scratch, I didn't have a bruise, I didn't have a sore hand, my head hadn't hit anything—I had stayed pinned in that seat. I got out of it and Jim Bob backed up and he asked me, 'Are you all right?' from the top of the hill. I said, 'I'm doing just fine—but if you're still up there when I finish climbing this bank, you're going to be in bad shape!' So he drove off—left me standing in the creek. I climbed up the bank and here comes a state cop who was one of my dad's friends and he scooped me up and of course I made the excuse that I was distracted by something that was going on in the car and I went off the road."

The wreck left Jack determined to get another car. He saved his earnings and a short while later a relative sold him a '51 Plymouth that had been abandoned in a field after its engine had blown. Roush found another engine in a junkyard and brought it home, where he rebuilt it, guided by a repair manual and the knowledge gained from lawnmower motors and a father who was gifted with his hands.

After high school, Jack enrolled as a math major at Kentucky's Berea College, leaving his street-racing Plymouth to his brother, Frank. But by his junior year, he was back to his old tricks with a '54 Dodge, which he had salvaged from a junkyard and equipped with a large Chrysler V-8 engine to boost the power. Roush street-raced the Dodge, and also competed formally for the first time in drag races at a track near Berea. He drove on used snow tires, beating competitors who could afford racing tires that were new.

Roush at first had helped his parents pay for his education with part-time jobs as a janitor, a freight clerk, and a jackhammer operator. But when he was an upperclassman, he opened a business fixing and selling used cars. Lacking a garage, he worked under a shade tree next to the mobile home where he lived, but his talent for resurrecting old cars was greater than his open-air shop suggested and his business became lucrative. By the time he graduated, in 1964, Roush had saved enough to pay cash for a new car and an apartment's worth of furniture when he moved to Detroit with his wife, Pauline, whom he'd met and married in his third year at Berea, and their baby daughter, Susan. Having watched his father twice go into debt and then twice have to dig his way out, and heeding his mother's admonition to "make your money before you spend it," Roush took pride in never having to borrow money during his young adult years.

Detroit in 1964 monopolized the domestic automobile market, and Roush took a job at Ford, which had recruited him while he was in college. He worked as an assembly plant quality-control supervisor but hoped for a promotion to a research department dedicated to the development of internal-combustion systems— engines. Told that he could improve his chances by earning an advanced degree, Roush entered a master's program in the mathematics department at Eastern Michigan University; attending classes at night and then during a year's sabbatical from the automaker, he graduated in 1970. Roush now had his diploma— but no offer of a position in research. Instead, Ford executives wanted to steer him toward plant management. "But I wasn't willing to trade the investment that I'd made in myself—the potential that I knew I had—for what I considered to be a reduced opportunity to be creative with my mind and productive with my hands," said Roush. So he left Ford for a research job at Chrysler. But he didn't like Chrysler's corporate culture or his long commute, and he soon quit.

The corporate path had frustrated Roush, but he had not wasted the last six years. During that time, Roush outfitted a 1960 Falcon with a high-horsepower engine, and sometimes he or his brother would race it at a drag strip—or take it to a back road or remote section of expressway, where, for a $100 or $200 purse, they would go up against another street racer. While at Ford, Roush also had joined The Fastbacks, a group of fellow employees (including a nuclear physicist and a chemist) who raced high-performance Mustangs and other jazzed-up Fords on drag strips around the country. Roush worked the pits and he occasionally drove, but his primary role was engineering and technical support. He specialized in increasing horsepower, and word of his sorcerer's touch earned him a growing reputation in the racing world. Roush began to make money on the side building other racers' engines—enough money to partially underwrite the nationally touring Fastbacks and to buy his first set of valve- and seat-grinding equipment, which freed him from reliance on outside machine shops and gave him superior control of the final product. Roush's entrepreneurial instincts had resurfaced. He was determined to independently support himself and his family, which now included a second daughter, Patricia.

In partnership with Wayne Gapp, a Ford engineer with similar ambition, Roush in 1971 formed a company devoted to building engines and drag-race cars—some of which they sold, and some of which they raced themselves, winning championships and many races around the country in the five years they were together. Roush drove less often than Gapp, but when he did, he brought the same analytical eye that Kurt Busch would many years later. "I would walk the drag strips that we were racing on," Roush said, "and I'd see where the trees were, I'd see where the bumps were, I'd see where the risks were, and I'd put on my seat belt and helmet and say: 'OK, dumb ass, this is what you want to do.'"

By 1976, ego conflicts and disagreement over the future of their company prompted Gapp and Roush to split; Gapp kept the competition side of the business and Roush the racecar- and engine-building division. Jack Roush Performance Engineering, based in the Detroit suburb of Livonia, achieved revenues of $800,000 in its first year. Roush would never drive professionally again, and years would pass before he returned to competition as an owner.

But his business grew. Roush had never needed much sleep nor did he desire long vacations or hobbies; instead, he routinely worked seven days a week, often until after midnight, an ethic he had inherited from his father, who became his partner for a while in the late 1970s. Having failed as an entrepreneur (although averting bankruptcy and managing to pay all of his debts, his son would have you know), Charles had ended his career as the plant manager for Welded Wire Products, the largest manufacturer in Manchester, Ohio. He left retirement to work for his son for a period of eighteen months—"my right-hand man," Jack would call him.

Roush had maintained his contacts at Ford, and in 1978 the automaker asked him to become the general contractor for a custom pace car that would appear at the 1979 Indianapolis 500. With America's clean-air movement of the early 1970s, Ford had withdrawn from all involvement in domestic racing, fingered by some as a source of pollution, but now the automaker was easing back in—in part to help bolster its appeal to a younger market, which had made its Mustang such a success in the 1960s. For his pace car, Roush took an assembly-line Mustang and transformed it into a fast machine that impressed not only Ford but car fanciers in general. Many ordered pace cars of their own—and Roush's connection to Ford strengthened.

Ford turned to Roush next in 1981, when the automaker decided to sponsor a U.S. road-racing team. The company paired Roush with a German owner who had European experience, and the resulting firm, Zakspeed-Roush, won several races competing for the International Motor Sports Association, whose most notable race was the 24 Hours of Daytona. The Germans had final say on technical matters, however, which became a contentious issue when engine parts began to fail and Roush's advice went unheeded. Roush and Zakspeed parted ways in 1983. But Roush still had his own company, and his experience had convinced him that road racing was not the future of American racing.

NASCAR, he now believed, was the future. Its audience was growing, and not only in the south, as drivers such as Richard Petty and the young Dale Earnhardt were attracting millions of fans.

But Roush in 1983 was not ready to compete. He had limited experience outside of drag racing, and while Jack Roush Performance Engineering continued to grow, he lacked the financial resources to mount a credible effort at the Winston Cup level. Roush intended eventually to compete in several NASCAR divisions, but he wanted to start at the top.

So once more, Roush became a racecar owner. With a new subsidiary, Roush Racing, he built his own engines and cars and hired drivers to compete with them in IMSA and the similar Sports Car Club of America's Trans-Am Series. Initially, Roush spent his own money, but even at this relatively obscure level racing was expensive. Edsel Ford II, an executive with Ford Motor Company's Lincoln-Mercury division and a fan of Roush since his drag-racing days, offered to sponsor his friend for two races, in 1984—but continued support would require winning, which would return value to the automaker as a form of advertising. "If I haven't made a statement that justifies sponsorship," Roush told Edsel, "I've got five gallons of gas and a book of matches and I can fix my problem and get on with my life."

Roush Racing secured a manufacturer's title for Ford in the Trans-Am series in 1984, and the next year won the first of ten 24 Hours of Daytona races, some with celebrity drivers like Paul Newman and Bruce Jenner taking a turn at the wheel. Ford was in for the long haul, and with the automaker's backing, a succession of championships in IMSA and Trans-Am followed. Said

Roush, "I was gaining momentum, I was gaining credibility, I was gaining acceptance, I was making money, I was buying equipment, I was educating myself, and I was growing with my people—many of whom had experience that was beyond my own." He was finally ready for NASCAR.

As Roush Racing grew to include teams in NASCAR's three highest levels, the parent company was also expanding. With former Ford engineers Bob Corn and Ron Woodard, Roush in 1981 had started an engineering and design firm called Engine and Control Systems; in 1989, he merged it with Jack Roush Performance Engineering to create ECS/Roush, which a year later became Roush Industries. The new title capitalized on the emerging brand power of the Roush name, and also reflected the company's expansion beyond engine development into fields including vibration and noise control, graphics, aircraft parts prototyping, and production of street vehicles like the Stage 3 Mustangs—vehicles off the Ford assembly line that Roush technicians modified to near-racing form. By 2001, Roush Industries and its subsidiaries had achieved nearly $300 million in annual revenue and employed more than 2,000 people in the United States and abroad. Roush remained chairman, but was assisted by three top executives: Evan D. Lyall, who had joined the company directly from high school and was now the chief executive officer; Douglas E. Smith, an auto industry veteran who was the chief operating officer; and Geoff Smith, the president of Roush Racing.

Roush's devotion to his work affected his family, including his last child, Jack Jr., born in 1972. The Roushes occasionally vacationed in Colorado, at Disney World, and elsewhere, but more often than not the father spent weekends at the track—usually without his children or his wife, who did not share his passion. "With all my racing and building my business," said Roush, "I have not been an average family man."

But Roush decided to become more involved with his son when Jack was six and a half years old; it was the late 1970s and

Roush had stopped drag racing, which freed up more of his weekends. He bought his son a go-cart, registered him in a carting league run by a Ford employees' recreational club, and took the boy to a fenced area behind one of his shops, where he laid out a small practice course with pylons.

"Of course, Pauline thought this was wonderful," said Roush. "I hadn't spent much time with the girls up to that point. She figured that I might be turning over a new leaf: Here I am getting ready to go spend some of my weekends with Jack, with the prospect that the girls could go and have their programs, too. I felt her approval."

Pauline joined Roush and young Jack the first evening of practice, and liked what she saw: The little boy she still rocked to sleep in her arms every night noodling around on his go-cart. But the boy was a quick learner, and when Pauline next visited, two nights later, she witnessed something different: a kid getting his fist taste of real speed. "Jack's got it up on two wheels," said Roush, "turning both left and right, sliding it back and forth. He's really got the hang of this thing—we'd gone through about five gallons of gas, and all but worn out a first set of tires. Pauline said something extraordinarily unpleasant to me—I think it's the only time she ever showed anger with her disapproval—and slammed the car door and left. She realized that she'd been duped, that really I was just getting ready to go racing again, and that it was not going to be just some real gentle, easy social thing."

Young Jack's first practice with others, on a quarter-mile oval, demonstrated the boy's ability—and his emotion. He was fast but not the fastest, which led him to complain to his engine-building father. "Dad! Dad! Two of them passed me!" he said. "I've got to have more horsepower!" Roush laughed at the irony. "Here I've spent my life trying to find the horsepower to satisfy all these professional drivers I worked with—and my six-and-a-half-year-old is on me the first five minutes I have him in his racecar."

Working into the small hours of the morning, Roush put more

muscle into the small Briggs & Stratton engine: enough to more than double its speed, from 3,000 to 7,000 revolutions per minute. And with Jack Sr. serving as mechanic and pit crew, Jack Jr. won the local championship for his age group his first year. He took the title the next two years as well—and Roush himself raced, taking the championships in his adult category.

Jack Jr. was ten when his father's involvement with Zakspeed brought him back to the racetrack. Roush offered to hire someone to take his place with his son's go-cart program—but Jack Jr. would also have to become more involved. "It's time to start working on the car and do more than driving," Roush said. But speed had not gotten its hooks into the son as deeply as the father. Music and computers were Jack Jr.'s love, and racing without dad lacked the appeal of the earlier days. "He didn't know if it would be as much fun without me," Roush said.

So Jack Jr. stopped racing to indulge his own passions, which led him as a young adult to found an Internet search-engine company with friends. Patricia earned a master's degree in creative writing after moving to San Francisco, where she was employed at a computer firm. Only Roush's eldest child, Susan, shared his interest in automobiles: She managed his collection of racing memorabilia and more than two hundred trucks and cars, including a '51 Ford that Roush had restored in the likeness of the first car he ever raced. Starting in 1998, Susan handled Roush's involvement in the History Channel's Great Race, which a Roush-sponsored car won in 2001.

The Kmart 400, the 14th points race of the 2001 Winston Cup season, was run on Sunday, June 10, at Michigan International Speedway, about an hour and a half southwest of Roush Industries' Livonia headquarters. That morning, Mark Martin visited the Pfizer hospitality tent outside the two-mile-long speedway. The many doctors, nurses, and Pfizer salesmen in attendance constituted a markedly different demographic than the crowds visiting Jeff Burton at a CITGO event.

Following his fourth-place showing in the Coca-Cola 600, Martin had finished ninth in the previous week's race at Dover, advancing four places in the point standings, to 14th. Martin liked the Michigan speedway, with its gentle turns and long frontstretch and long backstretch, which permitted speeds near 200 miles per hour—and with four Winston Cup wins there and another eight finishes inside the top five, it was a track where he had enjoyed considerable success. Although Martin's car had not handled to his liking in his final practice the day before the race, crew chief Jimmy Fennig had made adjustments after practice ended, and Martin was hopeful of a good race, which might allow him to advance further in the standings.

The first question that the Pfizer crowd posed to Martin concerned women racers. Included in the field at the Kmart 400 was Shawna Robinson, a thirty-six-year old mother of two who hoped to become a regular competitor in Winston Cup racing after a noteworthy career on non-NASCAR circuits. Robinson faced a substantial challenge: In more than half a century of Cup racing, only fourteen different women had ever even made a race, a total of only seventy times. Only one woman had ever led a lap, and the best finish by a woman was fifth—more than a half-century before, in 1949. With its redneck roots still visible, many in NASCAR continued to cast a skeptical—and sometimes derisive—eye toward women in motorsports.

Martin played off that attitude in his opening answer. "I think it would help the scenery an awful lot with female drivers!" he said, to laughter.

But Martin was no chauvinist, and he quickly turned serious. "There's not any reason why we don't have more except just kind of maybe a cultural thing," he said. "I know that my son is nine years old and he races Quarter Midgets and there are a lot of girls that drive the Quarter Midgets—and drive really well. But I think that as they get older, a lot of them wind up going in different directions. They have pulls toward a lot of other things—career things, family things." Martin said he supported more women racing in NASCAR. "I think it can be done—it just hasn't been done that much lately. Maybe in the future—I mean, there's no reason why you couldn't."

Martin expounded on the usual topics that surfaced in these sessions—weight loss from dehydration during a race, the G forces experienced rounding turns, safety at extreme speed—and then a man tossed out a question Martin rarely received, but which he himself had been pondering as the year unfolded.

"If you didn't have points to chase, would you race every weekend?" the man said.

"Well that's a good question," Martin said. "Three years ago, yes. But I'm not sure right now." He described the long second half of the season ahead. After the final weekend off, for the Fourth of July, racing would continue for twenty straight weeks, starting on July 7 with the Pepsi 400 at Daytona International Speedway. Sponsor obligations and testing, including at the new Chicagoland Speedway, in Joliet, Illinois, where Martin would head after today's race, would fill many of the weekdays between races.

"When you're in your twenties, you know," said Martin, "it's all fun and games. But the older you get—you see your kids growing up, you see things slipping away, sacrifices that you make to become successful. Everybody does that in their careers—but at some point you step back and look at it and say 'Uh-uh, I don't know how much more I want to miss.'"

One family moment that often crossed Martin's mind was the race at Watkins Glen, New York, on Saturday, August 8, 1998. As the race was in progress, an airplane piloted by Martin's father, Julian, crashed in Nevada, killing Julian; Julian's wife, Shelley; and their eleven-year-old daughter, Sarah. Word of the crash did not reach Martin until after he had returned home on that Sunday night. The son buried his father in Arkansas on the following

Wednesday, and then traveled the next day to Michigan, where he raced on August 16, finishing fourth. But despite media accounts depicting him as a duty-bound iron man, Martin did not compete ungrudgingly—and the choice he had been forced to make that weekend troubled him still.

Shortly before the Kmart 400, Martin discussed his feelings when his father died. "There was no right thing to do—it would have been wrong to miss the race, and it was wrong to run the race," he said. Winston Cup racing forced other choices and demanded sacrifices that Martin found increasingly onerous. "I don't call the shots in my life right now. My commitments, my schedule, my sponsors, my team, my car—they all call my life. I have had no control over where I go or what I do, that's how I feel, anyway." Like Jeff Burton, Martin—who would turn forty-three years old the following January—did not intend to be racing full-time when he was fifty. He had announced no retirement date, but his contract with Roush Racing ran through the year 2005 and it was unlikely he would extend it; already, he had retired from the Busch Grand National Series, in which he had also competed part-time since Jack Roush had hired him for Winston Cup. "I've never had one since I was fifteen years old—but I am gonna have a life," he said. "And then when somebody dies in my family, I'm going to be able to be by their side for one, two, three, four, five days—whatever it is. I'm not going to be excused from crises and funerals."

But that all lay in the future. Martin had not won a race in more than a year, and his craving had not abated.

Inside the Pfizer hospitality tent, Martin's reflections on his own career led to questions about his son. Martin brightened and said: "This sport—we're always out of control. You have so much personnel, so much equipment, so many things going on, so much management. It's like a huge, huge company. It's a lot more fun to race with my son than it is to race myself—a lot more. It's nothing but racing: There's no business to it."

As Martin returned to the track, a security guard who didn't recognize him asked if he had the proper credentials.

"Sometimes I wish I didn't," Martin replied. He was a man in torment.

Except for Mark Martin, the June 3 race at Dover had been another disappointment for the Roush racers: Matt Kenseth had finished 16th, after a NASCAR penalty for pitting out of sequence; Kurt Busch finished 39th, after crashing; and Jeff Burton followed his win at the Coca-Cola 600 with a 31st-place showing, which resulted not from penalty or accident but a poorly handling car. Fresh rumors spread about trouble inside Roush Racing.

And this time, Kenseth was the focus. So many reporters now believed he was conspiring to leave Roush, perhaps to drive for Richard Childress, who earlier had been rumored to be wooing Burton, that Kenseth in Michigan made a rare decision to seek out the press to put the rumors to rest. Fidgeting uncomfortably and speaking in a soft voice, he faced the microphones in the speedway's media center.

"How long is your contract at Roush Racing?" one reporter asked.

"A couple more years," Kenseth said. "I'm happy at Roush Racing. I'm not happy with the way we're running, but I think there are a lot of teams that aren't happy with the way they're running. . . . All of the rumors about me going to Richard Childress and all that, I didn't know where they started."

Pressed by another reporter, Kenseth conceded that people he would not name had approached him about driving for some other owner—not Childress—but he attributed those casual contacts to the ordinary course of business. "People will always mention things here and there like 'If something happens to your deal, think about maybe giving me a call.' But there's never been any talks that were more serious than that."

But then Kenseth gave a cryptic response to a straightforward question.

"Do you feel any kind of debt to Jack Roush?" a reporter said.

"That's kind of a hard question to answer," said Kenseth. "First of all, Mark Martin is the one, not Jack Roush, who saw me and got me hooked up with Jack Roush. I think Mark bugged Jack for probably a year or a year and a half at least before we ever got anything going, so it was Mark that really got this thing going for me and got me to Winston Cup racing."

This was classic Kenseth: just stating the facts as he knew them. But reporters construed his appearance that morning as less than a ringing endorsement, and the rumors continued.

Kenseth finished 15th in the Kmart 400, ahead of Mark Martin, who was 16th, and Kurt Busch, who came in last after losing control of his car on the 16th lap and crashing, alone, into the wall. Jeff Burton recovered from his Dover low by placing seventh, which moved him up four spots in the point standings, to 17th. He, Martin, and Kenseth were now all within 200 points of the top ten.

But the attention was on other drivers after the Kmart 400 ended. Placing 34th, Shawna Robinson became the first woman since 1988 to complete a Winston Cup race. "I'm not going to be real excited about running at the back all day, but at the same time, when I was in traffic and in groups I didn't feel like I was in the way—I learned and I ran with them and that was good," she said. "The main thing was I needed to finish—and I didn't crash." Robinson, who had failed in her previous attempt to qualify for a Cup race this season, said she would try again in July at the maiden competition at Chicagoland Speedway, and then in

August at the Brickyard 400 at Indianapolis. Credible performances might secure the sponsorship she sought to run the full
schedule in 2002.

Another attention-getter was Dale Jarrett, who placed 18th
and fell from first place in the standings, which he had held since
his March win at Darlington. Jarrett still drove in pain, but he
refused to sit out a race, as his doctor had advised to allow his
injured rib muscles to heal. "We can't take a day off—we're
gonna lose points if we do that, and basically take yourself out of
a chance to win a championship," Jarrett said. NASCAR's rules
would have allowed him to yield his wheel to a relief driver, but
he declined, as most drivers would, explaining, "We might find
somebody who can drive that thing better than me—and I don't
want them to know that!" Jarrett laughed, but he took the matter
seriously; like anyone who had made it this far in NASCAR racing, he knew of the many instances when replacements had
indeed won the primary driver's job. And Jarrett was hardly
alone in his bravado: Mark Martin, for example, had raced
against medical advice, most recently in July 1999, when he suffered a broken wrist, rib, and knee during practice for the Pepsi
400; Martin had to be lifted in and out of his car, but he started
and finished the race. The following week, Martin required knee
surgery—and two days later, he was back in his car for the next
competition, in New Hampshire.

But the biggest news out of the Kmart 400 was the winner,
Jeff Gordon, who replaced Jarrett as the points leader. With the
exception of one week early in the season, Gordon had not held
first in more than a year and a half—uncharacteristic for the
driver, who had captured his first Winston Cup championship in
1995, the year he turned twenty-four; his second championship
in 1997, when he became the first driver to win more than $6
million in a season; and his third in 1998, when he recorded
seven poles and thirteen wins, a feat that only Richard Petty had
equaled. But then, in September 1999, Ray Evernham, Gordon's

longtime crew chief, had quit to spearhead Dodge's planned reentry into NASCAR racing after years of absence. Through a disappointing 2000 season, Gordon had learned firsthand how delicate team chemistry was.

With his win the previous week at Dover and now at Michigan, Gordon was back in familiar territory. But almost thirty now, he had gained wisdom in his time away from the top. Commenting after the Kmart 400, Gordon downplayed the growing talk that 2001 could be his year. "We've got some momentum, but we have to stay focused," he said. "We can't get overconfident." Things changed stunningly fast in racing, as the Roush drivers this year could well attest.

Summer beckoned, and the Cup circuit moved from Michigan to the resort town of Long Pond, Pennsylvania, for the Pocono 500, held on June 17 at Pocono Raceway; it was Father's Day, a holiday for men, but NASCAR men raced.

On the morning of the race, NASCAR held a press conference to showcase its Winston Cup rookies. The only one missing was Kevin Harvick, who had shuttled all weekend between Pocono and Kentucky Speedway, where he was entered in Saturday night's Busch Grand National race, the Outback Steakhouse 300. Harvick won—and then returned to Pocono, via helicopter and jet, sometime after midnight. No one could begrudge him sleeping in.

Addressing the reporters, the other rookies all spoke of the unexpected difficulty of Winston Cup racing compared to the lesser series in which each had excelled before. Asked to rate their seasons, all gave themselves mediocre grades—and offered varying degrees of insight into their performances. "You really can't say what you've done well because you don't know—but you know when you've done bad because they're all going to tell you you done bad, you know?" said Ron Hornaday Jr. Kurt Busch was more articulate in his analysis: "It's just been a bunch of highs and a bunch of lows," he said. "That's what we have to work on: building consistency."

Reporters raised the subject of Harvick, who led in the Cup Rookie-of-the-Year contest and who held ninth in the overall point standings, all the more impressive considering that he had not competed at Daytona, and thus had one less race to his credit. Jason Leffler attributed much of Harvick's success to the people and machines that Dale Earnhardt's death had provided him. Said Leffler: "He jumped in a perfect situation where the car runs real well and he's got some good guys behind him. He don't have to carry the car that hard—the car's already there." Busch was more magnanimous. "He's definitely had the weight of the racing world on his shoulders ever since Daytona," said Busch. "He's done a miraculous job every week."

Ricky Rudd won the Pocono 500, and Jeff Gordon was second, which kept him first in the point standings. For only the second time in 2001, three Roush drivers placed in the top ten—and the fourth, Busch, finished 13th, beating Harvick, who coasted home in 15th after running out of gas on the final lap. Busch was the best rookie of the day.

Jack Roush had decided not to celebrate with his drivers. He wanted to beat the traffic out of the raceway and get to his jet, parked at a tiny airport a few miles away. He was heading to Greenville, South Carolina, to join the History Channel's Great Race, a cross-continent competition in which he had entered several of his lovingly restored antique cars. But Roush did have time for quick congratulations, and he extended them driver by driver.

"Nice job," he said to Busch, who he found in his hauler lounge.

"Everybody in the top ten but us?" said the rookie.

Roush confirmed that Martin had finished fifth, Kenseth sixth, and Burton tenth. "But you won something," said Roush, "the rest of them didn't."

"Rookie points."

"You won rookie points."

"It's just a drop in the bucket," said Busch.

"But it was a win. You won something!"

Gordon placed third in the next race, on June 24, at Sears Point Raceway in Sonoma, California, one of only two road courses on the Winston Cup circuit, widening his lead to 126 points over Jarrett, who crossed the finish line in 26th. Martin and Burton recorded top-ten finishes, and Kenseth came in 21st; Busch ended the race in 23rd, behind Harvick, who was 14th. Racers took their final weekend off until late November, and then competition resumed on July 7 with the Pepsi 400, a Saturday night race at Daytona International Speedway.

Predictably, remembrances of Dale Earnhardt and renewed discussion of safety issues accompanied the Winston Cup community on its first visit to the speedway since the death of The Intimidator. The Pepsi 400 also brought fresh evidence of NASCAR's continuing impact on the wider culture. Serving as the race's grand marshal, Britney Spears, dressed in a skintight starspangled jumpsuit, gave the call to start engines. Publications such as *Entertainment Weekly* covered the event, and the comparison was drawn between NASCAR's real-life thrills and those in *The Fast and the Furious,* a movie about street racing that had grossed more than $100 million in its first three weeks of release. Twenty-seven-year-old Paul Walker, one of the stars of the film, called automobile racing "an adrenaline fix" of the sort that others his age experienced in extreme sports. A generation that did not know war had turned to other outlets to satisfy its youthful yearning for adventure.

Dale Earnhardt Jr. struck a similar theme: "There's so much appeal to young people," he told *Entertainment Weekly.* "The sounds. The speed. The danger. Going to a race is like going to the biggest damn circus in the world, or a rock 'n' roll festival. It's like sensory overload." Bill France himself could not have written a better endorsement of the sport for the youth market, which was critical to NASCAR's continuing growth.

But Junior was no shill for NASCAR—he spoke his mind, just as he lived his unconventional life without apology. His music tastes ran to Notorious B.I.G. and Third Eye Blind—and also Elvis and Barry Manilow's "Mandy." He wore baggy jeans and his baseball cap backward, and he sometimes dyed his hair. He owned four computers, on which he played racing and S.W.A.T. games—and connected to the Internet. He hung out in nightclubs and bars, sometimes taking the stage to jam with the band, and he had turned the basement of his house into a lounge for his friends that he called Club E. He liked to sleep late, especially after a long night of partying.

And he idolized his father, who had divorced his mother when he was three, then raised him from the age of six. During the 2000 season, Junior had written a series of monthly essays for nascar.com, and his October offering was a tribute to Dad. "This man could lead the world's finest army. He has wisdom that knows no bounds," Junior wrote. "His friendship is the greatest gift you could ever obtain." Junior said that the highlight of his racing career was his father joining him in Victory Lane after he won The Winston in 2000.

He claimed he never saw his father cry—but Junior cried when Earnhardt died. In the ensuing weeks, the son would walk past Earnhardt's office, looking for him while knowing he was of course not there. And while his death did not deter Junior from racing, he maintained that it did mature him. "I had this little bit of a little brat in me somewhere," he said several weeks after burying his father. "That's all gone."

Junior did not compete ruthlessly, like his father, nor did he share The Intimidator's cocky attitude off-track. Even before Earnhardt died, the soft-spoken, polite Junior seemed oddly vulnerable for a racer. His father's death swelled his already substantial fan base, which, judging by the applause at drivers' introductions, was among the largest in NASCAR, and the press wrote glowing accounts of his handling of the tragedy and its aftermath. So it was hardly surprising that Junior, who stood 11th in the points but had yet to win in 2001, was the sentimental favorite returning to Daytona for the Pepsi 400.

As if following a script, Junior indeed won—and Michael Waltrip, who had beaten him by a hair to capture the ill-fated Daytona 500, placed second. At eighth, Jeff Burton was the best of the Roush drivers; Matt Kenseth was 16th, Mark Martin 18th, and Kurt Busch 30th.

Junior embraced Waltrip in Victory Lane as fireworks erupted and a spotlight casting a numeral "3" appeared in a giant cloud of smoke. Speedway officials had planned the display as a post-race tribute to The Intimidator—and now here was his son, basking in the glory.

"I never would have imagined this would happen," Junior told reporters. "I can't sit here and understand it. I can't believe this is happening to me."

Journalists proceeded to pen odes to Junior. For a sport still grieving the loss of its icon, it all seemed too good to be true.

Maybe it was, some soon began to whisper. Maybe the race had been fixed. The whispers quickly flared into a firestorm of open questions, and by July 9, two days after the race, NASCAR was caught up in another controversy.

What better way to divert attention from the still-lingering safety issue, the conspiracists theorized, than to have Junior win at the track where the season began on a tragic note? Dale Earnhardt had been Bill France's close friend and a leading partner in NASCAR's past success—wasn't Junior also a critical piece of the future, his fortunes vital to the sport's continued growth? Wouldn't an emotional fairy tale benefit TV ratings and ticket sales, including the following week at NASCAR's maiden race in the Chicago market, where motorsports historically had ranked far behind baseball, football, and basketball?

Conspiracy theories might find less fertile ground in other sports, but cheating had been a part of NASCAR culture from its earliest days, when the rule book was only a few pages long and ill-trained inspectors lacked the expertise or inclination to approve all of a racecar's untold thousands of components. And while inspections had become more rigorous over time, short of tearing each vehicle and its engine apart it was impossible to guarantee that every car at every race met the rules. Lore held that several of NASCAR's drivers and owners had cheated, including some of the biggest stars. And some conspiracy-minded individuals believed that certain NASCAR officials themselves had been involved in changing outcomes. They cited such questionable penalties as those against Mark Martin in 1990 and Greg Biffle in 1999, and they questioned the controversial Pepsi 400 in Daytona on July 4, 1984: President Ronald Reagan happened to be attending, and Richard Petty, well past his prime, happened to record his 200th and final win.

Those suspecting a fix in the Pepsi 400 cited Earnhardt Jr.'s dominance: he led 116 of the 160 laps, and no one passed him. Perhaps, the speculation went, the aerodynamic profile of his No. 8 Budweiser car had been illegally altered by fractions of an inch that inspectors missed—assuming they weren't in on it. Another theory held that Junior had gained an advantage by means of an illegal restrictor plate: NASCAR carefully controlled and distributed them for a race, and if Junior's had slightly larger holes, more air would reach the engine, and horsepower would be increased. No one assumed that Junior had participated in, or even knew about, any such schemes. They suspected someone in the NASCAR hierarchy.

Fix was all the talk of NASCAR the week before the race at Chicagoland Speedway. Junior reacted first with anger, sharing his thoughts publicly on a radio program hosted by 1973 Winston

Cup champion and now NBC broadcaster Benny Parsons. "A reporter came up and asked me that," Junior said. "I came as close as I ever have to knocking him straight out."

But Junior was a gentle sort.

"It really hurt my feelings that people would think that," he said. "I mean, aside from the days that I had my father with me, that was the greatest day of my life. I just can't believe that people would step on it like that. That really taints it so much that I almost can't really enjoy it."

Kevin Harvick won the Tropicana 400 at Chicagoland—and Kurt Busch finished eighth, his best showing since Talladega. "It was a great day for the No. 97 Sharpie Rubbermaid team. The crew did a fantastic job," said Busch, who also praised his rival. "Kevin Harvick and the No. 29 team did everything right today and they had a great racecar. It was wonderful to see a fellow rookie do so well at a brand new track. Hopefully we'll have our chance later on this season." Chicagoland also proved rewarding for Mark Martin, who came in sixth, and Matt Kenseth, who after starting in 37th place finished the race in seventh, his third-best showing of the year. "That was a great run for this team," said Kenseth. "The guys did great in the pits, my spotter Mike Calinoff did a great job, and I held on to the end." Only Jeff Burton, who finished the Tropicana 400 in 18th, left Illinois unfulfilled.

Four days later, racers for the first time in 2001 visited New Hampshire International Speedway in Loudon, a track, like Daytona, where the memories were still painful. It was the weekend of July 22, when the New England 300 would be run. A year had passed since Kenny Irwin Jr.'s death, and it was fourteen months since Adam Petty had died. None of Irwin's relatives attended the New England 300—but Petty's parents, Pattie and Kyle, driver of the No. 45 Sprint car, did.

Kyle had followed a different path from his father, Richard, the most revered driver in NASCAR history. He sported granny glasses and wore his hair in a long ponytail, despite hints from sponsors to clean up his image, and he became impassioned when talking about his many charities, notably the annual fundraising cross-country motorcycle ride that he had established. He was not a great stockcar driver like his dad. In two decades of Cup competition, he had never finished higher than fifth in the point standings, and he had won just eight races, the last in 1995. Kyle's greatest racing prominence had been as a manager—he was the chief executive officer of Petty Enterprises, the family business.

Adam, born in 1980, was the first of Kyle and Pattie's three children. Adam started racing go-carts when he was six, moving up to a class of small racecars called mini-sprints when he turned twelve. For his fourteenth birthday, Kyle gave him a stockcar chassis—and a challenge to finish building the vehicle. Adam worked on it for a few weeks, then quit. Kyle waited patiently; the Petty legacy certainly weighed on the boy, but he alone would have to decide if he wanted to carry it on. A few months later, having found football and baseball not to his liking, Adam told Kyle: "Let's get the thing together."

A legacy combined with talent is a foundation of early success, and Adam progressed quickly in stockcar competition. He won his first race in the American Speed Association, in April 1998; only seventeen years old, he became the youngest winner in ASA history, a title previously held by Mark Martin. That October, debuting at Lowe's Motor Speedway in front of his extended family, Kyle beat Cup veteran Mike Wallace in an Automobile Racing Club of America event. "Winning this ARCA race is the biggest thing that has ever happened to me," Adam said. "Having my dad in my pit tonight with my mom on the back straightaway, and my brother and sister and my grandmother and grandfather and all my aunts and uncles here and all the Winston guys watching, it's unreal." Adam's great-grandfather, Lee Petty, was a three-time Winston Cup champion in NASCAR's early days, and writers began to proclaim the first four-generation dynasty in all of American sports.

A tall, handsome teenager with a pleasing smile and a ready laugh, Adam did not let the Petty name swell his head; fellow drivers praised his down-to-earth attitude, and he made friends, not enemies, on and off the track. Adam ran his first full season in Busch Grand National in 1999, finishing 20th in the standings. He started the 2000 Busch Grand National season intending also to compete that year in at least five Cup races, to gain experience for 2001, when he would run the full Cup slate and compete for Rookie of the Year. Kyle, at forty, would continue to drive his own Cup car, but his nineteen-year-old son's career had become his focus.

Kyle did not race for almost a month after Adam died on May 12, 2000, and when he returned to his car, it was only for a few Cup races. Then he handed his Cup duties to another driver for the remainder of the season—and drove his son's No. 45 Chevrolet in Busch Series competition through the end of 2000, as a memorial—and with the belief that Adam would have wanted that.

Time had not brought much solace to Kyle and Pattie. In the lone interview they granted on the one-year anniversary of Adam's death, Kyle spoke of the many reminders of his son that he found at the racetrack and at home, and of driving Adam's street car every few days to keep the battery charged. And Kyle had not disconnected adampetty.com from the Internet: Visitors to the site found it much as it had been before his death, with a biography and photographs of a vibrant young man, and race results through the spring of 2000. The site's news page included a preview of the race weekend when Adam died, but no obituary or accident story. Only a message directing memorial donations to Kyle's charities hinted that Adam raced no more.

"I don't really see that it's gotten any easier," Kyle said in the anniversary interview. "I don't really even feel like we've had time as a family to get away from it and heal. You had Adam's accident and then you had Kenny's. And then you had Tony (Roper's) and then you had Dale's. It seems like the continuation of a bad dream." Said Pattie: "It's gotten worse for me to see how much harder each week gets, to see Kyle suffering each week without him." During the interview, Kyle cried.

With other Petty Enterprises drivers still competing, Richard Petty had returned to New Hampshire International Speedway in July 2000, the first weekend of Cup racing for him since his grandson's death. But Kyle and Pattie had not visited the track since burying their son, and until a few days before the July 2001 New England 300, they weren't sure they would.

Ordinarily among the most accessible of drivers, Kyle asked in a written statement not to be approached for comment when he arrived in Loudon. He explained that his affection for the Bob Bahre family, who owned the speedway and who had been devastated by the tragedies of 2000, had compelled him—and more importantly, the memory of his son. "Adam would want me and the 45 team to come here and race," Kyle said. "I love Adam, we all love Adam, and miss him terribly." Kyle had repainted his red car black, and written a love note on the side: "Adam Petty, Forever in Our Hearts."

One emotion Kyle maintained that he had not experienced was regret: Adam was pursuing what he loved, and he had understood the dangers. When Kyle's other son, nineteen-year-old Austin, decided to start racing mini-stockcars at Lowe's Motor Speedway in the summer of 2001, Kyle approved.

Other racers shared this perspective.

Weary though he sometimes was after almost three decades of racing, and contrary to Arlene's wishes, Mark Martin nonetheless envisioned his son following in his footsteps, assuming racing proved to be in Matt's blood. Martin noted that participants in many other sports get injured and die, and he drew a parallel to pilots who encourage their children to fly knowing that their passion can be deadly. "Other people in life have the same kind of (issue)—it's not just me and it's not just racing," Martin said. "You do the best you can to manage the risks. I think racing is a pretty safe sport. I've been in it a long time, taken a lot of hard hits, and with the exception of a bum knee, I'm pretty good for twenty-seven years."

Even Jeff Burton would not forbid his children from racing, nor would Kim; like Martin, they believed parents should guide career choices, but not make demands. "I don't want Harrison to feel like just because he's my son that he needs to drive, and I don't want Paige to feel like that," said Burton. "But if either made a decision and they understood the whole lifestyle, then I would support it. It would also suit me fine for that not to be the case."

Speed was a potent, and sometimes contradictory, addiction—for drivers and their spouses alike.

The Roush racers had arrived in Loudon hoping to continue their momentum from Chicagoland. But collectively, they disappointed again in the New Hampshire 300, which Dale Jarrett won. Jeff Burton did finish 11th, but Matt Kenseth placed 16th, Mark Martin 18th, and Kurt Busch 42nd, after his overheated engine blew up on lap 80.

With his seventh-place finish, Harvick was again the top rookie. He had claimed the honor in six of the last eight races, and now held a solid lead over Busch in the contest for Rookie of the Year. And that was not the only arena in which Harvick was impressing the racing community: He had advanced to seventh place in the overall Winston Cup standings (compared to 22nd for Busch), and he continued to compete in Busch Grand National, madly crisscrossing the continent on some weekends to fit in all of his practices, qualifying laps, and races in the two series. Harvick often slept only a few hours curled up on an airplane, yet despite his demanding schedule he insisted he was not exhausting himself, and his hold on first place in the Busch standings seemed proof. Except perhaps for owner Richard Childress and Harvick himself, few would have predicted such dominance. Although he had finished third in the 2000 Busch season and been named the series Rookie of the Year, he had never finished higher than 12th in his three prior seasons in the Craftsman Truck Series.

Of all the Cup rookies, only Kurt Busch realistically had any shot now of catching Harvick—and if his performance in the New England 300 was an omen, it was a long shot. Busch couldn't help comparing himself to his rival, and when he did, he discerned two significant differences: Harvick's greater experience, and his equipment and personnel. But Busch nonetheless respected his rival's accomplishments. "He's got a lot on his shoulders with that (Busch Grand National) program and running for the championship in that—and yet being expected to fill a legend's shoes," Busch said. "He's done everything he's supposed to have done so far this year and that's where I've lacked." Kurt Busch was nothing if not a gentleman.

Although Busch was becoming more accustomed to the rigors of Winston Cup competition, the unfamiliarity of the tracks, the duration of the races, and the complexities of a Cup racecar still vexed him at times. And there were no byes, no possibility of sitting out the rotation; even when his car was handling poorly he had to race, struggling to at least avoid wrecking even as he pondered what adjustments of tire pressure, shocks, springs, sway bar, and the like might improve his car's performance during the next pit stop. In the heat of July, Busch's high finishes in the spring races at Talladega and California seemed a distant memory.

"So you have the challenge of driving an ill-handling car and then still trying to remember what it's supposed to handle like so that you can make those adjustments," Busch said. "And then when you do get the car fixed, you've got to change your driving style once again, to what the car's going to do for the next 90 laps or so. And each of those laps it changes, because the tires wear out, the fuel goes away, there's the draft at the speeds that we run. Then there's track position: where you're at out on the race track. And there's the deciding factor of everything: what cars are around you." The best veteran racers managed all of this almost instinctively; they entered the zone. Busch so far this year had been an infrequent visitor—and the frustration had caused him to lose his temper several times. Following one poor qualifying effort, Busch had slammed his hauler's door, breaking it; on other occasions, he had cussed. After his wreck at Dover, he had briefly argued—live on national TV—with rescue workers sent to bring him to the track medical center for the checkup he didn't believe he needed, even though he knew that NASCAR regulations required it.

Many of those close to Busch provided encouragement: among them, his parents; Harry McMullen, who kept telling him that he was in but the first year of a long, exceptional career; and spotter Bruce Hayes, who predicted: "Someday will be our day. It's coming, it's getting closer." Melissa Schaper, his live-in companion now, found ways to shake him from his occasional irritability, and get him to eat on days when he lacked an appetite.

Jack Roush, meanwhile, maintained his enthusiasm for the young driver he considered as almost a second son.

"If we put the things around him that he needs and we manage him with support and with instruction that is timely," Roush said, "he can win a race tomorrow."

But Roush was not one to hold hands or utter daily words of support; contentment, he knew, did not beget great racers.

CHAPTER 8
LONG HOT SUMMER

The weekend after New Hampshire, drivers returned to Pocono Speedway for the Pennsylvania 500. It was Sunday, July 29. Bobby Labonte finally won, Dale Earnhardt Jr. came in second, and the Roush racers again enjoyed mixed results. Mark Martin finished seventh and Matt Kenseth 14th—but Jeff Burton came home 36th after an accident, and Kurt Busch finished 37th after an improperly tightened wheel fell off in the closing laps of the race. As Busch had steered his crippled No. 97 Ford Taurus back to pit road, the wheel had rolled down the frontstretch and crossed the finish line before coming to rest—a darkly comic journey that the TV cameras followed on close-up. Busch accepted partial responsibility for the mishap: Hopeful of a top-ten finish, he hadn't taken the time to return to pit road for investigation of an unusual vibration he felt just before the wheel came off.

"I was so sick and tired of having bad finishes, failing and folding at crunch time," said Busch. "I was just in denial. I wanted to finish the damn race."

Busch had put Pocono behind him when he arrived a week later at Indianapolis Motor Speedway for the August 5 running of the Brickyard 400—but if the opening practice session, on Friday, August 3, was an omen, it would be another long weekend for Busch and all of the Roush racers. The fastest of the four, Mark Martin, was only 24th best of the fifty-four drivers attempting to make the race at the world's most famous track, and Busch ran 36th, four miles per hour behind the practice leader, a disturbing deficit. But there was still one more practice run before the qualifying heat, and the mechanics had plenty of time to tune the cars. As they got down to business, Busch and Jack Roush shifted their interest elsewhere: Kurt's younger brother, Kyle, was making his debut as a Roush racer that evening at Indianapolis Raceway Park, a small speedway a few miles away from its bigger cousin. Kyle would compete in the Craftsman Truck Series, where Kurt had been Rookie of the Year.

Roush set off in his rental Lincoln for Raceway Park. It was late afternoon and traffic was sluggish—but he had arranged for an escort by three motorcycle police officers who wore sunglasses and black boots, and understood Roush's place in racing. Lights flashing and sirens wailing, the officers led Roush out of the speedway and onto the congested city streets. Leap-frogging ahead of one another, the officers stopped traffic at intersections, forced cars to the side, and, when all else failed, beckoned Roush to follow them at speeds approaching seventy miles per hour down the wrong side of the road. The twenty-minute trip, a race in its own right, excited Roush—and he was especially impressed by the one officer who rode his motorcycle standing upright on the seat most of the way. "Some people need to take risks, you know," Roush said when the officers had delivered him to Raceway Park. "Some of us gotta have one every day!"

Roush parked his Lincoln in a preferred spot, instructed the officers on when they should return, and walked toward the tunnel that connected to the infield. This was a different place than Indy, with its luxury boxes and gourmet menus, and seemingly from a different time: Vendors sold chili pies, corn dogs, lemon shake-ups, and pork butt on a stick; spectators not wanting to sit on metal stands could rent cushioned seats for five dollars; and a billboard for a country-and-western radio station declared, "Love Your Country!" Roush knew Raceway Park well: Long before he became one of the powers of NASCAR, he had drag-raced there with Wayne Gapp. Almost every Winston Cup driver had also competed at Raceway, or on tracks like it across America, usually on Friday or Saturday nights, family time, as they started the climb toward the pinnacle of their sport.

Roush entered the infield, where qualifying was about to begin, and conferred with the managers of his Truck program. They had started their season with the winners of the most recent Gong Show, Chuck Hossfeld and Nathan Haseleu, who were both in their mid-twenties, but Roush had tired of their lackluster finishes—and their inability to attract a major sponsor. To confirm that the drivers were at fault, not their vehicles and crews, a few weeks before Roush had substituted Greg Biffle and Kurt Busch for them in a Truck Series race—and Biffle and Busch, who had dominated in 2000, had nearly won. With no sponsorship and no buzz around which Geoff Smith might have marketed them, Hossfeld and Haseleu were doomed. Unwilling to wait for another Gong Show, Roush had first hired Eddie Wood's nineteen-year-old son, Jon, who had grown up around his family's Winston Cup operation, essentially a wing of Roush Racing now. And now Roush had hired Kyle Busch, who had turned sixteen years old in May and completed his sophomore year of high school in June. He would be the youngest driver in Truck Series history.

Kyle had come to Roush's attention through Kurt, who had mentioned the previous year that he had a kid brother who raced. Encouraged by their elder son's success, Tom and Gaye Busch had put Kyle behind the wheel of a Legends car when he was thirteen, three years younger than when Kurt had started. Lending credence to the existence of a racing gene, Kyle achieved the same quick success as Kurt in the Las Vegas area, and the

Busches, attempting to accelerate his career, soon allowed him to compete in a more powerful class of cars known as Modifieds. Kyle was an instant sensation, and his success moved Nevada sportswriters to lavish praise: "Kyle Busch, despite his youth, but mostly because of it, is the most talked about driver in local racing circles," wrote a columnist for the *Las Vegas Review-Journal* in July 2000. "He's almost legendary in Legends, those half-ton replicas of 1930-era cars with 1200cc motorcycle engines. He's also proving grand in Grand American Modifieds, as well as IMCA Modifieds, those thunderous, big-engine behemoths that top out at 100 mph." The columnist marveled at Kyle being only sixteen.

Except in the summer of 2000, he wasn't: He was actually fifteen, a year shy of the minimum age requirement for Modifieds. As the *Review-Journal* later learned and reported, Tom had presented a falsified birth certificate claiming his second son was born a year earlier than he actually was. Tom was contrite when caught. "I guess I shouldn't have said he was sixteen," he told the newspaper. "I don't want to look like a felon who doctored up car titles. I just wanted Kyle to become a better driver." Kyle was forced to withdraw from modified competition in 2000, but he returned in May 2001, when he really turned sixteen.

Roush did not condone deceit, but he considered the Busches' actions to be a pardonable, even reasonable, sin—and in any event, he was profoundly impressed by the results of the two test sessions his Truck Series managers staged for Kyle after he decided to replace Hossfeld and Haseleu. Like Kurt on his final audition, Kyle drove with a sophistication that belied his age. "He's been unbelievable in maturity and his poise and his judgment and his competitiveness," said Roush. If Kyle fared well at Indianapolis Raceway Park and in six or so more races through the 2001 season, Roush planned to enter him in the entire 2002 Truck season. (Kyle would combine his junior and senior years of high school into one, utilizing an intensive curriculum and sum-

mer classes, which he was already taking.) Assuming Kyle fulfilled his promise, Roush envisioned him racing a year or two in
the Truck Series, two or three years in the Busch Grand National
Series, and then on to Winston Cup—when he was twenty or
twenty-one years of age. If the scenario held, Kyle would put
Kurt in the category of late bloomer—and prove Roush an early
leader in what some were beginning to call NASCAR's youth
movement.

But Jack Roush's aspirations alone were not sufficient to per-
suade NASCAR officials that Kyle Busch belonged in the Truck
Series. NASCAR's minimum age was sixteen years—but no drivers had ever regularly competed at Kyle's age, and NASCAR
would let him race only after being satisfied that the teenager was
no hazard to himself or others. With faster and more powerful
vehicles, more seasoned drivers, and considerably longer races on
speedways that he'd never seen, Truck competition would be
more demanding than anything the boy had experienced on the
tracks back home. NASCAR officials were keeping a close watch
over Roush's latest protégé at Raceway Park, but so far they had
found nothing alarming. In fact, they had been impressed: During practice earlier in the day, Kyle had been fourth fastest,
demonstrating unusual cool in advance of the Power Stroke
Diesel 200.

Evening neared. Roush greeted Tom and Gaye Busch and
spoke briefly to Kyle, a dark-haired boy who was as tall and thin
as his brother. Kyle strapped himself into the No. 99, the same
vehicle Kurt had raced only a year before, and fired up his
engine. The official signaled the OK, and Kyle sped onto the oval
track, two-thirds of a mile long, for his two qualifying laps.

His first lap would prove 23rd fastest of the forty-three drivers
attempting to make the thirty-six-car field that constituted a
Truck Series race. But on his second lap, Kyle, hoping to pick up
a tenth of a second or two of speed, lost control and wrecked. He
was unhurt, but his car was too damaged to race, which forced

him into a backup vehicle. And that meant he would have to start last.

"It's going to be ugly," Roush said, a prediction he did not share with Kyle. Instead, he attempted to calm the boy by informing Kyle of his modest expectations. "To finish is to win," Roush said.

Kurt had missed the motorcycle escort to Raceway Park, but he and Melissa found their own way there as the grandstands began to fill. Although seven years separated them, Kurt and Kyle had kept a strong rivalry when they were growing up in Las Vegas. "I always had to put him in his place and just be the big brother and more or less kick his ass in everything!" Kurt explained. Tom and Gaye encouraged fraternity, however, especially in matters of racing; in the late 1990s, when he still lived at home, Kurt had shared his wisdom with Kyle, and the two had occasionally gone head-to-head on the Legends circuit—a diversion for Kurt, who by then was racing full-time on NASCAR's Southwest tour and dominating the competition. Kyle beat Kurt only once, an intolerable outcome for the older brother. "I couldn't handle that," Kurt said. "The next race I flat-out waxed him. That was just to spite him." But Kurt was a Winston Cup driver now, and he offered Kyle encouragement as Roush and the Busches awaited drivers' introductions. Kyle's Truck debut reminded Kurt of his own, in February 2000 at Daytona, when he had started last in his backup car after wrecking his primary vehicle in practice.

Craftsman Truck races attracted an eclectic mix of racers, and the Power Stroke Diesel 200 was no exception. Winston Cup regular Bobby Hamilton, who held 18th place in Cup standings, was looking for a little Friday night fun, and former Cup driver Ted Musgrave, who had driven for Jack Roush in the 1990s until Roush fired him for not meeting his expectations, sought a showing that might help resurrect him to NASCAR's highest level. Kyle would also be racing against Truck veteran Joe Ruttman—

who, at fifty-six, was forty years his senior. And there were the aging dreamers, racers like Larry Gunselman, a thirty-six-year-old Californian who was running a limited schedule in the No. 63 car that had been the late Tony Roper's. Gunselman was sponsored by Waterloo Tool Storage, a division of an Iowa-based company that billed itself as "the world's largest manufacturer of tool storage products for the consumer and professional markets." Pfizer or CITGO it was not.

It was nearing 7 o'clock. The announcer proceeded through the introductions, saying of NASCAR's newest Truck Series driver: "We're going to be hearing this name for years to come. Let's welcome Kyle Busch!" Kyle crossed the stage, acknowledged the applause with a wave, and walked to his car, where his parents wished him luck before departing for the grandstands. Kurt, who would watch with Melissa, Roush, and team manager Max Jones from the pits, gave some final advice: "Make sure you keep your mind focused and give 100 percent concentration for the two hundred laps. Don't wear yourself out too quick." Kurt closed by repeating what their father always said before races back in Nevada: "Bring it home in one piece." It was an admonition to be safe—and also to avoid costly damage that the Busch family's budget could ill absorb, at least during the boys' early racing days.

"Are you ready?" the announcer's voice rang out. The crowd roared that it was. "Are you ready? Gentlemen, start your engines!" Fireworks shot into the air against the setting sun as the drivers completed their warmup laps.

Like his brother, Kyle had a knack for moving quickly through the pack. By the end of the second lap, he had passed six drivers, and after thirty laps he had passed ten. The pit cart TV was tuned to ESPN, which heralded his rapid rise, best of any driver in the race. Roush gave a thumbs-up: so far, no ugliness, only a sixteen-year-old who was preternaturally assured.

Darkness fell, and the race continued under the lights. Kyle steered clear of several wrecks and he brought his car through his pit stops without incident and, by lap 138, he was running in eighth. The announcer compared his charge to a performance by his Winston Cup brother.

Not every driver had been so fortunate. Roush's other Truck driver, Jon Wood, who had been running near the front, was hit from behind and lost five laps to repairs—and the driver who crashed into him, Ronnie Hornaday III, twenty-two-year-old son of the aging Winston Cup rookie, was done for the night. So was Larry Gunselman, who stood silent and alone in a dark area of the infield as his small crew picked at the carcass of his wrecked car, which carried a small decal memorializing Tony Roper. Gunselman's entire season had unfolded disastrously, with overheating, engine failures, and accidents foiling him in seven of the thirteen races in which he had competed. Roper's death had opened the door of opportunity, but without a finish better than 16th in the Truck standings and with his thirty-seventh birthday approaching, that door could soon close.

Once he found the zone, Kyle Busch stayed in it: The three-quarters point of the race came and went, and he kept eighth place. A late shuffle dropped him to ninth, but from then on, no one could pass him. Roush's radio had broken, so he asked Kurt to use his to send his brother a message: "Bring it home. Don't get tired." Roush was smiling. What a pitch he and Geoff Smith would have for the Newell Rubbermaid executives who were in town this weekend for the Brickyard 400. They already sponsored one Busch, and now a convincing case could be made to sponsor another.

The checkered flag flew, and Kyle came home ninth, which earned him winnings of $9,350—pocket change now to his brother, but a fortune for him. Roush and Kurt reached the teen as he was climbing out of his car. Unsteady on his feet and sweating profusely, he managed a grin. "That wasn't too bad," said Roush, shaking his hand. "I think you came out a little short on what it cost to repair that truck. We'll send you a bill Monday!"

Kurt hugged Kyle and handed him a bottle of chilled water. "Good job," he said as they went to find their parents. Kurt had tears in his eyes. A line that he seemed to remember from an Austin Powers movie had crossed his mind: "That's my baby boy," the line went.

Kyle returned with Tom to Las Vegas to race on Saturday night in a local meet. Kurt's crew, meanwhile, had made progress preparing the No. 97 car for the Brickyard 400. The car handled better in Saturday morning's practice, enabling Busch to improve his speed by almost five miles per hour—to 21st fastest, best of the Roush team. But qualifying an hour later was another let-down: He would start the race at 34th, behind Burton, Kenseth, and Martin. Busch hoped his crew could work some magic before the final practice, scheduled for late afternoon.

Newell Rubbermaid had scheduled an autograph session for the midday break, and Busch drove himself, Melissa, Gaye, and Roush account manager Kathy Kalin on a golf cart to the sponsor's arcade, just outside Indianapolis Motor Speedway. Newell sold an extended family of consumer products, and marketing executives had created the concept of a "block party" to present them in entertaining fashion to race fans. Visitors to the arcade could shoot hoops, test their lug nut-tightening skills, examine an actual No. 97 Sharpie Rubbermaid Ford Taurus, and attempt to destroy with a bat a plastic storage bin that Rubbermaid advertised as unbreakable (battered and dented though it was, the bin was whole when Busch arrived). With his girlfriend beside him and his mother in the background, Busch signed autographs in an area filled with toys, garbage cans, coolers, Venetian blinds, lawn furniture, car seats, and many other mostly plastic items. This was domestic bliss as the marketers at Newell Rubbermaid imagined it.

From the block party, Busch went to his motor coach, the weekend home he shared with Melissa. Gaye prepared lunch while the couple played with Jim, the young cairn terrier they had bought last month in a pet shop near New Hampshire International Speedway—about the only welcome outcome of the New England 300 weekend, as it turned out. "It had that doggie-in-the-window look," Busch said. "It's the same type of dog as Toto in *The Wizard of Oz*." With children still in her future, Melissa wanted a puppy.

The couple had met in the spring of 1998 at a speedway in Lake Havasu City, Arizona. It was a Saturday night, and Busch, having finished his race, was standing outside his trailer when two pretty teen-aged girls approached.

"Can I speak to Kurt Busch?" the blonde one said. Melissa's truck-driver father raced part-time, and she often accompanied him to the track, collecting autographs from the various racers when opportunity arose. She had never met Busch, but assumed from his considerable local reputation that he must be substantially older than the nineteen-year-old kid that she saw drinking a soda outside the Busch trailer.

"Yeah, hold on, let me get him," Busch said.

Kurt went into his trailer and reemerged a moment later.

"Hi, I'm Kurt Busch," he said.

Melissa's face reflected her surprise. "Oh, my God, how embarrassing!" she said.

But Busch was amused—and attracted. Watching Melissa approach, he had imagined seeing a glow, a sort of halo, over her head. "This could be the one," he thought, before she had spoken a word.

Melissa, who was fifteen, accepted Kurt's offer to join him for a late-night dinner at a nearby Denny's, and the next day, Kurt stopped by her house, which happened to be in Las Vegas. "She came out looking like a million bucks," said Busch. "She didn't just come out in a T-shirt and shorts." Busch treated her to an ice cream when the ice-cream truck drove by, and a few days later he invited her on their first date, a Garth Brooks concert. Busch hadn't been seeing anyone; racing filled his days, and his nights belonged to the Las Vegas Valley Water District.

For her part, Melissa, a high school freshman when they met, worried about their age difference. "After our first date," she said, "I was like 'Wow, this is him!' But I was a little shy for a little while. I always thought about him, though, like every day: 'Should I call him? Nah, I'll just leave him alone, wait for him to call me.' He did."

Dates led to going steady, and when Roush hired Busch for the Truck Series, Melissa joined her boyfriend, who paid her airfare, at all the races that her high school schedule allowed. They continued that arrangement when Busch began competing in Winston Cup, and Melissa moved in with him after she graduated. When they weren't on the road, they lived in an apartment near the No. 97 shop—and spent their leisure time golfing, dining out, watching movies, and making plans to buy a house. "Just the general type relationship," said Busch. "We never seem to have a dull moment."

Following that afternoon's Brickyard 400 qualifying, Busch and Melissa would join Gaye and motor coach driver Scott St. John for a quiet dinner in Indianapolis. It was August 4, Busch's twenty-third birthday.

Sunday, August 5, dawned sunny and hot. Kurt Busch spent part of the morning talking about the Busch brothers with a reporter from *USA Today,* and after the drivers' meeting he changed into his fire suit, ate a light lunch, and walked onto the frontstretch, where *Tonight Show* host Jay Leno had just addressed the more than 250,000 spectators, the largest crowd on the Winston Cup circuit. A NASCAR fan and collector of classic automobiles, Leno would drive the pace car for the Brickyard 400. He considered it a high honor, for this was America's preeminent automobile racetrack, opened in 1909, a year before NASCAR founder Bill France Sr. was born.

Busch also felt the weight of history at the two-and-a-half-mile-long speedway, where he had never raced before. Built of 3.2 million red bricks that were later paved over, except for a venerated strip still visible at the start/finish line, Indy had hosted many of the world's finest racecar drivers since the first Indianapolis 500, on Memorial Day 1911. Jeff Gordon had won NASCAR's inaugural race at Indy, 1994's Brickyard 400, and Dale Earnhardt had won the next year. "It hits you hard when you first show up and make your first lap," Busch said. "This is why there is a sport today. It didn't start in Daytona—it started here."

It was 1:15 P.M., fifteen minutes to the start of the race.

Speedway officials paid tribute to Earnhardt, a minister delivered the invocation, the national anthem was sung, and four F-16 fighter jets and a B-52 bomber flew over the crowd. Busch kissed Melissa and climbed into his car. "Remember, Kurt—we have to finish," crew chief Ben Leslie said over the radio. After the back-to-back disasters of New Hampshire and Pocono, merely completing the Brickyard 400 would be an accomplishment.

Leno led the field around the track, and Chuck Conway, chairman of the board and chief executive officer of Kmart, waved the green flag—Jimmy Spencer, who drove the Kmart-sponsored No. 26 car, had won the pole.

Adversity struck almost immediately. Halfway through the second lap, rookie Andy Houston crashed, taking out several drivers, including Mark Martin and Matt Kenseth. Martin went to pit road for repairs. Sixth fastest in Saturday's final practice, Kenseth's car was damaged beyond his crew's ability to fix it at the track, and he would be credited with a 42nd-place finish—ahead of only Houston, who had wrecked his own car along with Kenseth's. Short of getting injured, Houston could not have closed an already bad weekend on a worse note. On Friday, McDonald's, the sponsor of his No. 96 Ford, had announced that it was dropping him, leaving his future in Winston Cup racing in grave doubt. Houston had failed to make eight races, and now had failed to finish six—an abysmal record, even for a rookie.

Thirty-five laps later, another rookie, Casey Atwood, got caught up in a wreck and lost his chance of a respectable showing. But Kurt Busch was moving steadily toward the front in a beautifully handling car—Leslie and the crew indeed seemed to have found the magic. Busch was in 11th on lap 57, and when the race leaders returned to pit road for fresh tires and fuel on lap 64, he stayed out—in order to complete a lap in first place. Leading a lap was worth five points in the overall standings, and every point counted.

Martin and Kenseth had started the race in cars that had been redesigned after the April aerodynamics meeting—and watching them get mangled had dismayed Jack Roush, who thought both had a chance of winning. But he took comfort in Busch, and also Jeff Burton, who had started 22nd and progressed rapidly toward the front. Roush was further encouraged by the gas economy of his engines. Just past the halfway mark of the race, he calculated the fuel mileage and concluded that Busch and Burton could finish the 160-lap event with just one more refueling—while the other leaders would likely need to come to pit road twice. Assuming no engine blew and racing continued without another caution flag (when everyone could freely gas up), superior fuel economy might bring Roush his second win of the 2001 season. "If it stays green, they're toast—we got 'em!" Roush said.

Three-fourths of the way through the race, Busch was running third and Burton was fourth—and the raced continued under green. But with twenty-nine laps to go, the yellow caution flew. NASCAR officials claimed to have spotted debris on the track, but many drivers questioned its existence—and one who should have been in a position to see it, Steve Park, who had been holding a substantial lead, all but accused NASCAR of fabricating the presence of debris to cheat him out of a win. "It seems

like when we have such a big lead, there's always a debris caution," Park said. "For some reason, the leader of the race never
sees it."

When green-flag racing resumed, Burton had dropped out of
the top ten. Busch was in sixth, behind Rusty Wallace—and gaining, his lap times several tenths of a second faster than leader Jeff
Gordon. "Just concentrate, hit your marks, and you can pick 'em
off one at a time," Leslie radioed. "You've got a real shot at this
thing. You just need to be nice and smooth."

Soon, Busch was on Wallace's rear bumper. Busch was faster
in the corners—but the crafty Wallace kept boxing him out. So
Busch tried to get by on the straightaways—but Wallace was
faster there. He drove for Roger Penske, and Penske-built engines
in early August 2001 generated more horsepower than any in
Winston Cup competition, as even Jack Roush had to concede.

"Great job today—couldn't be prouder," Leslie said. "We've
got about twenty laps to go here. We just need to be nice and
smooth."

But Busch was frustrated. The handling of his car had pleased
him all day—but not its power. The end of the race loomed, and
he still couldn't pass Wallace. And if he couldn't pass Wallace, he
couldn't win.

"We finally have a racecar," Busch said. "Now we need an
engine."

Roush, who always monitored the radio traffic, was furious
when he heard that. Since the failures at Atlanta in early March,
engines had remained a contentious issue inside his company—
and the situation had puzzled outsiders, who were used to Roush
engines being at the head of the class. Concluding that the new use
of certain lighter components had led to the failures in March at
Atlanta, Roush's technicians had temporarily reverted to heavier
materials—which had brought greater durability, but at the
expense of the additional horsepower that lighter pistons and other
parts where NASCAR allows innovation can bring. Following the

post-Texas brouhaha, Roush's specialists had rededicated themselves to horsepower, and with design modifications had narrowed the gap with its competitors, even Penske, who had achieved his gains through the use of nontraditional materials. The gap had not entirely closed, but the technicians were still hard at work and Roush was confident he would achieve parity by the end of summer.

Roush kept his anger at Busch to himself for the moment. But spotter Bruce Hayes had an inkling of what awaited the rookie when the race ended. Switching to a channel he knew the boss didn't monitor, he urged Leslie to get to Busch before Roush did. Maybe Leslie could soften the blow. But Roush moved fast, and Leslie would not beat him.

The checkered flag flew, and Jeff Gordon—who had turned thirty the day before—won his third Brickyard 400, increasing his lead to 160 points over Dale Jarrett in the championship contest. Busch finished fifth. Neither Leslie nor Roush was there when Busch got out of his car—but Dan Zacharias, a reporter who worked for a Ford-hired firm, was, with his tape recorder and a request for the customary post-race quote. Zacharias's transcripts of statements from all of the Ford drivers were distributed to the press every race weekend.

"We always seem to play the fuel-mileage game and it never turns out," Busch said. "You sacrifice horsepower for that and it seems like it never turns out. It turned out [only] once so far this year: at Charlotte."

A moment later, Roush reached Busch.

He pulled the young man toward him, so that onlookers would not be able to witness what was about to transpire. Gripping Busch's forearm with all his strength, Roush leaned into his driver's face like a drill sergeant with a raw recruit. "I spent thirty-five years of my life getting ready to put you in a car of that caliber!" Roush screamed. "You have the best car I have, the best engine I have! I don't want any negative press!"

Needless to say, Busch did not raise the topic of engines when he went to the formal post-race press conference as the Brickyard 400's top rookie. "This is quite a unique track and it's my pleasure just to even drive here," he said. "It was just a great invite by Jack Roush to give me this opportunity. This is where racing started and this is quite a treat."

By the time Busch returned to his hauler, Roush's reprimand was no longer uppermost in his mind. It wasn't quite a win, but fifth place at the world's most famous race track still felt mighty good. "That's what I like," he said as he stowed his top-rookie cap with the four others he had earned. Busch changed into his street clothes and went to find Melissa. A warm summer night lay ahead, and he planned to treat her to an ice cream after they got back to Charlotte.

Jeff Burton took 15th in the Brickyard 400—then placed second at the following weekend's race, the Global Crossing@The Glen, at Watkins Glen, New York, one of only two road courses on the Winston Cup circuit. Martin finished 15th, Kenseth 23rd, and Busch 29th. Gordon won again, widening his lead to 194 points in the point standings—over Ricky Rudd now, who with his fourth-place finish at Watkins Glen pulled ahead of Jarrett, who came in 31st.

With their serpentine twists and right-hand turns, road courses challenged many Winston Cup drivers, who spent nearly all of their time on ovals, where all the steering was to the left. Unlike Mark Martin and Jeff Gordon, who had dominated the competition at Watkins Glen and Sears Point the last few years, Burton until recently had been mediocre on road courses. But with his third-place finish in 2000 at the Glen and now his second at the 2001 Global Crossing, he seemed on his way to joining the road-course elite. "We're happy with today's finish," said Burton. "We had good pit strategy, and Frank did a great job of getting us up front. Pit strategy is real important here, and Jack gives us a good engine with great fuel mileage and we try to take advantage of that. We had a fast car, and I thought we had something for Jeff Gordon on that last lap. I gave him all I had, and that just wasn't enough."

Given Burton's early season, Jack Roush would take it. "They did great, and I'm real proud of them," he said.

The following Sunday, August 19, saw the second race of the year at Michigan International Speedway: the Pepsi 400 presented by Meijer. Sterling Marlin won, but Rudd finished 42nd and Jarrett 37th, enabling Gordon—who placed seventh—to extend his lead to 298 points in the championship contest, a formidable although not invincible margin with more than a third of the season remaining. Fourth at Michigan was Matt Kenseth, with his best performance of 2001. "We haven't had the greatest year, by any means, but it was good to come here and run up front," he said. "It was a big morale booster." Martin finished eighth, his tenth top-ten showing of the year, and Burton, hampered by radio failure and an ill-handling car, came in 16th. Busch's engine blew a quarter of the way through the race, consigning him to dead last—but he wisely did not discuss engines in public after the race except to note that his had failed. Privately, though, Busch was downhearted.

In any other year, Gordon's march toward a fourth championship would have preoccupied the NASCAR community in the days following Michigan—but once again, safety issues dominated. On Tuesday, August 21, NASCAR finally released the findings of its investigation into the death of Dale Earnhardt. And this time, it did not dispense with the matter in a conference call that ended without questions.

NASCAR in the preceding weeks had named a new vice president of corporate communications and had hired other public relations specialists, including Bill Greene, former director of communications for the U.S. House Budget Committee. Their influence showed. For the Earnhardt investigation announcement, NASCAR had orchestrated a slick press conference featuring slides, film footage, and distribution of two thick volumes entitled "Official Accident Report, No. 3 Car."

But the heart of the conference, held in Atlanta, was the presentations by NASCAR's lead consultants: Dean L. Sicking, a professor of civil engineering at the University of Nebraska and director of the school's Midwest Roadside Safety Facility, and Dr. James H. Raddin Jr., director of the Texas-based Biodynamic Research Corp. These were no slouches: Sicking's curriculum vitae ran to thirty-five pages, and Raddin, a graduate of the Massachusetts Institute of Technology, had headed the Air Force's School of Aerospace Medicine and participated in the investigation of the terrorist downing of the Pan Am 747 jet over Lockerbie, Scotland, in 1988. Even NASCAR's staunchest critics could not impugn such credentials.

The consultants' work, which cost more than a million dollars, seemed as exhaustive as the limits of science and the available evidence allowed. They examined the interior and exterior of Earnhardt's car, with particular attention to his seat belt system, steering wheel, seat, roll cage, engine compartment, and nose. They measured the skid marks, reviewed videotapes of the accident, and analyzed the telemetry—the electronic signaling system indicating position and speed that NASCAR used for scoring, and broadcasters used for their live coverage. They crashed a Winston Cup car similar to Earnhardt's, ran a separate sled test with a crash dummy, and simulated the February 18 accident on a computer. They subjected Earnhardt's helmet to a computerized tomography scan, and his seat belt to DNA and microscopic analysis. They reviewed the medical examiner's report—although the Volusia County attorney instructed the medical examiner not to discuss the case, and under the new

Florida law the consultants were prohibited from viewing the autopsy photos.

Sicking, Raddin, and the other experts who had worked with them reached four major conclusions.

First, they maintained that Earnhardt "most likely" died of a blow to the lower back of the head, which caused a basilar skull fracture. Dr. Barry S. Myers, hired by *The Orlando Sentinel* to review Earnhardt's death, had also concluded that a basilar skull fracture had killed The Intimidator.

Second, the NASCAR consultants concluded that Earnhardt's skull fracture probably was not caused by the whipping motion of his head, as Myers believed, but rather from violent contact with his steering wheel or another part of his car. (Whether NASCAR's investigators would have concluded differently if they had been able to view the photos, like Myers, was a question that could not be answered.)

The third conclusion was that one belt of Earnhardt's five-belt system broke at some point during the crash. A footnote to the report said that while NASCAR did not doubt the sincerity of emergency medical technician Tommy Propst, who claimed that the seat belt was unseparated, "his recollection is mistaken." Besides discrediting Propst, this finding proved further damaging to the reputation of the belt manufacturer, Simpson Performance Products—whose president, Bill Simpson, already had resigned after months of fan harassment and what he maintained was NASCAR's campaign to make him the scapegoat in Earnhardt's death. Simpson noted that the belt had been installed improperly, but the NASCAR consultants disagreed that this had contributed to its breaking.

The consultants' final conclusion was that no single factor caused Dale Earnhardt's death. Rather, a rapid chain of actions and reactions together were responsible: the initial contact with Ken Schrader's car, the violent movement of Earnhardt's head that resulted, the severity of impact with the wall, the breaking of the seat belt, and the lifting of Earnhardt's helmet partly off his head, which exposed it to injury. In other words, no one still knew precisely what killed Earnhardt—nor would anyone ever now.

During the question-and-answer period that followed the presentations, the consultants sidestepped the issue of whether a HANS or similar device might have saved Earnhardt—but given that his head went into sudden, violent motion, it seemed logical to assume that a restraint system at least would have improved his chances of survival. Sobered by four deaths from nearly identical head injuries over the last year and a half, many Winston Cup drivers now wore a restraint, including one whose example could not be ignored: Jeff Gordon, who had discussed on *Larry King Live* his belief that his HANS device had saved him from serious, perhaps life-threatening, injury when he crashed in May's The Winston. Yet some drivers, especially in NASCAR's lower divisions, continued to spurn head restraints. Whether they were uninformed or just plain stupid, they continued to cling to a lethal tradition.

Many of NASCAR's critics surely thought that it would mandate head restraints now that the Earnhardt investigation was concluded—but NASCAR did not. Asked in Atlanta why NASCAR still only recommended them, Mike Helton said: "We think there's still some things we need to understand completely. Mandating them completely at this point is not a wise thing to do based on production schedules of the parts and pieces themselves and the understanding of the entirety of their uses." With photographs of car parts stained with Earnhardt's blood in the reports that his staff was distributing, this sounded like nonsense. The real explanation, some believed, was that NASCAR feared its own legal liability if equipment it mandated were to fail, and injury or death followed.

And this wasn't the only area in which NASCAR declined to seize the day. Helton announced that NASCAR would hire a full-time medical director to help local doctors improve emergency response at the tracks—but the director would not assume duty until the beginning of the 2002 season, even though there were still thirteen races left in the Winston Cup season. So-called black boxes to record crash data would be installed in every Winston Cup car—but also not until 2002. Other possibly promising advances, such as soft-wall technology and energy-absorbing bumpers, would be analyzed by NASCAR at a research center it had recently opened—but no such measures would be immediately adopted, for fear of unforeseen ramifications. "Those things are being studied," Raddin said, "but we need to be very cautious as to how they're implemented so we don't try to fix the last accident and end up creating a number of other accidents in things that are being handled very well right now." Raddin's rationale was sound, but it did not address the larger issue: Why NASCAR had not vigorously pursued soft walls and the like months or years before. None of these ideas was new.

Many racers praised the Earnhardt report and NASCAR's response, if only for the fact that NASCAR had demonstrated in unprecedented public fashion its willingness to address driver safety, albeit on its own terms and at its own pace. "All in all, I thought it was very well done and very thorough," said Jeff Burton. "They have over the last—really I want to say twelve months—but especially the last five months, bit by bit, given us information and made themselves available so that we can make our cars better."

But the critics only found fresh reason to fault Helton and, by extension, Bill France Jr., who was not in Atlanta. Jason Whitlock, a writer for the *Kansas City Star*, noted that NASCAR had not even mentioned the aerodynamic and restrictor-plate rules that made for exciting but dangerous racing at Daytona and Talladega. "Maybe if France Jr. and Helton outlawed restrictor-plate racing we would never see another driver wildly blocking a pack of four or five cars from chasing the leaders," Whitlock wrote, in an allusion to Earnhardt on his final lap. "But if that were to happen, it's difficult to imagine NASCAR's TV ratings continuing to blow through the sky."

"Tuesday's two-hour news conference should be the last we hear of why Dale Earnhardt's life was lost," wrote Gil Lebreton of the *Fort Worth Star-Telegram*. "What about the safety of the ones who are still driving?"

Two days after the Earnhardt report was released, Cup drivers arrived at Bristol Motor Speedway for the second and final time in 2001. Unlike March's Food City 500, a Sunday afternoon affair, this weekend's race would be held under the lights on a Saturday night. Many racers and fans considered it the most thrilling event of the Winston Cup season, and it attracted spectators who ordinarily would be unlikely to travel to the hills of eastern Tennessee, moonshine country—including this year the attorney Johnnie Cochran and Pixar Animation Studios executive vice president John Lasseter, the director of *Toy Story* and *A Bug's Life*. A fervent NASCAR fan, Lasseter owned an actual Winston Cup car that had been retired from Roush Racing's active inventory.

But Kurt Busch was more mindful of another notable who would be there: Joseph Galli Jr., the head of Newell Rubbermaid. Galli's company not only sponsored Busch's car—it owned the rights to the August 25 race, the Sharpie 500.

Newell Rubbermaid and Roush Racing had planned a busy weekend for Busch, and on Thursday he cruised with Melissa in his midnight-blue Stage 3 Mustang over the Blue Ridge Mountains from North Carolina into Tennessee. That evening, Busch signed autographs for two hours at a NASCAR fair that filled the streets of downtown Bristol. The next day, he mingled with Sharpie employees in one of his sponsor's luxury boxes high above the speedway. And in a three-hour period before the race on Saturday, he signed autographs in a Roush Racing souvenir trailer, dropped by the Newell Rubbermaid block party, then visited two hospitality tents and two luxury boxes.

Wherever he went, Busch spoke diplomatically, answering a question about Jack Roush with this assessment: "If you've done something wrong, he'll be sure to let you know about it—but he's a great guy to work for." Busch's answer to a question about Roush engines, however, hinted of a simmering discontent. "They haven't developed the power that every other team has developed," Busch said. He did not get into engine failure during his hospitality appearances, but the blown engine the previous week at Michigan still bothered him. And mechanical failures were only part of the discontent that he felt now. With a few exceptions such as the Brickyard 400, Busch was dissatisfied with his car's handling—and now, like Burton and to an extent Martin, he believed the new Goodyear tires were affecting him. He also believed he suffered from his crew's relative inexperience; compared to the men around Martin, Burton, and Kenseth, his group was indeed green. Still, Busch placed no small measure of blame on himself: his own inexperience, he knew, hindered him in his quest for more speed.

On the eve of the Sharpie 500, Busch stood 24th in the standings, about where he had been since late May. He ranked ahead of many veterans, including Kyle Petty, former champion Terry Labonte, Daytona 500 winner Michael Waltrip, and Rick Mast, who the week before had run his 349th Winston Cup race of a career in which he had never finished a season higher than 18th. But Busch found no consolation in such comparisons. He measured himself by his own expectations, and the consistency he had hoped for this year eluded him. He hadn't been able to put together two back-to-back strong finishes in months, and since the Pocono 500 in June, he hadn't qualified higher than 23rd.

Busch's other aspiration, becoming Rookie of the Year, was also fading. It was still mathematically possible for him to overtake Kevin Harvick, but only if his racing improved dramatically and Harvick's unexpectedly declined, neither of which seemed likely at the end of August.

"It's very discouraging to watch this other rookie just run away with the Rookie of the Year chase when I did it to people last year in the Truck Series. Now I'm on the flip side of the coin," said Busch. Although it wasn't true, he believed that he had sorely disappointed Roush, the man who had been so impressed with his talent and extraordinary learning skills.

"Whether I'm the right man for thirty years [at Roush Racing], I don't know," said Busch. "But what I've been able to do thus far is adapt to different situations, whether it be people, racecars, or racetracks, and give the performances to exceed expectations—and that's something that I've failed to do so far this year. It's been tough to swallow, tough to take in stride: just to be an average-type rookie."

Of the many discoveries of Busch's maiden Winston Cup year, one was the least welcome. "It's a very humbling sport," Busch said.

Mark Martin had learned that lesson almost before Busch was born, and as he sat in his hauler awaiting the start of the Sharpie 500, he expressed frustration at his own performance in 2001.

Since late spring, Martin had advanced only two places in the point standings, to 12th, placing in jeopardy his record among active drivers for the most consecutive season finishes in Winston Cup's elite top ten—twelve seasons, from 1989 through 2000. In the NASCAR media guide, which was updated weekly, Martin now appeared in the "Would You Believe?" column for the longest winless streak of his Cup career, forty-nine races. Martin's best showing in 2001 was fourth, at Talladega and Charlotte. He desperately longed for a win, for the feel of something good in his veins.

"I don't want to finish my career out hoping and praying that I can break into the top ten with a good day," Martin said. "That's not satisfying to me—it's humiliating. And I don't enjoy being humiliated."

Martin enumerated a few of his many racing achievements: thirty-two Winston Cup wins, forty-one Cup poles, four International Race of Champions (IROC) titles, four American Speed Association titles, the all-time record for Busch Grand National wins. "I haven't forgotten how to drive," Martin said. "I'm the same guy that stood 'em on their ear—the same guy. When I get in that car tonight, I'd drive it right straight to the front, be leading in twenty-five laps, if the car was good enough."

But most of the vehicles he had driven all year were not good enough to win races, Martin maintained. Several factors had contributed, including the well-known ones of horsepower, aerodynamic design, and the new Goodyear tires—but something less easily quantified, and infrequently discussed, was also involved. "Everybody wants it to be mechanical," Martin said, "like a machine and you just go fix the machine and then it operates properly and it's better than everybody else's machine. It's not that." Rather, it appeared to be some subtle shift in the dynamics of driver and crew—team chemistry—and Martin's own struggle, similar to Burton's, to reconnect to his vehicle, to find the feel that brought so many victories. A longtime master of existence on the edge, Martin had lost something vital.

But only temporarily, he hoped; a racer since the age of fifteen, he had experienced the many moods of his tempestuous passion, and he knew better than to seek improved fortune with another owner, as someone younger or foolish might have. Martin was nothing if not loyal.

"I have been in torment for twenty-seven years—or at least for the last fifteen, trying to live up to expectations, my own expectations," said Martin. "Jack Roush is the same way. He shares in that pain. I'm not mad at Jack Roush because of where I'm at—and I'm not thinking of conspiring, I haven't met with my attorney to see about getting out of my contract, none of that. I'm just taking the beating, trying to take it like a man, and working as hard as all the rest of the people within the organization to try to work ourselves back around to the front of the pack."

Much of the press and many of the conversations this year about Martin concerned the joy he found with his son on the Quarter Midget circuit. Now, a new theme was emerging: the possibility that the satisfaction he derived from Matt's racing had dulled his own desire to win, a sort of inverse proportion of emotion and commitment. Martin dismissed that theory—but some writers did not. "In the Worst of Times, Martin at His Happiest," was the headline on one story about Mark's involvement with Matt.

Martin understood that journalists could be fickle, but for more than a decade he had been able to count on the unbending loyalty of his fans, and until practice the day before, he had seen no evidence that their feelings might be changing, too. But during his laps on that Friday, a man held up a message that Martin had never seen directed at him: QUITTER, the sign read.

As the sun set, leaving behind a hot summer night, the master of ceremonies introduced Galli and the evening's other dignitaries. The drivers crossed the stage, then circled the track, each riding in the back of a Chevrolet pickup truck, the official pickup truck of NASCAR. Children dressed in the colors of the flag sang "God Bless America," the crowd of almost 146,000 removed their hats for the national anthem, and fighter jets swooped low over the crowd, prompting Jack Roush to exclaim, "That's horsepower!"

Martin had qualified in 31st, which meant he would pit in unfamiliar territory: the back straightaway of the half-mile speedway, a serious but not insurmountable disadvantage, as Elliott Sadler, winner of the spring race at Bristol, had proved. "You guys remind me we're on the backstretch, because I'm dumb enough to forget," Martin said over his radio as the race began.

Despite his poor qualifying, Martin was satisfied with his car for one of the few times in the season—and he became downright pleased as the race progressed. "The car's pretty good," he said on the thirteenth lap, when he steered clear of the first crash of the Sharpie 500.

Martin dodged trouble again on the twenty-fifth lap, when Brett Bodine wrecked—and Jeremy Mayfield, caught up in the resulting fracas, nipped the rear of the No. 6 Viagra car. Martin sustained no damage, and lost no momentum.

"Twelve car said sorry for the bump—he got shoved into you," said Chris Morris, Martin's spotter.

"No problem, he's cool," said Martin. Like Burton, Martin raced clean.

With Morris's encouraging voice in his ear, Martin took aim at the cars in front of him, passing them one by one. "Clear, buddy, clear," said Morris. "That's the way to do it. Just let him know you're faster."

And Martin was. By the sixtieth lap, he had advanced nine spots, to 21st. "Our times are pretty good, Mark," said crew chief Jimmy Fennig. "When you're in the open you're as good as the 30 car." That was Jeff Green, the race leader.

The fourth caution flag flew on the eighty-fourth lap, when seven cars, including Kurt Busch's, tangled. It was developing into a regular Bristol free-for-all, more exciting still under the electric glare of lights, but so far Martin had escaped the mayhem. He was in 19th, moving steadily toward the front.

"Some of those guys are losing their patience, so we'll be all right," said Fennig. Fennig knew patience intimately; a Milwaukee native, he started in racing as a mechanic at the age of seventeen, and spent the next decade and a half as a stockcar crew chief (and one year as a driver) on dirt and asphalt tracks throughout Wisconsin. Fennig became Martin's American Speed Association crew chief in 1985, and was his chief again the next year, when Martin won his fourth ASA title. After several years with other Winston Cup drivers, Fennig rejoined Martin at Roush Racing in 1996, and the two had been together since.

The Sharpie 500 continued, and Martin kept advancing. He was in 11th on lap 100, eighth by lap 125, and seventh by lap 150. "Car's real good," he said. If he stood this course, he had an excellent chance of winning. Nine caution flags had flown by lap 200, but Martin remained untouched.

Thirty-two laps later, his right-front tire blew.

Martin smacked the wall hard, but he managed to return to his pit, where Fennig quickly determined that his suspension was too badly damaged to race. The crew could not repair it on pit road—and there was some doubt it could be repaired at all, but Martin was determined to try. Fennig ordered the car off pit road, and he and his mechanics got to work with a saw, a hammer, a crowbar, a blowtorch, and screwdrivers and wrenches. Bristol's lights cast an otherworldly glow on the scene, and Martin, sitting stone-faced with his helmet in his lap inside his crippled Viagra car, looked like a man strangely imprisoned. "It hurt me really bad," he later said. "There was nothing but ugliness inside me." Another race would pass without a win.

The carnage continued as Martin sat. Among those involved in a succession of wrecks were Dale Earnhardt Jr., Bill Elliott, Ricky Craven, and Johnny Benson, who safely escaped his car after a fire erupted beneath it. After more than forty-five minutes of fevered repairs, Fennig judged Martin's car raceable. Its battered body held together with tape, the No. 6 returned 164 laps behind the leader. Amazingly, it handled almost as well as it had before the accident. Martin could hardly believe it.

"Y'all are my heroes, man!" he said. "That's awesome."

"We might be able to pick up one more spot," Fennig said. In fact, Martin picked up two. Having returned to the Sharpie 500 in 39th place, he soon drove to 37th. On some laps, he was faster than leader Tony Stewart.

"Pretty good: running with the leader, wrecked!" said Martin.

Stewart won the Sharpie 500, Harvick took second, and Gordon came in third, widening his lead over Rudd in the point standings. At 15th, Burton was the best of the Roush racers at Bristol; Busch was 25th, a decided improvement over his initial run at The World's Fastest Half Mile; and Kenseth took 33rd after hitting the wall near the end of the race. Despite his finish, Martin maintained 12th place in the point standings.

"It is such a shame that we had to blow a tire and ruin the great run we had going," Martin said. "The Viagra crew members were heroes tonight to get me back on the track and running as fast as the leaders."

Martin certainly had not quit—but a prominent sportswriter who had seen the QUITTER sign that the man had held up during practice on Friday had decided to explore its meaning in a column.

Kurt Busch's objective for the next race, the September 2 Mountain Dew Southern 500 at Darlington Raceway, was to qualify and finish respectably—20th or better would fit the bill. He had not forgotten his inaugural weekend at the treacherous speedway, back in March, when he had started 27th and finished 30th.

So Busch did not expect to contend for the pole; having drawn 37th in the order for Friday's qualifying, he watched as drivers such as Rusty Wallace and teammates Burton and Martin, all of whom had enjoyed success at Darlington, turned in fast times. Kevin Harvick was fast, too.

But on his turn, Busch topped the thirty-six drivers who had gone before.

Eight were still to qualify, and Busch kept his eye on the scoring tower as they completed their laps. Jimmy Spencer was slower than Busch. Ricky Craven was slower. Todd Bodine— slower. Now it was down to the final entrant, Jeff Gordon, the driver of the No. 24 DuPont Chevrolet. Gordon was the acknowledged king of Darlington: He had captured four poles at the track, most recently in March, and he had won five races there.

A TV broadcaster joined Busch on the front stretch as Gordon started around. "Oh, this is going to be close!" the broadcaster said. "What's it going to be at the start/finish line? Can't do it! Kurt Busch has won the pole for the Mountain Dew Southern

500!" Gordon's time, 29.286 seconds (167.916 miles per hour), was twenty-three thousandths of a second slower than Busch's.

"You guys have been promoting this deal about drama," Busch told the broadcaster. "This is drama! This is unbelievable, to go out there and pull a lap like that and have the 24 chasing you—he's Mister Drama himself. I'm just ecstatic. I can't believe it. Just to have this whole program behind us, to even drive in Winston Cup—I've got to thank this guy right here." He meant Roush, whose smile was as big as his rookie's.

"Were you nervous?" the broadcaster said.

Busch wasn't—he brimmed with the excitement of having beaten everyone, of having won at speed. No full-time Winston Cup rookie, not even Harvick, had won a pole in the 2001 season. Few drivers ever did in their first year of Cup competition.

"You can expect anything from a Mount Everest–type peak to a Death Valley–type low in Winston Cup racing," said Busch. "There's nothing that really can prepare you for this—or you can compare it to."

Mark Martin hugged Busch, and Roush did, too. Roush said that based on the 2000 Truck Series, he had begun the 2001 Cup season expecting Busch to win a pole at some point—but that expectation had fallen away as the year had unfolded. "I'd settled in for a long siege," Roush said. "I figured this was going to be harder than I thought it was going to be initially, and that we were not going to get a pole this year. Kurt and Ben have been working really hard. They've been hunting and pecking all over the map on setups and things and I can't believe it happened here today. It's just wonderful!" It seemed as if Busch's day had finally arrived, his engine difficulties behind him.

Starting from the pole, Busch led the first twenty-four laps of the Mountain Dew Southern 500, and again on laps 81 through 130—and he was running second, behind Gordon, when his alternator quit on lap 233. To conserve electrical power, Busch shut off the special brake-cooling fans mounted in Cup cars on tracks like Darlington, where brakes are subject to heavy use. But losing the fans compromised his braking, and Busch brushed the wall a few laps later and was forced to pit for repairs. When he returned to the race, he was in 27th—a lap down. He had made the lap up and advanced as high as 18th when a tire blew, sending him back to the pits again. Busch finished the race in 39th.

It was at about this point that Busch began repeating the old saw that if he didn't have bad luck, he wouldn't have any luck at all.

Ward Burton won the Mountain Dew Southern 500, with Jeff Gordon taking second and extending his lead in the point standings over Ricky Rudd to 342. Mark Martin took 20th in the race, and Matt Kenseth came in 23rd. With his sixth-place showing, Jeff Burton was the best of the Roush drivers for the second race in a row.

This wasn't the only indication that Burton might have turned the corner. The day before the Southern 500, he had made one of his occasional starts in a Busch Grand National race, the Southern 200, also at Darlington—and he had won, beating Harvick, the series' points leader, and fellow Roush racer Greg Biffle, who was all but assured of being named the series' Rookie of the Year.

Burton credited dogged effort, not some miraculous discovery, for his brightening prospects; he had not visited a sports psychologist as he endeavored to reconnect to his machine, only adhered to the time-honored ethic of try-and-try-again. "We're just working our asses off," Burton said. "We'll probably look back on this two years from now and not really understand what we were doing wrong. I really believe that. There won't be one thing that we all of a sudden come up upon and say, 'Oh my God, that is why we were running bad!' It won't be like that. We've just got to keep working."

Like Gordon, Burton had raced long enough to understand that one outstanding weekend could inspire false confidence, which could jeopardize success—and he was determined to keep his team emotionally grounded. "I don't like cocky people, especially people who aren't successful," Burton said. "That really pisses me off. For us to be cocky now would be ridiculous."

Cockiness, however, was becoming an increasingly publicized issue for another celebrity. As autumn approached, many drivers were beginning to believe that Kevin Harvick had gone beyond confidence to arrogance, which made enemies in Winston Cup racing. They based their judgment on several incidents on and off the track—and on Harvick's sense of superiority, expressed in statements to reporters and articles that his staff wrote for his Web site. Many in the NASCAR community had heralded Harvick as the salvation of stockcar racing after Dale Earnhardt's death, but the honeymoon was over.

The end may have come in the heat of Bristol, with the ruckus surrounding Harvick's aggressive racing during the Busch Series race the Friday before the Sharpie 500. Gunning for the lead, Harvick had bumped Jeff Green out of his way. Green spun, but managed to avoid wrecking—and after the race he was livid, more so because he and Harvick were Winston Cup teammates, both driving for Richard Childress in the elite series. "Anybody can turn somebody sideways to pass them," said Green, who finished second behind the man who had spun him. "I don't know if I could sleep tonight." Harvick made light of the situation, playing off the primary sponsor of Green's Busch Series car, Nestlé Nesquick. "I guess he drank too much chocolate milk and his stomach hurt," Harvick said. "He should know by now I'm not very patient. He should've learned that last year. When it's time to go, it's time to go. You've gotta do what you've gotta do."

The next weekend, during the South Carolina 200, Harvick tangled with Chad Little, the ex-Roush racer who drove in Busch Grand National now. Upset with Harvick's aggressive driving, Little tracked the driver down after the race—and a fistfight in the garage area ensued. Deeming Harvick more at fault, NASCAR fined him $10,000 and placed him on probation through the end

of the year (Little was fined $5,000 and given the same proba-
tion). Little wasn't the only driver Harvick had annoyed in the
South Carolina 200: Jeff Burton criticized him for complaining
that Burton wouldn't let him pass in the closing moments of the
race. Harvick was a lap down and wanted Burton to let him make
it up, but Burton blocked him, saying it would have hurt his
chance for the win. Burton found an irony in Harvick's complaint: When Harvick had been in Burton's shoes in a Busch
Series race in May, he had refused to let Biffle make up a lap. "He
made a big deal about it," Burton said. "He called Biffle everything but a son of a bitch on the TV and on the radio afterwards."
At Roush Racing, the drivers stood together.

From Darlington, the Cup circuit moved to Richmond, Virginia, for the Chevrolet Monte Carlo 400, on September 8—and
once again Harvick crossed a veteran driver. With the race winding down, he bumped leader Rudd to take over first. Rudd nearly
went into the wall, then spent the remainder of the race with
Harvick's number. He nailed him at the very end—with a bump
that moved the rookie aside to give the veteran the win. "What I
gave him was a clean love tap," Rudd said. "What he gave me
was a cheap shot trying to wreck me, so there is a difference."

Burton shared in the growing sense that Harvick intended to
play only by his rules—that he seemed not to care that even
Earnhardt, as aggressive a driver as NASCAR had ever seen, realized that a degree of give-and-take was essential to sustained success in such a tight fraternity as Cup racing.

"Most drivers in Winston Cup are very respectful of each
other—for the most part, we don't just knock people out of the
way on purpose," said Burton. "Kevin Harvick has decided that
it's OK to do that and that pisses me off. What he doesn't understand is that gratification for a few minutes isn't going to out-
weigh all the trouble that he's created for himself. I think he's a
very good racecar driver, but I think he has forgotten how hard it
is and he's become overconfident and self-centered."

Mark Martin was somewhat more restrained in his assessment of Harvick. "I think he's just an arrogant kid that has the attitude of 'get back and let me show you how this is done,'" Martin said. "Dale Jr. didn't do that. Stewart didn't push people out of the way. And you know what? He's probably really a good guy. He probably is—but he could be the same [driver] if he'd just be a little bit more humble."

Harvick remained unmoved, all but implying that he was genetically predisposed to pugnacity since he'd been aggressive since his toddler days on a Big Wheel. "Frustrated competitors, tired of staring at the back of his car, fire any number of complaints in his direction: He drove too high, he swung too low, he tapped a rear bumper too hard," wrote a member of his staff on his Web site. "Staunch supporters of other drivers don't like him. They lodge [*sic*] a chorus of boos into the air when he is introduced. They bash him on message boards and applaud his mistakes, no matter how rare. They know he is a constant threat for the win, and it's oh-so-irritating."

Whether Harvick was a constant threat to win could be debated—but his driving and his controversies unquestionably contributed to NASCAR's sustained popularity. Football season was upon America, and NASCAR's TV ratings had never been higher.

As racers prepared for the season's second contest at New Hampshire, set for September 16, Burton had deeper concerns than some belligerent rookie. With his ninth-place showing in the September 8 Chevrolet Monte Carlo 400, Burton had climbed from 13th to 11th in the Winston Cup standings. He had no possibility of winning the championship, of course, but he was close to breaking into the top ten for the first time all year, just 119 points behind Johnny Benson, who had fallen steadily from the third-place position he'd occupied in March and April. Misfortune had also benefited Burton: Steve Park, sidelined with a head injury since an accident at Darlington, had left the top ten.

The Winston Cup top ten was more than a convenient ranking of NASCAR's best drivers: At season's end, it was a badge of honor, the NASCAR equivalent of a baseball pitcher with twenty wins or a batter with a .325 average. Only the top ten drivers (and the Rookie of the Year) were invited to speak at the annual Winston Cup banquet at New York's Waldorf-Astoria Hotel. For Burton, who had started the season as the title pick and then foundered so badly, wearing a tuxedo in Manhattan would bring special satisfaction—and alert other drivers to his intentions for 2002.

"If we can speak at the banquet, then it puts us in a position of showing strength—of togetherness, of a never-say-die attitude— and our competitors will watch that," said Burton. "We'll make a statement, verbally and visually, that we are a factor. And I think that's important. People need to respect you, they need to understand that you're a force and that they're going to have to deal with you."

What Burton said also held true, of course, for Mark Martin and Jack Roush. For twelve straight years, longer than any driver and owner still active in NASCAR, they had been honored in Manhattan in December.

CHAPTER 9

EXTREME RISKS

On the morning of Tuesday, September 11, Jeff Burton drove his daughter to school, then dropped by his racecar shop, his usual routine whenever he was in town. He had just left the shop when a strange conversation on his car radio caught his attention.

"You won't believe what we're watching," the deejay said. "An airplane has just hit one of the World Trade Center towers."

Burton, who held a pilot's license, immediately recalled the propeller plane that slammed against the White House in 1994. *It's some crazy son of a bitch in a Cessna 172,* Burton thought. *A nut on a suicide mission.*

But the deejay and his on-air partner began to talk about a jet, so now Burton figured the tower had been struck by a small private jet, perhaps one like his own. When the deejays quoted an eyewitness who said the tower had been struck by a commercial jetliner, Burton was baffled. *What in the hell,* he thought. *I gotta see this.* He headed for home. He hadn't reached Lake Norman when the deejays reported that a second jet had struck the other Trade Center tower. Now Burton knew that something more than the final act of a deranged person was unfolding. America was under attack.

At home, Burton joined Kim by the kitchen TV. Both towers were burning, but it appeared as if only a few floors at the top of each were involved. Then one of the buildings crumpled to the ground in a doomsday cloud of dust and debris—and a short while later, as people could be seen jumping to their deaths, the second tower followed. *Oh my freakin' God!* Burton thought. *I'm watching thousands of people die and it's not a movie—it's live, it's the real thing.*

As the morning advanced and the attack on the Pentagon and a fourth jet crashing in Pennsylvania further shocked the nation, Burton called his mother and his brothers to confirm that they were safe—and he and Kim discussed what they would tell their daughter, Kimberle Paige, when she returned from school. "You want to isolate children from those things," Burton said, "but it's hard to isolate them from evil. It's hard to say, 'OK, Paige, it's not that big of a deal,' because it is a big deal." When Paige got home, the Burtons spoke in a language she understood: They told her that very bad people had "wrecked" airplanes into big buildings in New York and Washington and that many people had died. The Burtons said that they were scared—and it was OK for a little girl to be scared, too. But they did their best to keep her from the TV, with its ghastly images repeated over and over.

Burton stayed at his house the rest of Tuesday, watching the news late into the night—and he was similarly captivated on Wednesday. "You weren't watching it to see the gruesome scenes," he said. "You were wanting to pull something out of it, trying to understand. You go through this range of emotions: Let's go kick somebody's ass, you're not going to mess with us like that, we've got to make a stand. Then you go through: God, think about the parents, and the children."

As the week continued, Burton endeavored to put September 11 in a larger context. He could never forget how the 2001 Winston Cup season began, with the death of Dale Earnhardt, which had closely followed the deaths of the three other drivers in 2000; taken together, those single deaths and now the deaths of thousands had given him fresh appreciation for his blessings and put dreams of buying yachts and speaking in Manhattan in perspective. "I think I understand more so—not just from Tuesday, but from before then—what's important in life," Burton said.

Looking beyond the blessings of family and friends, Burton, like so many, was saddened and angered by what the terrorists had accomplished on one pristine late-summer morning. "I grew up in a time just before 'the lockdown,'" Burton said. "I'd leave my house in the morning when I was probably twelve years old and go play all day, and my parents didn't go with me everywhere I went. I don't see as much of that today, and that's sad—and what happened Tuesday shut that down even more. It takes away your feeling of safety and that's a terrible thing."

Within hours of the attacks, Major League Baseball canceled its games, and many other sports soon followed suit. "It doesn't take a rocket scientist to figure out sporting events are absolutely meaningless compared with what's going on in Washington and New York," said home run king Mark McGwire. "For people to think it's OK to play sports this weekend is absolutely asinine."

The National Football League and NASCAR, however, demurred. The Winston Cup circuit was to return to New Hampshire for Sunday's running of the New Hampshire 300—and all NASCAR initially did was cancel the practice and qualifying sessions scheduled for Friday, September 14. Race fans in their campers and RVs set off for Loudon, and race teams scrambled to make travel arrangements. With all but military aircraft grounded, the trip north promised to be a logistical nightmare. And some racers weren't a day's drive down the coast in North Carolina—some were stranded out west, where they had been testing or fulfilling midweek sponsor obligations.

But this was NASCAR, which had gone forward with races

hours after Adam Petty and Kenny Irwin Jr. had been killed—
and which had not skipped a weekend after its biggest star had
perished. Drivers themselves were divided on the wisdom of running the New Hampshire 300: Some wanted to commemorate
the victims of September 11 by rescheduling, while others
believed postponement would be a victory for the terrorists. Burton saw both sides. "I am very conflicted," he said. "I don't know
what the right thing to do is."

Thursday dawned, airliners remained on the ground, and neither NASCAR nor the NFL gave any public indication of a change
of heart; the morning wore on, and the first fans pulled into the
campsites at Loudon as hastily chartered team buses prepared to
leave Charlotte. Then, shortly before noon, NFL commissioner
Paul Tagliabue made an announcement: Major-league football
was postponing its games.

More than an hour later, Mike Helton announced that
NASCAR was rescheduling the New Hampshire 300, along with a
Truck Series race that had been set for Texas Motor Speedway.
Jack Roush's two Truck teams were already ten hours on the road
to Texas when word reached them.

"It is time for families to come together," said Helton. "We felt
that postponing this weekend's races was simply the right thing to
do. We join the nation in mourning those who lost their lives and
we pray those wounded recover fully." Helton did not explain why
NASCAR needed more than two days to discover the moral high
ground, but during an interview he did reveal that Bill France had
spoken to Tagliabue before deciding to postpone the New Hampshire 300. In any event, NASCAR rescheduled the race at the hard-
luck speedway for November 23, the day after Thanksgiving,
extending the Cup schedule by one extra week. Assuming terrorists
did not strike again, the next race would be the MBNA Cal Ripken
Jr. 400 at Dover Downs International Speedway in Delaware. The
future Hall of Fame baseball star Ripken, who was playing his final
season for the Baltimore Orioles, would serve as grand marshal.

Like drivers, fans split on the wisdom of postponing. "NASCAR did the correct and sane thing," a man wrote in one of hundreds of e-mails to nascar.com. But another wrote: "I can't believe that you fell to the mercy of the terrorists. . . . Instead of having the race and showing them YOU ARE NOT AFRAID of them, you could have had a memorial service at the track."

Many of the comments sent to nascar.com concerned personal inconveniences, not philosophical differences. One fan asked if Mike Helton had ever been to New Hampshire in late November. Did NASCAR intend to attach snowplows to the racecars? Was this some clever way for the track owners to avoid refunding ticket money? What about those who had bought tickets to the November 18 NAPA 500 at Atlanta, believing it was the season finale, perhaps the race when the championship would be settled? What about fans who had to work on the day after Thanksgiving?

An outsider reading only these sentiments would not have guessed that NASCAR fans considered their sport to be the toughest of any. On this matter, some of them sounded like whiny, spoiled children.

Drivers and their families were still settling into their motor coaches in the Dover infield when President Bush addressed Congress and the American people on Thursday night, September 20. Renewed patriotism gripped the land, and it was on colorful display the following morning when the garage opened for the start of the three-day race weekend for the MBNA Cal Ripken Jr. 400.

Owners had decorated their cars to reflect America's new mood, and flag decals on quarter panels and deck lids abounded— along with memorials to the dead and messages of support for the rescue teams still at work in New York and Washington. Burton's No. 99 CITGO car, already painted in red, white, and blue, bore the slogan "United We Stand"—and Matt Kenseth's car, the No. 17 DeWALT, was one of several with a "God Bless America" decal.

Most striking of all was Ken Schrader's No. 36 M&Ms car: Sponsor Mars Candy Co. had erased every trace of its product from the car, substituting an American flag that covered the vehicle from nose to rear bumper. In light of the millions of dollars that sponsors paid for advertising, it was a magnanimous gesture.

Many teams, including Roush Racing, announced fund-raising programs for the victims of the September 11 attacks; and many drivers, including Burton and his teammates, had agreed to donate a percentage of their royalties on merchandise sales. The media center was blanketed with press releases conveying the sentiments of drivers, owners, and sponsors. Some expressed a sort of naive disbelief that America was a terrorist target, including driver Hut Stricklin, who said: "To think that there are wackos like that living in the United States and the world." Others, such as Dale Earnhardt Jr., extended sympathy to the survivors: "I have an idea of what each of those family members or whoever who might have lost a cousin or brother or mother or a son feel," said Junior. And some drivers wanted the public to know that terrorism was not about to cow them: "I sure don't feel like crawling in a hole and hiding because of what these people have done," said Tony Stewart.

But privately, many racers were anxious—if not outright scared. So much had changed.

Nearby Dover Air Force Base, where teams ordinarily parked their planes, had been closed to all civilian traffic—and a mortuary on the base, it had been widely reported, was still processing remains unearthed from the Pentagon rubble. Everyone entering Dover Downs was subject to search, coolers and backpacks were banned, and more police officers were on patrol. Speedway officials declined to disclose specifics of their security plan, except to note that it had been developed in consultation with the FBI, and that the focus was less on foiling a lone assailant with a gun than on "one guy blowing up one hundred," in the words of speedway president Denis McGlynn.

Heightened security notwithstanding, it was difficult not to imagine that Sunday's expected crowd of almost 150,000—what would be the largest gathering of the weekend in the land— would surely be a tempting target for terrorists. The facts that the race would be broadcast live on national TV and that federal authorities had issued a terrorist alert for the weekend only raised apprehensions further. In many haulers, TVs ordinarily tuned to ESPN were kept on CNN.

"I do not feel safe," said Mark Martin. "That's just not how I want to go."

Asked if he was worried, Burton said: "You'd be crazy not to."

Returning to his hauler after Saturday morning's practice, Burton discussed with Kim his desire to visit firefighters and police in New York, an idea inspired by boxing great Muhammad Ali, who had toured Ground Zero the day before and then joined entertainers in a nationwide telethon. Like Burton, Kim was anxious about being at Dover—and she remained concerned for Paige, who had been experiencing nightmares. And like her husband, Kim lamented the loss of a degree of innocence: Sadly, their children would grow up in a world where it now seemed danger could be around any corner. It definitely was not the South Boston, Virginia, of their youth.

The conversation later turned to Islamic fundamentalism, and how militants within that religion teach their children to hate Americans—in part, Kim maintained, because of American wealth and the rights that American women enjoy. Burton, who regularly joked about how he cooked more often—and much better—than his wife, could not resist a jab.

"And you're teaching Paige to hate cooking like your mom did to you," he said.

Kim did not skip a beat. "Honey, that's what they make take-out for," she said.

"You're gonna be screwed when we get on the C rations," said Burton.

The events of September 11 may have darkened it, but Burton had not lost his humor.

Burton pulsed with energy on race morning, the same as always. He had seen the recent news reports about the possibility of terrorists spreading anthrax from aircraft, and he joshed his spotter, Chris Farrell: "If you see a crop duster coming in over Turn Three, you might want to let us know." Farrell, a studious young man, wasn't quite sure if Burton was kidding. Then Burton traveled to the CITGO hospitality tent with Becky Hanson, who confided that when she had heard a strange noise the night before in her hotel's ventilation system, she feared it indicated an act of chemical warfare.

At his CITGO appearance, Burton made his usual jokes, including the crowd favorite explaining how his brother Ward had a noticeably thicker accent than his own. ("He grew up on the southernmost part of the house. I used the milkman theory for a while, but my mother didn't like that.") But Burton turned serious when asked whether racers would need snow tires at the rescheduled New Hampshire 300. "I assure you it's not what I want to do," he said. "But compared to what's caused us to have to run the race in November, who cares? It's no big deal."

For others, though, it was a big deal. An increasing number of drivers and crew members were griping about losing their Thanksgiving holiday—ordinarily the start of the off-season, which lasted less than three months and was crammed with car-building, testing, and sponsor-related obligations. But France and Helton were standing firm. At the weekly drivers' meeting, which followed the hospitality appearances, Helton laid to rest the wishful notion that NASCAR might cancel the race—or run it on a weekday in October, as some had suggested. "We know it can be very cold in New Hampshire on November the 23rd, we know that Friday is after Thanksgiving, and we know that Thanksgiving is the biggest traditional family American holiday outside of the Fourth of July," said Helton. "We know it's not a popular decision, but we're going to do it." NASCAR maintained that it had selected that Friday in order to have Saturday and Sunday as backup dates in case of bad weather—but many in the NASCAR community didn't buy that. NASCAR statements to the contrary, they believed that France was sacrificing their Thanksgiving for Helton's sake—the rumor was, Helton's stepdaughter was getting married on Saturday, November 24. It wasn't anywhere as big a controversy as those that had preceded it during the last year, but NASCAR had touched off more acrimony.

Bobby Labonte led everyone in the Pledge of Allegiance, and the meeting gave way to the drivers' chapel service. In his sermon, chaplain Dale Beaver asked racers and their crews to join the new war that the president had declared. "Put on all of God's armor so that you will be able to stand firm against all strategies and tricks of the devil," said Beaver, reading from the Book of Ephesians. "For we are not fighting against people made of flesh and blood, but against the evil rulers and authorities of the unseen world." Beaver did not specify what role racecar drivers should play, but he urged them to be ready to "die well," as Jesus Christ their savior had.

"And since we died with Christ," Beaver read from Romans, "we know we will also share his new life. We are sure of this because Christ rose from the dead, and he will never die again. Death no longer has any power over him."

The season that began with Dale Earnhardt's final lap moved improbably toward its conclusion.

Numerous seats would be empty when baseball and other major-league sports resumed their schedules in the days ahead, but the MBNA Cal Ripken Jr. 400 was a sell-out—the nearly 150,000 spectators who awaited the green flag by chanting "USA! USA!

USA!" and waving the nearly 150,000 flags that the speedway's owners had distributed for free. Ripken spoke, country-and-western star Tanya Tucker sang the "Star Spangled Banner," and one red dove, one blue dove, and forty-eight white doves were released into the air—not as a peace offering to terrorists, track officials said, but as a symbol of farewell to the victims of September 11. But birds were about the only airborne objects that day: Federal authorities had banned all traffic over the speedway except for a TV-camera helicopter, and no military jets conducted the usual crowd-pleasing pre-race flyover.

The drivers started their engines and set off on their warmup laps around the mile-long concrete oval.

"The pace car is rolling," said Chris Farrell. "God bless America."

Burton was starting 22nd, better than his Roush teammates, who all had required provisionals to make the race—a situation that had led Burton to crack that he had won "the Special Olympics of qualifying." Kurt Busch had been so maddened with his poor qualifying laps on Friday that he had stormed off exclaiming: "Fuck it, I quit. Tell Jack to get another driver."

But Busch had been the fourth fastest of all forty-three drivers in Saturday's final practice, and he wasted little time in moving from the very end of the field to the middle of the pack. After only twenty-seven of the four hundred laps, Busch, who had finished 39th in the spring Dover race, was running in 20th. Martin and Kenseth also quickly moved to the middle, and Burton held his own. But none of the drivers was satisfied with the handling of his car, and all hoped to improve their performance during pit-stop adjustments.

Busch never got much of a chance: On lap 96, his engine began running roughly, and twenty laps later, it died altogether, ending his day on a depressingly familiar note. A dozen laps further in, Martin, who had advanced to 19th place, was hit when he braked to avoid a wreck; forced behind the wall for repairs, he was almost a hundred laps down when he finally returned to the race. Kenseth didn't escape bad luck, either: Just past the halfway point, his engine began to overheat, and he lost ten laps while his crew fixed the problem. Kenseth would finish the race in 29th, Martin 32nd, and Busch 41st—the third time in the last five races that Busch had been 39th or worse, a trend that was rapidly depleting his reserve of provisionals.

From his seat on top of Martin's pit cart, Jack Roush watched another disappointing day unfold—and another engine fail, at a point in the season when he thought Roush Racing had left its motor troubles in the past. But Roush still had one strong horse in the race; by the time the next caution flag flew, on lap 227, Burton had moved up to 11th. Burton pitted for fresh tires, and was in 13th place when he returned.

"One hundred fifty to go, man! Rock 'n' roll!" said Frank Stoddard. "We've got the fastest car on the track! Let's go get 'em!"

A few laps later, the handling on Burton's car began to deteriorate.

"It's too friggin' loose," Burton radioed to Stoddard.

Stoddard hoped the situation would stabilize on its own, as sometimes happened. "You're doin' fine, baby," he said. "Just keep maintaining with me. Your lap times are still the same as the third-, fourth-place cars." While he could be excitable and high-strung before a race, Stoddard was often Burton's calming influence once the green flag flew.

"It's getting worse and worse," said Burton.

"We've got about fifty laps 'til a pit stop," said Stoddard. "Just keep maintaining. Nice and smooth."

"I am just so fucking loose!"

"Everyone is saying the same. I don't know if someone is putting oil out or what, but everyone is real loose coming out of Turn Four—fishtailing."

"God damn it!"

"Hang on!" Stoddard shouted. "Hang on!"

But Burton had lost all patience—he decided he had to make

his pit stop even though the green flag was flying and his competitors would stay on the track. They would lose precious time and probably any good chance of winning, but without adjustments, Burton would have no chance at all.

"Let's do it, guys," Stoddard said.

It was lap 341. Burton's men gave him fresh tires and fuel and tweaked the suspension, all in 14.47 seconds—impressively fast, but not surprising. They were, after all, the 2000 World Pit Crew Champions.

But their effort was for naught.

"Frank, I am loose as shit," Burton said when he was back in the race. "Every time we fucking gamble it bites us right in the ass. We just pissed this thing away."

"No, we didn't. We're in 21st position. We're one lap down."

"We're more than one lap down."

"Two laps."

"It's just completely fucking loose now."

And that wasn't the extent of Burton's woes. With only minutes left in the race, Burton's engine began to expire. A valve spring had broken.

"What the hell is going on?" Stoddard said.

"It's blowing up," said Burton.

"What do you want to do?"

"You've got to realize when you're whipped."

"Then let's just take our whipping like a man."

Stoddard urged Burton to drive the final few laps slowly, in the hope of keeping his wounded engine going. He wanted Burton to have the dignity of finishing.

"Don't go wide open on the gas," said Stoddard. "I know you know what you're doing, but I want you to bring this thing home for me."

Burton let several cars pass him as he hobbled around the speedway.

"Easy on it now," said Stoddard. "We've almost made it."

"Coming to the checkered flag," said spotter Farrell.

Burton crossed the finish line in 21st place, well behind winner Dale Earnhardt Jr., who drove his victory lap holding an American flag.

"This is a really tough break, guys," Burton said over his radio.

His frustration had eased, and as he had many times before in this season, he sought to lift his crew's spirits: "We ran so much better than we did here earlier in the season, so that's something positive. You guys worked hard all day, and now we'll just get ready for Kansas next week."

Despite his troubles, Burton managed to advance 30 points closer to the top ten: Johnny Benson, who held tenth in the point standings, had finished 31st after an accident near the end of the race.

Burton left Dover drained, from eight months of racing and twelve days of unprecedented national crisis. At Lake Norman in the week ahead, Burton would repair to his basement den, the place where he kept his trophies and his draftsman's tools, his escape the night after his poor finish in Atlanta all but ended his championship hopes for 2001. Except for driving Paige to school each morning, Burton spent two days on his couch sleeping, watching movies, and eating popcorn and pizza. He took no calls and accepted no visitors; even Kim knew to keep her distance while her husband renewed his strength for the stretch drive of this daunting Winston Cup season.

With no pending appearance in Victory Lane and having nothing immediately to say to any of his drivers or mechanics, Jack Roush decided to make a quick getaway from Dover Downs International Speedway. He wanted to beat the traffic. Roush had often commented that the one thing that could send him into early retirement was the congestion after a race—which with upward of 150,000 spectators, many of them inebriated, could last for hours.

The moment the last racecar had exited for the garage, Roush sprinted across the track. Dover Downs' vice president and director of auto racing, Melvin L. Joseph, a longtime friend, had let Roush park his rental car in one of the speedway's premium spaces—and he had assured Roush that police officers would help him quickly on his way. Roush hoped to be able to reach his jet in time to fly home to Michigan before the sun set. A couple of hours alone at 25,000 feet was one of the few things that might take his mind off this latest round of engine trouble.

Roush beat the crowd and got quickly into his car, a Mitsubishi. Roush disliked Japanese cars—he had once paid an employee who foolishly drove one his week's wages in yen—but the rental company had no Fords, and Roush was left without a choice. He started the import and had moved only about 30 feet when a police officer held up his hand and said: "Stop."

"What do you mean, stop?" Roush said.

"My commander is down here and he says no cars are going to move in this area until most of these people are out," the officer said.

Roush's heart sank. Melvin Joseph's VIP parking lot was near the start/finish line, at the confluence of several major pedestrian exit lanes.

Roush asked to speak with the officer's commander. He explained the situation, but the commander was unbending. Because of today's heightened security, he said, a different traffic pattern was in effect and no cars from this area would be allowed to move until the speedway had emptied.

The crowd was beginning to descend. One man wearing a cap with the colors of the flag recognized Roush—and decided to tease him about his car.

"Jack," he cried out, "what are you doing in that Mitsubishi? We oughtta burn that son of a bitch!"

The fan evidently was kidding, but the police were taking no chances; no terrorist incidents had marred the race that day, but the authorities remained on edge. Hearing the possible threat, two officers rushed the fan, handcuffed him, and dragged him away. He was a tall man, and Roush watched his patriotic hat disappear into the distance.

This is going to be a very long day, Roush thought.

By now, a sea of people was surrounding his car. Roush removed his signature fedora, but it was too late: Fans had recognized him, and they were beating on the trunk and hood. They wanted autographs.

Roush locked his doors, rolled down his window, and began to oblige.

More than an hour passed, and Roush wore out three Sharpies signing caps, shirts, flags, arms, a leg, the top of a shaved head. One woman wanted him to sign her T-shirt along the line of her breasts, but Roush refused—unless, he explained, he could do so without touching her. The woman, who was wearing a sports bra, took off the shirt.

Eventually, an officer approached Roush's car. He wanted Roush to back up so that he was out of the way. Roush refused.

"Let me tell you something, pal," Roush said. "I'm having a really good time here, and I'm not moving. I may spend the night here—I may be signing autographs tomorrow. Don't bother me. Go away."

A second officer then threatened to summon a tow truck.

"You better send two," Roush said, "because I've got four-wheel brakes on this car—and if you jack up one end of it, I'm just going to put them on and you're not going to move me."

Prompted by a call from an official who had overheard the standoff on a scanner, the police eventually agreed to let Roush leave. He did, but not before lecturing the commander on the danger he believed police had created—and not before promising a telephone reprimand from someone in authority after he had informed Melvin Joseph of what had transpired on his VIP lot.

*

One quarter of the Winston Cup season remained after Dover. There would be no Cup title for Roush Racing in 2001, and probably no Rookie of the Year, but Roush hoped that not only Burton would be at the head table at the Waldorf-Astoria this year—he still hoped that Martin, who held 12th in the point standings, and Kenseth, who held 15th, would make it, too.

But those hopes could not be realized with unreliable engines. And so when he returned to Michigan, and then embarked on his regular Tuesday trip to North Carolina, Roush once again was a man on a crusade. And what he found was that a system he himself had put in place was flawed.

At the time of the MBNA Cal Ripken Jr. 400, Roush Racing maintained two major race engine-building centers: the original facility in Livonia, Michigan, and a newer one in Mooresville, North Carolina, that had opened after Roush's entry into NASCAR. Livonia's specialists built engines for Winston Cup and Craftsman Truck cars—and they operated Roush Racing's primary engine-research labs. Mooresville's specialists initially built only engines used in Busch Grand National competition by Roush racers (and many competitors who bought or leased engines, including 2000 champion Jeff Green); but in recent years, Roush had given Mooresville the additional duty of building some Winston Cup engines, too. Roush believed that all of his racers would benefit from this sort of internal competition, and also from the plethora of competitors' Cup shops near Charlotte. "Every wall has got a stethoscope to the other side listening for some bit of intelligence, some secret, some trick," said Roush. "I felt by having a [Cup] engine shop down there that I'd have something better than I could with a more concentrated, single effort."

Under the system in place through the Dover race, Martin's and Burton's Cup engines were built in Livonia, Kenseth's and Busch's in Mooresville. Roush concluded that the failure of Burton's engine during the Ripken 400 probably could not have been avoided—manufactured by an outside vendor, valves sometimes broke—but the failure of Busch's motor was caused by an avoidable assembly error in Mooresville. And this wasn't the first time a Mooresville-built Cup engine had failed, a fact that had led Busch and Kenseth to feel that on some weekends they had been stuck with inferior engines—a feeling that did not enhance the esprit de corps. So on the eve of the next race, at the new speedway in Kansas City, Kansas, Roush decided to shift all Cup engine production back to Livonia. Instituting the latest findings from the research labs would also be enhanced, since directives henceforth need travel only from building to building, not state to state.

"For the rest of the year, you guys need to concentrate on your Busch Grand National engines," Roush told the men in Mooresville, "on building great engines for Greg Biffle and the six to eight other customers that we've got. Let me go back and reestablish confidence with the 97 and the 17 and get them on the same page as the 21 the 6 and the 99." (Livonia also built the engines for Elliott Sadler's Wood Brothers' No. 21 car.)

The sudden swing would tax Livonia's resources, requiring tens of thousands of dollars in unbudgeted overtime pay in a period when the country was slipping into recession—but Roush never scrimped when engines were at issue.

For all of the Roush drivers but Kenseth, who placed 32nd, the Protection One 400 at Kansas Speedway on September 30 was a welcome bounceback from Dover: Martin finished sixth; Busch finished ninth, after starting 40th; and Burton, refreshed from his two days of hibernation, came in 11th after starting 26th. Jeff Gordon won the race, and Johnny Benson had another poor day, enabling Burton to pull within 11 points of tenth place in the point standings. Martin also moved closer to the top ten—he was only 50 points away from Benson now, in 12th place. For one week, at least, a mood of relative satisfaction settled over Roush Racing.

But elsewhere in NASCAR, discontent and uncertainty were rife: The annual ritual known as Silly Season, in which owners, drivers, sponsors, and even crew members jockeyed for new relationships, was under way. Silly Season was NASCAR's version of free agency.

Among the drivers in play that autumn were Jeremy Mayfield, the 22nd-place driver who was abruptly released from Penske Racing two days after the race at Kansas. Jimmy Spencer was looking for a new deal, as were Robert Pressley and Kevin Lepage, who had not found a permanent home after being released in 2000 from Roush Racing. The future of Steve Park, idled since his head injury in early September, remained in question—and with each passing week, Park's substitute, Kenny Wallace, seemed more likely to land a full-time job with Park's owner, Dale Earnhardt Inc. But with the exception of Kurt Busch and Kevin Harvick, whose long-term futures were secure, the 2001 rookies faced the worst uncertainty: Jason Leffler was losing his Cup job, Andy Houston was dropping down to the Busch Series in 2002, and Ron Hornaday was rumored to be returning to the Craftsman Truck circuit, where his twenty-two-year-old son raced.

Rumors always multiplied during Silly Season, and predictably some of the old ones about Martin, Burton, and Kenseth leaving Roush Racing resurfaced that autumn. But the fact was, none of the three was looking—or even tempted.

As the gossips speculated once more on his future, Jeff Burton traveled to New York to visit with grieving firefighters and police officers. Bobby Labonte and his crew chief, Jimmy Makar, joined Burton. The 2000 champion, Labonte had been feted the previous December in Times Square and at the Waldorf-Astoria—but no publicity attended his visit this time. He and Burton had refused to allow media coverage or advance publicity; they had come to lift spirits, not pose for pictures.

Station by station, the racers went, meeting with men and women who had answered the call of duty on September 11—

and who had lost friends and fellow workers in the collapse of the World Trade Center towers. Some recognized the racers and some did not, but all seemed to appreciate their out-of-town guests. "We heard story after story after story of heroic acts, of devastating acts, terrible stories of children that don't have a father or don't have their mother anymore—brothers that have lost brothers, and sisters who have lost sisters," said Burton.

At every stop, people asked if Burton, Labonte, and Makar had visited the place where thousands had died. They had not, and did not intend to. "That was a little more than I thought I wanted to deal with," said Burton. The thought of so many bodies still lost in the rubble deeply disturbed him.

But the firefighters and police kept insisting that the racers go, and finally Labonte said to his friend: "We need to go do that."

"All right," said Burton, "let's do it."

Burton grew unsettled as they approached the scene. "We weren't going to the outer perimeter of it—we were going onto Ground Zero," he said, " and whether we wanted to deal with it or not, we were going to be standing in the midst of it. And I was nervous about what I was going to see, and what I was going to smell, and what I was going to think."

The trio walked past National Guardsmen onto the debris, where smoke still swirled and the air still smelled burnt. Burton was stunned by the magnitude of destruction, which no camera could adequately capture. Even the small details horrified him: the wheel to an office chair he spied in the wreckage, the donuts still in their case in a nearby restaurant whose windows had all been blown out. Said Burton: "You start realizing that these people were just doing their deal: They didn't assault anyone, they didn't flip off anyone, all they did was get up in the morning and go to work. I'm standing there with Bobby Labonte, Jimmy Makar—you know, tough guys—and there was a point where I had to not cry. I said: 'I can't do that, I'm not going to let anybody see me do that.'"

Not long after returning from New York, death brushed by Jeff Burton once more. It was Thursday, October 4, and Winston Cup drivers had completed their qualifying laps for the following Sunday's UAW-GM Quality 500 at Lowe's Motor Speedway. Drivers for the Automobile Racing Club of America had taken to the speedway for a race, and Dale Earnhardt's older son, Kerry, was battling Blaise Alexander Jr. for the lead with four laps remaining when their vehicles collided. Earnhardt's car flipped and burst into flames, and Alexander's hit the wall. Alexander died instantly of head trauma.

A well-liked man of twenty-five who had wanted to be a racer since he was a young boy, Alexander drove for owner Felix Sabates, for whom Kenny Irwin Jr. had raced. Racing had consumed Alexander from his childhood in Montoursville, Pennsylvania, the town that was home to sixteen high school students and five adult chaperones who had died in the 1996 crash of TWA Flight 800 off the coast of Long Island. His goal was Winston Cup racing, and he had raced since 1997 in NASCAR's Grand National division and also in ARCA, where he had recorded one win and eight top-ten finishes in the 2001 season. Alexander was buried on a hill facing the building that had been his first race shop—in a cemetery two blocks from his parents' home. "I believe young Blaise is smiling because he knew he had won, he had crossed the final finish line," said the priest at his funeral. "And God was there, waving the checkered flag of victory." Sabates was similarly fatalistic: "When these guys strap themselves in a car, they know their lives can be over in a few seconds. Look at the guys in the World Trade Center. They didn't expect to die. When the good Lord decides that's what he wants for you, there's nothing you can do about it."

Although he owned a head-restraint device, Alexander was not wearing it when he died. He was not unusual in this regard: Resistance to the devices had continued after Dale Earnhardt's death. The reasons varied. Dale Earnhardt Jr. did not like how the devices felt, and Tony Stewart complained of being claustro-phobic. Jimmy Spencer worried that a HANS device could break his neck, not save it. "Will it leave you crippled? Is it going to leave you a vegetable?" Spencer declared in August. "Personally speaking, if I'm in a bad accident and it takes my life, then that's fine. I just don't want to become a vegetable." But Spencer and Junior had eventually relented, and by October the only regular Cup driver still holding out was Stewart.

Still, several Cup drivers wore head restraints only during races, and then only at certain of the faster racetracks; some driv-ers at other levels of NASCAR, and in other automobile racing leagues such as ARCA, never wore them at all. Alexander's death brought renewed calls for NASCAR and other sanctioning bodies to mandate restraints.

"I have lost patience with the people in this industry who are dragging their feet," said H. A. "Humpy" Wheeler, the president of Lowe's Motor Speedway, on the Friday after Alexander died. "Action has to be taken quickly because this could happen again tomorrow, it could happen Sunday, it could happen next week." Wheeler was a frequent critic of NASCAR and Bill France Jr., and a prominent voice for improved safety, having helped advance, among other innovations, an energy-absorbing bumper nick-named the Humpy Bumper.

Despite his record of safety advocacy, Jeff Burton had sided with NASCAR in not supporting a mandate to wear head and neck restraints; a requirement for one or another product might stifle development of a superior product by another manufac-turer, Burton believed. But Alexander's death pushed Burton to rethink his stance. "Here's a young man that knew that he should be wearing something and he didn't take the initiative to figure out how to get it done," Burton said. "He wasn't dumb, he wasn't a daredevil, he just for whatever reason didn't get it done. Maybe to protect some guys that won't take that step, for whatever rea-son, we need to make it mandatory."

But Mike Helton was unmoved. "We're frustrated, the drivers are frustrated, everyone in motorsports is frustrated, but I've long maintained we will not react just for the sake of reacting," he told reporters on the day of the UAW-GM Quality 500. "I don't have a timetable and I don't think there is a timetable."

The drivers were already strapped into their cars for the start of the UAW-GM 500 when the big video screens at Lowe's Motor Speedway abruptly switched from a live feed of the pre-race ceremonies to NBC anchorman Tom Brokaw. It was Sunday, October 7, almost one month since the terrorist attacks on New York and Washington, and Brokaw brought the news that U.S. forces were sending bombs and cruise missiles into Afghanistan.

The crowd of 130,000 erupted. Fans waved American flags and repeated the chant heard at Dover, "USA! USA! USA!" They roared their approval when singer Lee Greenwood reached the line in "The Star-Spangled Banner" about bombs bursting in air, and again when Air Force jets screamed by on their customary flyover. And they stood to cheer when New York City firefighters, part of a contingent of some 5,000 firefighters from around the country who were attending the race, gave the command to start engines.

Sterling Marlin went on to win the UAW-GM Quality 500, and all four Roush drivers found reason to be pleased, if not elated. Kenseth rebounded from the disappointment of Kansas with a 12th-place showing, and Busch finished 22nd, no inconsiderable achievement considering that he had started 43rd after another poor qualifying effort had forced him to use another provisional to make the race. Martin finished in ninth and moved up one spot in the point standings, to 11th. Burton did him one better: With his fifth-place finish in the race, he displaced Johnny Benson.

Burton now was in tenth place, a member of Winston Cup's

privileged echelon for the first time since last year—an extraordinary accomplishment given how his season had started.

"We're not quitters and we're going to keep fighting," Burton told the media. "It's harder to work together when things aren't going well than it is when things are going well, and our guys have done a great job of sticking together through thick and thin." Clichés notwithstanding, Burton spoke the truth. Since the Daytona 500, the No. 99 CITGO team had not experienced a single defection—although not for lack of opportunity. In stockcar racing, jobs were always opening up with other owners, some of whom paid better wages and allowed employees more days off than Jack Roush—and who were not shy about recruiting, especially during Silly Season.

But events far from Charlotte overshadowed this latest chapter in Burton's resurrection, and war fever surfaced in all of the drivers' post-race interviews. "I just hope we're as good at war as Sterling was in the race today and we can kick their tail," said Dale Jarrett. Tony Stewart could have been a member of the U.S. Special Forces talking when he offered his opinion of Osama bin Laden. "It's time to finish this guy off, as far as I'm concerned," Stewart said. "Bring his head back on a stick."

To reach Martinsville, Virginia, you head north from Charlotte on Interstate Highway 85 on a trip that lasts more than two hours. You proceed past exits for Lowe's Motor Speedway and Dale Earnhardt Boulevard and then leave 85 for the highway that brings you to Winston-Salem, world headquarters of R. J. Reynolds Tobacco Holdings Inc. The road narrows to two lanes as you leave Winston-Salem. High-rise buildings give way to double-wide trailers and unkept ranch houses scattered between tobacco fields that are dusty and brown in the golden light of a midautumn afternoon, and one-man garages and Baptist churches seem to appear around every turn. GOD'S BEEN BLESSING AMERICA, reads the sign at one church, BUT WHEN WILL AMERICA BLESS GOD?

Martinsville Speedway materializes alongside the main road a few miles over the Virginia state line. It is the oldest track still in use on the Winston Cup circuit, and when it opened, in September 1947, three months before NASCAR was founded, it offered seating for only 750. But founder H. Clay Earles, a young tobacco salesman with an entrepreneurial bent, was onto something. Stockcar racing in its infancy was largely confined to fairgrounds and pastures, and the idea of a dedicated facility with stadium seating was an instant success, with more than 6,000 paying customers attending Martinsville's maiden race, even though most had to stand. Encouraged by his friend Bill France Sr., Earles progressively enlarged his speedway, adding more seats and parking lots and concession stands—and maintaining Winston Cup races while competing tracks in places such as North Wilkesboro, North Carolina, and Manassas, Virginia, lost them as NASCAR grew into a major-league sport with a fan base from coast to coast. "We like to see a man bring his wife and children to our events and be comfortable," Earles said. "Racing appeals to all ages, and many of our most avid fans are young folks and ladies."

By 2001, Martinsville Speedway seated 86,000 people, a tiny capacity by the standards of modern Winston Cup competition. The original dirt surface had long since given way to a half mile of gently banked paving, and twenty-six luxury boxes had been built—but freight trains still lumbered by on the old tracks directly behind the small backstretch stands, close enough that engineers liked to wave and blow their whistle on the morning of a race. Until 2001, the speedway lacked a garage building, or tunnel or a bridge to the tiny infield. Everyone had to wait for practice to stop before crossing over, and, as at Bristol, those inside when a race started were trapped until the end.

Friday, October 12, was the start of the Old Dominion 500

weekend. The fields surrounding the speedway were filling with campers, recreational vehicles, and pickup trucks as the afternoon wore on, and fans were drinking beer, grilling sausages and steaks, and roaming the midway grounds. The souvenir trailers were conducting a steady trade, and business was brisk at the Winston booths, where adult smokers received a free half-carton of cigarettes and a racing video in return for disclosing their name and address to R. J. Reynolds, owner of a vast consumer mailing list. Nearly everyone in the crowd of thousands was white, and most of the few that were not belonged to the speedway's maintenance and janitorial staff. The scene was not far distant from 1947, when doctors prescribed smoking to soothe sore throats, beef was considered the secret to vitality, and African-Americans still rode at the back of the bus.

But a closer scrutiny of the midway revealed more contemporary truths. Fans could connect to the Internet at the AOL/nascar.com pavilion, or apply for a credit card at the MBNA and Chase booths. Men could receive a free health screening at the Pfizer/Viagra Tune Up For Life tent—and also complete a form authorizing the pharmaceutical giant to send them information about Pfizer products. Among the optional items on the form were these questions: "Are you familiar with the term erectile dysfunction? If you were aware that you had erectile dysfunction, would you be willing to undergo treatment for it if your healthcare professional recommended it?"

This was also the post–September 11 world. As at Dover, fans were subject to search on entering the speedway, the police were out in greater numbers, and parked vehicles were prohibited under the grandstands. The leading news of the day was anthrax—and not an FBI warning involving crop dusters. An act of bioterrorism had killed an employee at the Florida headquarters of the *National Enquirer*'s parent company, and Tom Brokaw had just disclosed that an anthrax-laced letter sent to him had infected a member of his staff. Still rattled by the events of a month before, many people were now experiencing heightened anxiety.

Burton was among them. The foremost safety advocate of NASCAR's drivers, he had a new concern involving his well-being as a professional racecar driver: fan mail. For now, at least, he wasn't opening his.

"I'm certainly not a high-profile person the way that Tom Brokaw is," said Burton, "but we are athletes. A lot of people know who we are, and it appears to me that these people are targeting things that are symbols of America. And sports is a symbol of America." Burton had taken other measures to keep himself and his family safe, including enhancing the security of his jet, his motor coach, and his residence, where Kim had assembled first-aid supplies and laid in a supply of bottled water and non-perishable foods.

Martinsville Speedway's remoteness and relatively small size left Mark Martin less worried than he had been at Dover Downs, but he remained anxious, and he was spooked looking ahead to the next running of NASCAR's most famous race, the Daytona 500, the following February. "When you're sitting in the middle of 150,000 people and you know a little about what makes these people tick—that's a perfect, perfect opportunity, and in one way it makes as big or a bigger statement as the World Trade Center," Martin said. "You could make one heck of a statement by wiping 150,000 people out."

But Martin and Burton—and Matt Kenseth, Kurt Busch, and all of the Cup drivers, for that matter—were determined to keep racing and to continue with their daily lives. They vowed not to let the terrorists win. "They can kiss my ass," Burton said. "I am going to secure myself the best way I know how, but I'm not going to quit doing the things that I've always done. They aren't going to change my dreams, and they aren't going to change the things that I care about—they just are not going to do it."

*

When a man at Bristol Motor Speedway in August held up a QUITTER sign directed at Mark Martin, a writer who covered NASCAR for *The Sporting News,* set out to divine its meaning. In her column, which ran in September under the headline "Martin Says Racing Is No Longer His Top Priority," the journalist imagined herself inside the driver's head at the moment he spotted the sign. "Feelings of disbelief and anguish rushed through Martin's diminutive body, once solid but showing signs of wear from 25 years behind the wheel," she wrote. Quoting Martin, the journalist described the fulfillment Martin found in his son Matt's racing this year—and his frustration at his own. Starting in 1998, the year Mark Martin's father died, wrote the journalist, "slowly, Martin's will to win seemed to evaporate."

Martin took exception to the analysis when her column was brought to his attention. "I don't think that writers have the right to do editorials and then insert one sentence of quotes," Martin said. "That's not right—not if they're not going to include the whole conversation where that quote comes from so that it's put into context. That's tabloid writing."

But Martin was more wounded than irate—not only by the column, but also by the similarly unflattering letters to *The Sporting News* that followed. One was from a man in Virginia who claimed to have held up the QUITTER sign at Bristol. "Mark isn't giving the 100-percent effort his fans are used to," the man wrote. "But then, why should he care what his fans think? He is still pulling in the big bucks despite finishing outside the Top Ten." The possibility that someone might really believe he was a quitter ate at Martin, so on the Saturday of the Old Dominion 500 weekend, he invited reporters to meet with him at Martinsville Speedway's media center.

For almost an hour, Martin bared his soul.

He expressed his gratitude toward his sport, which had brought him the kinds of riches and fame a young kid from rural Arkansas could only dream of, and he talked of being "blessed" with an exceptional sponsor, owner, and crew chief. "A lot of drivers would quickly trade places with me for my performance this year—and, more than that, for the organization that I have behind me, the relationship that I have with Jack Roush and Jimmy Fennig and the people that we have," said Martin. He acknowledged his long winless streak and the 2001 season's failed expectations, and said that if he knew how to improve his performance, he of course already would have done so.

"The thing I'm saying is that there have been some things written this year that have hurt my feelings," Martin said. "I'm telling you right now, do not question my commitment or my will because it's the same as it always has been and it will continue to be because that's me."

Martin retold the familiar story of how he had raced the week his father died, and often after having been injured—and he revealed that the chronic back pain that surgery in late 1999 had relieved had returned this year, although physical therapy had recently resolved it again. And he told a new story, about his son Matt. "We were at the race track a few months ago," said Martin, "and between his heat race and the features, he got kicked in the eye. It was almost swelled shut: there was a slit there, just barely open, and he was almost in tears and everything. His mother and I tried to get him to go home, but he said he wanted to race because he wanted to get the points. He drove the race car and then we took him home. Of course, he had a lesser result than his expectation, so it was a very tough night. Racing deals you all kinds of blows. You have to race when you're physically in pain, mentally in pain, and emotionally in pain. The real winners race through all that—and it will also bring you the greatest high and the most joy of anything." He could have been a junkie, describing the cycle of addiction.

Martin said he considered it "most likely" that he would win again someday, bringing him redemption; but come what may, he said he wouldn't quit Cup racing before his contract with

Roush expired at the end of 2005. And it was conceivable, he had previously said, that even after he left Cup competition he would race part-time in some less demanding venue. He would long crave the thrill of a win, even if driving alone could never excite him again.

"When I say I don't love to drive a racecar," he told the reporters at Martinsville, "that means if no one was here and you had a racecar sitting on pit road and there wasn't a race coming up that I was testing for or trying to prepare for, I wouldn't drive the car. I don't like to make laps—I like to win. I like to sit on the pole. Driving a car fast is not where the thrill is for me. Beating the competition is."

Martin had run strongly in the two races preceding the Old Dominion 500, and with his sixth-place finish at Kansas City and his ninth-place showing at Charlotte, he had climbed to 11th in the point standings—and he was just 56 points behind Burton when he arrived at Martinsville, the scene of his last victory, in April 2000.

Martin did not win the Old Dominion 500, which was run on Monday, October 15, after rain forced postponement on Sunday—but he placed seventh, after leading several laps in the middle of the race. Kenseth also led several laps, but was reduced to a 36th-place finish after the freak failure of a rear-end gear. Burton finished fifth, solidifying his tenth-place position in the point standings. Kurt Busch came in 35th, but that number did no justice to Busch's performance.

Failing to qualify again on time, Busch had been forced to use another of his rapidly dwindling reserve of provisionals to make the race, and he had started near the end of the pack. But he drove like a man possessed, and on lap 240, having passed twenty-nine cars, he took over the lead from Martin. Busch kept it for the next thirty-seven laps and was running in second late in the race when Ricky Rudd, who was on his rear bumper, decided to put the rookie in his place. Second in the point standings,

Rudd remained in pursuit of Jeff Gordon for the Winston Cup championship, but having failed to gain much ground on the leader recently and with the season winding down, the forty-five-year-old Rudd sorely needed a win, and he wasn't inclined to let a twenty-three-year-old kid thwart him. So he bumped Busch out of his way. Busch's left rear tire went flat and a brake line was cut, forcing Busch to the pits for repairs and giving Rudd the chance to win—a chance Rudd lost when his engine died a few laps later. "We had an incredible racecar today," Busch said after the Old Dominion 500. "If nothing else, we showed the field that we can run with the best of them and sooner or later we're going to capture that first win."

Instead, another driver visited Victory Lane for the first time: Ricky Craven, who had gone 173 races before prevailing.

A native of Maine, the thirty-five-year-old Craven had come up through the ranks in New England—like the desert Southwest, a region that had never given stockcar racing a great champion. Craven competed in one Winston Cup race in 1991, then joined the circuit full-time in 1995, when he finished 24th in the point standings and was named the Rookie of the Year. He finished 20th in the points in 1996 and seemed on his way toward entering racing's elite when he suffered a serious blow to his head in a racing accident early in the 1997 season. Craven returned later that year, but continuing headaches and dizziness, symptoms of postconcussion syndrome, forced him out of Cup competition early in 1998. He recovered, and neurologists pronounced him fit to race again, but owners were reluctant to take a chance on a driver with a history of head injury and now a nickname of Crash Craven, and he raced only intermittently in 1999 and 2000. Craven often said he spent those years discovering a new appreciation for his wife and two young children, all the while looking for a full-time sponsor and owner (Tide Detergent and Cal Wells, who eventually signed him for the 2001 season). More so even than Mark Martin, Ricky Craven had

Beneath the scoring tower, Matt Kenseth's crew watches qualifying at Indianapolis. Crew Chief Robbie Reiser has his back to camera.

Mark Martin leads the pack at Atlanta Motor Speedway, where speeds routinely approach 190 miles per hour.

Fans always mob Mark Martin for autographs when he's at the track.

The new Chicagoland Speedway opened in 2001, and former Rookie of the Year rivals Matt Kenseth and Dale Earnhardt Jr. were there.

Angry at Kurt Busch's comments about the quality of the Roush racing engines at the Brickyard 400, Jack Roush spared no words on his rookie.

Despite damage to his car, Mark Martin continued on in the Brickyard 400 at Indianapolis Motor Speedway, on August 5, 2001.

The lights glisten off Matt Kenseth's car in the Bristol night race, the Sharpie 500 on August 25, which some consider NASCAR's most exciting event.

Against the long odds any rookie faces, Kurt Busch won the pole for the Mountain Dew Southern 500 in September at the treacherous Darlington raceway.

Mark Martin and Jeff Burton have been teammates at Roush Racing for years. Rumors that both were looking in 2001 to drive elsewhere proved false.

Most cars, including Matt Kenseth's, sported patriotic colors at the September 23 race at Dover Downs, the first since the September 11 terrorist attacks.

Kurt Busch pulls it out of a near-wreck at Dover during the MBNA Cal Ripken Jr. 400, which honored the baseball great.

Crew chief Ben Leslie and Kurt Busch. Leslie landed the job when Jack Roush replaced Busch's first Cup chief early in the season.

NASCAR chairman Bill France Jr. in the lobby of the Waldorf-Astoria hotel the day of the 2001 annual Cup banquet.

Mark Martin and wife, Arlene, and their son, Matt, confer before the start of the 2002 Daytona 500.

Joined by his mother, his brother Kyle, and his girl-friend Melissa, Kurt Busch walks to drivers' intro-ductions before the 2002 Daytona 500, ready for a new season to begin.

experienced racing's darkest depression—and now its most exhilarating high.

In his victory interview, Craven described his long journey: "If you want to speak in terms of extremes," he said, "there was a percentage of time spent feeling sorry for myself—and then you look at this side of things, and it's like I'm on top of the world! I mean, this is the greatest day in my life professionally! This is exactly what I've worked all my life for." Because of the rain delay, Craven's family had returned home before the race so the children would not miss a day of school, but Craven spoke to them by phone the moment he climbed out of his car. "My family is the joy of my life," he said of the conversation. "Every one of us does something for a living and, by God, I get to do something I love to do and I won! Life doesn't get any better than this right here."

Head injury remained topical as the racers left Martinsville for the fall race at Talladega: On Wednesday, October 17, NASCAR reversed its long-held position and mandated head restraints for all drivers in the Winston Cup, Busch Grand National, and Craftsman Truck Series. The edict was effective immediately, and applied to all races, qualifying laps, practices, and testing sessions—in other words, any time a driver was on the track. The devices would also be required on NASCAR's regional touring circuits beginning with the 2002 season.

In announcing the decision, NASCAR vice president George Pyne did not mention legal liability—nor Blaise Alexander and the many other drivers who might still be alive had they been wearing HANS or Hutchens devices. "The driving force for the mandate was the level of comfort among the teams and drivers in wearing the devices," said Pyne. "Initially, we didn't feel it was appropriate or the right thing to do to make our drivers feel less safe. But NASCAR has worked closely with safety experts, drivers, and manufacturers to address issues that led some drivers to feel that these devices might make them less safe. As time has gone on and teams have grown more comfortable with them, we felt it was the right thing to do." Even Bill France's harshest critics found reason to praise the mandate: Improved driver safety, NASCAR had finally decided, was worth the cost of greater liability in the event of an accident.

Of the Cup racers in mid-October, only Tony Stewart had never worn a head and neck restraint. "I'm not being bull-headed about this, but there is nothing right now that I'm comfortable wearing inside the race car," he said after NASCAR's announcement. "When I ran Indy cars, there was a time once when I had the foam headrest that goes around the rim of the driver's cockpit touch the top of my shoulders. I ran one lap, pulled in and bailed out of the car because I felt like I was getting trapped inside the car. It wasn't because of anything mechanical, it was because of my own anxiety that comes from being claustrophobic. That's how the HANS device makes me feel." Earning a living inside a space with barely more room than a coffin seemed a poor career choice for a claustrophobic, but there Stewart was.

After an angry exchange with NASCAR officials on the Friday of race weekend, Stewart reluctantly joined his peers in wearing a head restraint for the October 21st running of the EA Sports 500 at Talladega Superspeedway. Dale Earnhardt Jr. won—once again, amid controversy. A post-race inspection of his car revealed that it was an eighth of an inch lower to the ground than the rules allowed, a thin infraction that likely gave Junior a bit of additional speed, but NASCAR allowed the win to stand, while fining Junior's crew chief $25,000. Stewart took second at Talladega, and Burton placed third, an excellent day that nonetheless did not move him up from tenth in the point standings. Kenseth's fourth-place finish did advance him a position, to 14th in the point standings—but Martin, finishing ninth, remained in 11th, and Kurt Busch, finishing 29th, remained in 25th. With his seventh-place showing, Jeff Gordon moved 395 points ahead of Rudd in the point standings.

But yet again, safety overshadowed Gordon's drive to the title, which now was his to lose.

The spring race at Talladega had gone off without the big wreck that drivers had dreaded, and the EA Sports 500 seemed destined to be similarly favored when, on the last lap, as several drivers were battling Junior for the win, Bobby Hamilton made contact with Bobby Labonte. Labonte's car flipped, touching off a maelstrom that mangled almost twenty cars. No one was badly hurt, but the drivers lived through a moment of terror. Said Stewart, who raced with Labonte for owner Joe Gibbs: "When you come off of Turn Two after the checkered flag waves and you see your teammate's car upside down, it scares you to death. I'm just glad to be alive."

Once their terror subsided, many of the drivers were enraged, along with many crew chiefs and owners. Jack Roush called the wreck "horrific," and owner Robert Yates "barbaric." Jimmy Makar minced no words in his explanation of why NASCAR refused to modify the restrictor-plate and aerodynamic rules that allowed the cars to run so close together at Talladega and Daytona: "Look at the crowd," said Makar. "They loved it. Thumbs up, thumbs down. Who lives, who dies. We're a bunch of Roman gladiator geeks."

This time, however, racers did more than speak to journalists. After the race, many of them descended on the NASCAR officials' trailer to demand change. And this time, the NASCAR hierarchy did more than listen.

"We don't like these wrecks any more than the drivers," said Jim Hunter, NASCAR's new vice president of corporate communications. "We're sitting on the edge of our seats—certainly not like the drivers are—but I think everyone at NASCAR is sitting on the edge of their seat in an event where they're running that close. Even though we have tried to figure out how to fix that, we have been unsuccessful. So we have got to figure a way."

NASCAR did not intend to act unilaterally. Shortly after Talladega, Mike Helton invited representatives of every Winston Cup team to a meeting on November 1. Together, Helton said, racers would make superspeedway racing safer. "There's been some frustration in the past over the way we've handled things, and hopefully this will ease some of that," Helton said. "We recognize this is a different time, that things have changed and maybe we need to change a little bit as well."

In light of NASCAR's initial reaction to the death of Dale Earnhardt, this was a remarkable admission. NASCAR's long public relations nightmare was finally over.

Even before the start of the Checker Auto Parts 500 at Phoenix International Raceway on Sunday, October 28, Jack Roush had reason to celebrate. With young Kyle Busch nearing the limit of Craftsman Truck Series races he could run in 2001 and remain eligible for the Rookie of the Year title in 2002, Roush had substituted Greg Biffle in Friday's Truck race—and Biffle had won. Biffle won again on Saturday, racing in his regular series, Busch Grand National. The victory established a new record for wins in the series by a newcomer (five) and guaranteed Biffle Rookie of the Year honors. Roush considered Biffle an important piece of the future: He would run seven Winston Cup races in 2002, and join the circuit full-time in 2003.

Roush, of course, wanted a weekend sweep in Phoenix, which he had never achieved in his years of NASCAR racing. His best hope for Sunday was Burton, who had won the Cup race at Phoenix in 2000 in the same car he would drive in the Checker Auto Parts 500. Time apparently had taken nothing from the vehicle: Burton qualified in third, and was fourth fastest in Saturday's final practice.

The car, however, handled poorly early in the race, and Burton's crew made multiple adjustments in suspension and tire pressure as they sought to bring their driver to the edge. Burton wasn't satisfied until late in the race—but he nonetheless managed to lead several laps a third of the way through, and again at the two-thirds point. After momentarily losing the lead to Mike Wallace, Burton regained it on lap 279—and kept it through 312, the final lap.

"Float it in, baby!" Stoddard said as Burton headed toward the finish line. "Float it in!"

Burton won by 2.645 seconds, a commanding margin of some 500 feet. His crew waved an American flag and someone handed the driver one, which he held out his window as he circled the track and drove to Victory Lane. Wearing a captain's hat given to him by a visiting New York police officer, Jack Roush joined the celebration. Roush's racers had not only delivered the sweep this weekend—Burton had recorded Roush's 50th Winston Cup win. Only eight other owners had ever won more races in NASCAR's top series.

Interviewed after the Victory Lane celebration, Roush talked of the road his organization had traveled in the twelve months since Burton's previous win at Phoenix: "At this time last year, we were on a high note," Roush said. "Matt was securing the rookie championship, and Jeff was certainly on his way. Kurt Busch had a number of races he had done very well at and we made the best [car-building] effort we've made in thirteen years over the winter. I could not look back and add a person or replace a priority to try to get ready. We go to Daytona and we have a terrible crash. We have pause throughout the community. We've got to stop and reassess what we're doing and how we're doing it and why we're doing it . . . and then we've got the tire. The tire was the joker—it was the wild card this year."

Roush said that Goodyear's new tires had disrupted his drivers' connection to their cars; but with yet more evidence that it was being reestablished, he could afford a moment of humor. "Jeff and Matt and Mark and Kurt all said that their rear ends could not feel the car through that tire," he joked. "I don't know if other teams had that, but we've had to reeducate a part of their body that's got their brains in it!" The reporters in the media center howled. It was not every day that they witnessed the funny side of Jack Roush.

In his remarks, Burton expounded on tires, agreeing with Roush that he seemed finally to be regaining his connection—that when his car handled poorly now, more often than not he knew what was wrong and how to fix it. Then he praised Stoddard and the crew. "The sign of a person's integrity and a person's true character is when things aren't going well," Burton said. "Everybody gets along great when things are going fine—and when things aren't going fine, you really find out who is tough and you find out who is committed to the program. To the man, I don't know of anyone on our team that I've been disappointed in. I kept telling everybody that we aren't quitters and this is an example of that."

In the week following the Checker Auto Parts 500, the Ford Motor Company honored Roush, Burton, and Biffle with a full-page ad in *USA Today*. But there was another significant, if less well-publicized, development with Roush Racing to emerge from Phoenix. After starting 38th, Kenseth had finished fourth for the second week in a row, enabling him to climb one more position in the point standings, to 13th. In their quiet, Wisconsinite way, he and crew chief Robbie Reiser were putting it all together for the homestretch of the Cup season. Now, three Roush drivers stood a chance of finishing in the top ten.

But with his 19th-place showing at Phoenix, Mark Martin stayed 11th in the point standings. Kurt Busch, who wound up 22nd, also was unchanged, at 25th. With just four races left, Kevin Harvick was now assured of being named Rookie of the Year.

Busch began the season hoping the title would be his, but he had let go of that dream earlier in the fall, during the spell of disappointment that left him repeating the old saw that if he didn't have bad luck, he wouldn't have any luck at all. After his engine failed at Dover and Rudd knocked him out of contention at Martinsville, Harvick's brakes had locked part way into a pit stop at

Talladega—an unintentional event that momentarily blocked Busch, who had the adjoining stall, and cost him a good finish. Phoenix had brought more heartache. Forced to use the last of his provisionals to make the Checker Auto Parts 500, Busch had progressed from 41st place to almost tenth when, fewer than sixty laps from the finish, Jimmy Spencer intentionally spun him out. Busch was livid—but Roush, an older and more seasoned man, was sanguine: "It's a price that old dogs exact on young dogs every place on earth, a price paid for the rite of passage into adulthood. And the more exuberant, the more talented, and the more successful the young person is, the more likely he is to meet with the contempt and the disdain of the older people." Still, Roush did not dismiss the matter out of hand. "Kurt's having a rough year with his being junior in this senior league here," he told reporters after the race, "but he'll earn the respect and those guys will eventually give him racing room—and if they don't, they'll someday pay a price for it." Roush did not need to remind anyone that he had three other drivers, each a veteran, in his Winston Cup stable.

Hoping that superstition might bring results where minds and machines had come up short, Busch had placed a box of Lucky Charms cereal on his pit cart at Phoenix—but after Spencer spun him out, the cereal went back to his motor coach, where Melissa subsequently ate it. Whether cereal or raccoon penis bones, such strategies had their limits.

Still, Busch was guardedly upbeat before the next race, the Pop Secret 400 at Rockingham, North Carolina, on Sunday, November 4. With no provisionals left, he needed a fast qualifying lap to make the race—and he achieved a very fast one, eleventh best of the field. Having avoided the embarrassment of watching the race at home on TV, he went on to run seventh fastest in the weekend's final practice. And he demonstrated that this speed was no fluke from the moment the green flag flew.

Busch reached tenth place by the twenty-second lap of the Pop

Secret 400, and he took the lead on lap 176, maintaining it through lap 190, and regaining it on lap 270, two-thirds of the way to the checkered flag. He was running in second forty-two laps later when the needle on his engine temperature gauge began to inch up. Busch prayed that it was something his crew could resolve by removing tape from the front grille, which lets air reach the engine. Tape placement was a curiously delicate, if vital, proposition: too little, and a car's aerodynamic performance was diminished; too much, and an engine could overheat and self-destruct, as Busch had experienced firsthand in July at New Hampshire. A Cup car might cost $150,000, but three inches of a $3.98 roll of ordinary duct tape could spell the difference between pride and ruin.

Busch's crew stripped off tape on the next pit stop, but the needle continued toward the red. Sixty laps from the end of the race, as Busch was running in second, the last of his coolant turned to steam and his motor gave out. Oil leaked onto hot metal and ignited, causing flames to shoot from under the hood of the No. 97 car as it coasted back to pit road.

Busch jumped to safety—and was immediately met by Jack Roush, who implored him not to criticize Roush engines or Roush employees in his comments to reporters. Busch did not—but his car chief obliquely did.

"The motherfucking engine blew up!" said the car chief over the radio, monitored not only by Roush but by broadcast crews, NASCAR officials, and fans with headsets.

The comment enraged Roush, both for its semipublic nature and for the disrespect it showed to his engine builders. Roush found the car chief a short while later in Busch's hauler—and he fired him on the spot, something he'd never done before, usually preferring to sleep on any such decision. For Busch, who sorely needed stability to foster team chemistry, it was one more in a disconcerting succession of personnel changes: Ryan Young, his best tire changer, had abruptly resigned after the UAW-GM Quality 500 four weeks before to take a job with Jeff Gordon. Young's loss was personally disappointing as well. As a member of the 2000 Craftsman Truck Rookie-of-the-Year team, he had relocated to Charlotte with Busch and become his roommate and, Busch thought, his friend.

Roush in February had higher expectations for Busch than the 25th place he now held in the standings—but he wasn't about to give up on the young driver now. The season's results had so far been mediocre, but Busch's talent and ability to learn were beyond dispute.

"We've had some missteps in his judgments on the racetrack," Roush said, "and we've had some missteps within the team, which is a rookie team supporting a rookie driver. We've failed to capitalize a couple of times—and we've not adapted as well as we might have some other times. Considering his age and his potential, we're on track. I'd just hoped it would be easier." He'd hoped, too, that his engines would have served Busch better, and for this, Roush accepted some responsibility.

Many of Busch's lessons in 2001 were drawn from mistakes that Roush believed he would not repeat in 2002. Other lessons concerned racing's dark side, the torment that Martin and, to a lesser extent, Burton and Kenseth had experienced during their careers—but those lessons, too, would serve the young driver well in the future. Busch's career may have read like a fairy tale until 2001, but sooner or later, Roush knew, Busch had to learn that speed was a harsh master. Better it be sooner.

Said Roush: "That will be the profound lesson for this year: how extraordinarily difficult this business is. It will make him appreciate when things go problem-free—he will enjoy his success, and hopefully deal with it better through this humbling experience."

But philosophizing did not soothe the rookie. With three races to go, Busch felt tired, and uncharacteristically defeated.

CHAPTER 10

THE CHECKERED FLAG

Kurt Busch finished 23rd at the Pennzoil Freedom 400, at Homestead-Miami Speedway on November 11, but he still lacked sufficient provisional points to automatically make the race after that, the NAPA 500 on November 18 at Atlanta Motor Speedway, which would have been the season finale if not for the September terrorist attacks. Busch was subdued when he arrived in Georgia. His stomach hadn't been feeling right lately, and he wasn't sleeping well: Day or night, he couldn't get his mind off the humiliating possibility of being sent home.

"I haven't been myself for a good three weeks now," he said. "It's eating at me. I can't wait for the year to be over."

Busch might have found consolation in Friday's practice at Atlanta: His best lap was the 20th fastest of the field, which seemed to bode well for qualifying. But when practice ended, Busch was gloomy, telling Geoff Smith, who had joined him in his hauler lounge, that the lap had been nothing but luck.

In the season's waning weeks, Smith had emerged as a sort of mentor to Busch. The Roush Racing president had witnessed the rookie on TV criticizing Goodyear's tires after he hit the wall dur-

ing qualifying at Kansas City, and like Jack Roush, he had coun-
seled the young driver to contain his frustrations in his remarks
to the media: raw displays of emotion, Smith explained, would
not enhance Busch's public image, nor please his sponsors. Smith
had also urged Busch to employ constructive criticism, not pique,
when interacting with his crew. On more than one occasion,
Smith knew, Busch had disparaged his car as "junk"—an indirect
slur of Ben Leslie and the others on his team who had configured
it, and a denial of the pivotal role that Busch himself played in
setups.

Now, as Busch awaited the start of qualifying, Smith turned
fatherly. He praised Busch for not instinctively striking back at
the veterans who had gunned for him this year and said that he
eventually would earn their respect. He told Busch that the primary and associate sponsors of the No. 97 car had seen ample
evidence of his talent for speed, which confirmed the "blue sky"
potential that had been Roush Racing's sales pitch for the driver
who had started the season in a virgin-white car. Said Smith: "If
you can never get to the front, they wonder: 'Does he have it?
Have we done the wrong thing?'"

Not for the first time that autumn, Smith compared Busch to
Jeff Gordon, who would become the 2001 Winston Cup champion at Atlanta—but whose 1993 rookie year had been uneven,
like Busch's. "He was fast a lot of times—but it was wreck after
wreck," said Smith. "It was like, 'Well, this program is going to
take years.' But for him, it didn't take very long." And it wouldn't
take much longer for Busch to find his way, either, Smith predicted.

"That's good to hear, being that we're pretty far off our expectations," said Busch.

"You're far off your expectations," Smith said, "but you're not
far off from what I was thinking."

Busch was only momentarily soothed. He continued to compare his rookie Cup season, especially its plagued second half, to

his quick mastery of every other series in which he had competed, and he lamented his failure to win a race this year—the first season in his career that he had not experienced the exhilaration of Victory Lane. "I like to be successful," he said. "Whether I'm still bolting together water mains for the water district, I want to do it right—and make sure that the people that I'm working with and surrounded by are happy. It seems like I haven't done that."

Busch knew that Roush remained confident in his future—even the boss's body language, Busch believed, confirmed that to him. "It's something that I feel every time he looks at me and he smiles," said Busch. "I feel honored to have a project given to me by such a statured man." But Busch also believed he had let Roush down, and he hoped next year to make it up to the owner.

"I've never looked at the New Year as turning a new leaf over and creating a New Year's resolution," he said. "I've always just looked at it as another day to continue what I was doing because everything ran so smoothly. Now I can see in the professional world that many people do that—if they have a bad year, whether it's the economy, whether it's this, whether it's that. I'll use the new year as a fresh start and as a way to get motivation until Thanksgiving of next year."

One thing remained unchanged by his rookie season: his passion for racing. "I couldn't do anything else in the world," said Busch.

Having tasted speed at an impressionable age, he was forever addicted.

Shortly after 4 P.M. on that Friday in November, Busch strapped himself into his racecar. The NASCAR official gave the signal, and Busch roared off pit road on smoking tires. He was the 39th driver to run his qualifying laps, and so far most of those ahead of him had been fast, including Carl Long, who almost never made a race. Long was so severely underfunded that he could only try a few times a year—and when he did, he showed up with a crew too poor to afford uniforms.

"OK, man, I know you can do it," Leslie told Busch on his radio. "Just be smooth."

"Rolling out. Ten-four, buddy," said Busch.

The first of Busch's two qualifying laps was 29.854 seconds—36th fastest, square on the qualifying bubble. With drivers like Tony Stewart and Dale Earnhardt Jr. still to qualify, Busch almost certainly needed a faster second lap if he was to be assured of getting one of the forty-three slots.

But his second lap was only a few hundredths of a second faster, leaving Busch in 35th place. As he walked through the garage area back to his hauler, the next driver, Bobby Hamilton, ran a better lap. Busch was back on the bubble, a fact he learned from a computer inside his hauler.

"We're going home, aren't we," he said. "Perfect. Glad the engine stayed together." He was being sarcastic.

Busch went into his lounge, and while he was changing out of his fire suit, Bill Elliott pushed him off the bubble. Busch was indeed going home.

Leslie offered words of comfort, but Busch rebuffed him.

"I'm not taking that piece of shit to Loudon," he said, storming out of his hauler. "You can find someone else to drive it."

Leslie was a soft-spoken young man, but now he was angry, too. "If he's going to be that goddamn ungrateful," he said after Busch had left, "I'm not building him another car."

"I wish Jack were here," said Stephanie Smith, director of sponsor relations for Roush Racing. But the weather was sunny and warm, and Jack had left early to go fly vintage airplanes with friends.

"This is one call I'm not looking forward to making," said Kathy Kalin, who handled Busch's public relations. She had to break the news to Newell Rubbermaid, which now also would lack a presence Sunday at one of the season's highest-profile races, thereby suffering an incalculable loss of media exposure for which it so handsomely paid.

On hearing that the Roush contingent had been reduced to three cars, Jeff Burton took it upon himself to seek out Busch's crew and thank them for their work. Busch had already left with Melissa in a rental car for the five-hour trip back to Charlotte—but Burton could empathize with him, although he disapproved of his parting shot to Leslie. Burton remembered well the last Winston Cup race he himself had failed to make: the Purolator 500 at Atlanta in March 1996, when, like Busch, he was in his first year of Cup racing with Jack Roush. Had he seen Busch, Burton would have advised him to do his best to put the day behind him, although he understood that was easier said than done.

Burton had flown into Atlanta on a high note. After finishing 18th at Rockingham, he had placed fourth at Miami, best of the Roush drivers. Since the halfway mark of the season, the Pepsi 400 at Daytona, only Jeff Gordon had accumulated more points in the standings than Burton—and it was just 114 more points. Burton's return had so impressed *The Charlotte Observer*'s David Poole, one of the deans of motorsports journalism, that Poole had just contacted *TV Guide* to amend a forthcoming article containing his predictions for 2002: He had initially picked Burton to finish eighth, but now saw him in fourth. Other writers were beginning to believe that Burton would contend for the title the following year.

In any event, Burton now was guaranteed at least a tenth-place finish for the 2001 season—but his ambition was greater than that. Two races remained, and he hoped to run well enough in both to reach as high as sixth in the point standings. "We are in the attack mode," he said. He did not intend to coast now.

Nor did he intend to coast in 2002. His plan for the next year was to work even harder, with more test sessions and longer hours at the shop. "We're going to work our asses off," he said. "But when we're not working, I'm going to be spending time with my family." With Kim's support, Burton had visited a boat dealer the previous week near the Homestead-Miami Speedway. He was finally going to buy himself that yacht.

But Burton hardly considered a new boat to be the year's crowning reward. He found greater satisfaction in the role he had played in helping to improve driver safety, in his charitable causes, and in his reaching out to the victims of September 11. He said events on and off the track starting with the birth of his son Harrison Brian in October 2000 had given him a deeper under-standing of life.

"When you assess all the things that go on around you and you assess the things that go on in the world, you play this little, bitty, teeny, tiny, small, almost nonexistent role," said Burton. "But if you step it up and you go and try to make things better, then you play a much larger role—and that role can be in all different kinds of ways. It can be in humanitarian aid, it can be in doing some-thing at your local church, it can be in: 'Hey we got a race team that's struggling, let's go fix it.' Now you've affected a group. There's so many different ways that you can go out and make things better for you, your family, the people around you, and peo-ple you don't know—if you embrace it. And that's pretty cool."

Burton also made another important discovery in 2001.

"I have questioned how tough I am mentally in my life," he said. "Not that I think I need Prozac or anything like that—I'm just saying that there's times I've questioned how much mental power and how much resolve I really have. And I've learned that I have a lot."

Like Jeff Burton, Matt Kenseth began the Atlanta weekend with optimism. He had finished tenth at Rockingham after starting

40th—and his crew that weekend had wrested the World Pit Crew Competition title from Burton's crew, the 2000 winners, in record time. Kenseth had finished in 27th in the Pennzoil Freedom 400, but not because he drove poorly: An alternator fitting broke, which killed the battery of the No. 17 car, necessitating a pit stop that ruined his chances of winning when the new battery shorted and burned a hole in an oil line. "So for having to rebuild our car," Kenseth had told reporters in Miami, "we got the best finish we could out of it. I feel good about it because we ran really well. I thought we ran with the top five cars most of the day." Kenseth, however, held 13th in the point standings, with no chance now of reaching the top ten, even with a great day at Atlanta

Mark Martin was in similar straits. Following his four consecutive top-ten finishes from Kansas City through Talladega and then his 19th-place showing in Phoenix, he had come in 34th at Rockingham after getting caught up in the mess that Spencer's bumping of Busch had created. Miami was also a disappointment, with Martin finishing 24th after his car's handling deteriorated in the second half of the race. He had dropped to 12th in the point standings, with virtually no chance now of landing a speaking role at the Waldorf-Astoria banquet.

Martin was the kind of driver who lay awake at night pondering setups for his car, and thinking about his driving and his crew. As he examined the 2001 season, he could fault no individual. "I look at a bunch of extremely talented people who gave everything that they had to give—and who came up with a result that was less than what the whole group was capable of," Martin said. "We're all disappointed. We've all been much more successful."

Lately, Martin had been thinking that something must be done to rejuvenate the chemistry of the No. 6 team. It would involve shifting people, possibly including hiring someone from outside—but Martin had not, as yet, sorted out those details. He only knew that change had to come, or he might risk not winning in Winston Cup again.

"Something has to give," said Martin. "You can't keep doing the same thing and expect a different result."

By the NAPA 500, anthrax fears had receded and the fall of Kabul had given Americans reason to be optimistic about the campaign in Afghanistan. But the recent crash of American Airlines Flight 587 in New York had made travelers skittish again, and the government continued to caution that the war on terrorism was far from over. A long year just kept getting longer—and so did the 2001 Winston Cup season. On the road since before Valentine's Day, the racers and the reporters who covered them were punchy that November weekend in Atlanta.

"Just trying to get the season over so I can find a nice quiet place to commit suicide," sportswriter Monte Dutton said on Friday.

"Book me a room," another journalist replied.

As part of a promotion for the movie *Dr. Seuss' How The Grinch Stole Christmas!* Jimmy Spencer's car had been repainted and renamed: It was now the No. 26 Kmart GRINCH! Ford Taurus, surely one of the strangest epithets ever for a car. Hoping for coverage, a public relations specialist went through the media center distributing a contest form seeking reporters' choices for real-life people who could play the characters in *The Grinch Who Stole NASCAR.* The lead character, of course, was The Grinch.

"That's easy," said a writer. "Bill France."

Other strange touches were in evidence. Many still talked of snow in New Hampshire for the November 23 race, the season finale even though the long-range forecast called for unseasonably warm weather, and Saturday featured the running of an ARCA race whose name honored pigs: Pork The Other White Meat 400. Kerry Earnhardt won, and representatives of The National Pork Board treated him to grilled pork chops in Victory Lane. It was nothing if not a photo-op.

In preparation for their year-end wrap-ups, journalists interviewed Winston Cup stars. Dale Earnhardt Jr. held forth for almost an hour on his racing, his social life, and his father, and Mark Martin talked about his son, who was competing at Atlanta on Saturday afternoon in a class of cars called Bandoleros. The most surprising revelations, though, concerned Kevin Harvick.

Having raised the ire of several veterans with his aggressive driving during the summer, Harvick had continued to anger drivers as autumn had begun—and they had not held their tongues. "He's already made a name for himself. He's taking all that away from himself by being a bonehead week after week," said Todd Bodine, ordinarily a gentlemanly sort, after Harvick bumped him at Talladega. Bobby Hamilton was more blunt after Harvick administered similar treatment at Martinsville. Harvick might think he was turning into another Dale Earnhardt, said Hamilton, but he was only kidding himself. "He wouldn't make a scab on Earnhardt's butt right now," Hamilton declared.

Harvick had responded, but not on Hamilton's level. "Not only did he disrespect what I've done and our race team," said Harvick, "but he disrespected the Earnhardt family." If he seemed more restrained than he had during a summer of swagger, perhaps it was because owner Richard Childress had urged him to choose his words more carefully after receiving many e-mails criticizing the rookie—or perhaps Harvick finally heeded the bad press that kept mounting.

Meeting with reporters during the NAPA 500 weekend, Harvick at times sounded uncannily like Earnhardt, Hamilton's assertion notwithstanding. Asked about the extreme speeds that Atlanta Motor Speedway allowed (the qualifying record was Geoff Bodine's 197.478 miles per hour), Harvick said: "This is not a business where you need to worry about how fast you're going. You know the consequences if something goes really wrong. And if that's not what you want to do, maybe you should go play golf or something."

But at other times, Harvick came across as modest, if not chastened. Having just won the Busch Grand National championship, and assured of being named the Winston Cup Rookie of the Year, he acknowledged how fatigued his double duty had left him— "I'm really burned out," he said—a stark contrast to the summer, when he bristled at suggestions that such a merciless schedule had to exact a toll. Although he did not touch on it at Atlanta, Harvick in an interview published a few days earlier had even revealed that he had been so spent in early September that he had not wanted to leave his house: He felt, he said, like he'd been struck with a sledgehammer. Competing full-time in NASCAR's top two series, he would later reveal, had so exhausted him that at least twice he had required intravenous fluids. On one occasion, he would tell a reporter, "when we were standing outside my trailer and I was telling [the media] that I don't get tired, I had IV gauze on my arm."

Harvick reminded reporters of his last visit to Atlanta, in March, when he had qualified fifth and then won the race—but his purpose was not to relive glory, but rather to illustrate racing's vicissitudes. With his slow qualifying lap, Harvick needed a provisional to make the NAPA 500.

"Last time, we unloaded here and qualified in the top five," said Harvick. "It's pretty humbling when you come back and take a provisional."

Kurt Busch had gone home, but his crew had not. Jack Roush had demanded that they stay in Atlanta until after the race— ostensibly to help his other drivers, although their usefulness was limited since Burton, Martin, and Kenseth each had a full crew. In truth, Roush was making a point—punishment, some called it, for their role in failing to make the race. Roush did not, however, force Busch to return. He suspected that would have broken the young man's heart, and created a trackside spectacle that Roush Racing hardly needed. "Rather than him be totally miserable and make the people miserable around him—be exposed to the media and all—it was better for him to be out of sight," said Roush. "All of our pundits and our critics and people jealous of our sponsors feed off that stuff, you know. You can't give them that food."

Dressed in street clothes, the No. 97 team wandered the garage area purposelessly on the morning of the NAPA 500 while the rest of Roush's men tuned cars and moved equipment into position for the race. Burton made his last visit of the season to the CITGO hospitality tent (there would be no sponsor obligations on the racers' one day in New Hampshire) and then, after the drivers' meeting and early lunch, he joined Martin and Kenseth on pit road. The national anthem was sung, the forty-three drivers started their engines, and a pair of B-1B bombers flew over the speedway three times in quick succession, low enough that the thunder of their engines drowned out the racecars and sent chills down spectators' spines. Halfway around the globe, B-1B bombers had been pounding Taliban positions in Afghanistan.

Martin had qualified second, thus earning the outside of the front row, next to pole winner Earnhardt Jr.—but the handling of his car quickly went south, and by lap 40 of the 325-lap race, Martin had fallen to 30th. His crew eventually fixed the problem, but it was too late, and he would finish in 22nd, making it mathematically impossible to reach the top ten in the standings regardless of what happened in New Hampshire. Kenseth's performance in the NAPA 500 also was unfulfilling: Starting 23rd, he had reached as high as third when poor handling and a brush with the wall dashed his hopes. He would finish the race in 17th place, and remain unchanged in the point standings, at 13th.

Burton started strong in the race, moving from 34th to the front of the pack by the halfway mark.

"You're as fast as the leader," Frank Stoddard said. But the fresh tires Burton took on twenty-five laps later sent him into a funk; the crisp handling of his car had disappeared and it was now slip-sliding around the track.

"I'm all over the fucking place," Burton said. "These tires aren't worth shit."

"You just got to hang on best you can," said Stoddard. "Think about the long run like we had earlier." After several laps of wear, the tires on the previous stretch had achieved harmony with the car's setup, allowing Burton to connect to his machine. Stoddard expected it to happen again.

But Burton was impatient: He was neck-and-neck with Harvick, one of the drivers he had to beat today in order to advance in the standings.

"We just are junk!" said Burton. "I'm loose, I'm tight, I'm everything!"

"Ten-four," said Stoddard, "just keep doing what you can."

Shortly after, Burton found the edge. He passed Harvick and began pulling away. "Quicker than anything out there," said Stoddard.

But some while later, during confusion over whether to come in for a pit stop, NASCAR penalized Burton for speeding on pit road. He lost track position and his chance at winning—but he recovered sufficiently to finish in tenth place. Harvick beat him, though, and Burton remained tenth in the point standings. He would have one more chance to advance, in New Hampshire.

Bobby Labonte won the NAPA 500 after the late race leader, Jerry Nadeau, ran out of gas with less than a mile to go. But the top story from Atlanta concerned Jeff Gordon, who, with his sixth-place finish, claimed his fourth Winston Cup championship; only Richard Petty and Dale Earnhardt, with seven titles each, had ever won more. And Gordon was only thirty years old, with another two decades or more of racing conceivably still ahead of him.

Accompanied by his wife Brooke, a former Miss Winston, Gordon sprayed champagne, posed with his gold trophy, and accepted a giant mockup of the $3.6 million check that R. J.

Reynolds awarded the bearer of the Winston Cup. Speaking to journalists after his stop at Victory Lane, Gordon thanked the tobacco company and its cigarette brand. Then he thanked God—not only for the 2001 title, but also for seeing him and his team through their disappointing 2000 season, when some doubted he would ever be champion again.

"I just have to thank God every day for all the blessings that me and this entire team have been given," said Gordon, a born-again Christian. "Without the perseverance that God gives us, we wouldn't have been able to get from last year to this year the way we did."

It was 4:30 A.M. and dark as midnight when the haulers pulled into New Hampshire International Speedway on Friday, November 23rd, the day after Thanksgiving. Puddles in the garage area had frozen, and breath turned to fog as the crews began to unload their cars. But no snow lay on the ground, the sky was clear, and the forecast called for afternoon temperatures to break fifty degrees. Disparaged in advance as the Arctic 300, the rescheduled New Hampshire 300 would be run under tenable conditions after all.

But it would hardly be a typical race. Having decided to condense a weekend of competition into a day, NASCAR had canceled qualifying, and drivers would take the green flag in the order their owners held in the standings when the New Hampshire 300 had been postponed. Practice would consist of one 45-minute session, from 8:30 to 9:15 A.M., with the race beginning at noon. The speedway did not have lights, so one way or another, by nightfall everyone would finally be heading home for the off-season.

Kenseth and Busch were fast during practice—and Martin posted the fastest laps of the drivers for most of the abbreviated session, with Burton immediately behind him. Jack Roush was delighted: "I'm just filled with anticipation that something really good is going to happen today," he said. Martin had enjoyed success at New Hampshire, with seven top-five finishes in thirteen tries, and Burton had done even better, winning four races there—including the one in September 2000, when he led every lap, a feat last accomplished in Cup competition in 1978 by the legendary Cale Yarborough. Trailing Harvick in the standings by only 34 points, Burton could climb to ninth with a strong race today; an exceedingly strong race combined with terrible runs by Rusty Wallace and Dale Earnhardt Jr. might enable him to reach as high as seventh.

Roush already was looking beyond the 2001 Winston Cup banquet, which would be held a week after the New Hampshire 300; far from dulling his passion, the unexceptional year now ending left him itchy to start the next season. Each of his racers had matured in 2001, and the nagging engine and aerodynamic issues had been resolved or would be over the winter, Roush believed. Martin's and Busch's teams still lacked proper chemistry, but Roush, unknown to all but his innermost circle, planned a reformulation in the next few days. With only a modest measure of good fortune, the owner envisioned three and possibly all four of his Cup drivers speaking at the Waldorf in 2002—and Burton or perhaps Martin finally claiming the one title that still eluded him after fourteen years of NASCAR racing.

"Jeff and Mark are both contenders," said Roush. "Matt's a wild card and Kurt Busch should win a race next year and get another pole. He should for sure be in the top fifteen, and if we can have some luck going for us and if we don't misstep he could easily be in the top ten."

Busch's own aspirations for 2002 were more modest: He wanted solid runs week in and week out, and he wanted the same crew all season long. "I'd like to finish 15th every race to get us some stability," he said. "Just consistency all around—a consistent development toward something better." Maybe after such a sophomore season, he would be ready to join racing's elite.

Aware of the role he would have to play in helping to improve, Busch had met on the Monday after the NAPA 500 with Geoff Smith, Harry McMullen, and Ben Leslie. Busch conceded that he had behaved inappropriately when he failed to qualify at Atlanta, and after apologizing, he committed himself to controlling his temper and working to lift team morale. Busch planned to treat everyone to dinner and a night out during the off-season, but he would begin by talking individually to his men about his education during his first Cup season. He did not as yet know that Roush planned to shake up his crew.

As he waited alongside his racecar for the New Hampshire 300 to start, Busch was a wiser young man than he had been in Florida in February.

"Because of the lessons learned from day one til now, I think I'm much stronger, much wiser," he said. "Winston Cup for sure is a lot tougher than I imagined it to be."

Almost from the green flag of the New Hampshire 300, tires bedeviled the drivers. Expecting subfreezing weather, Goodyear had manufactured the batch with a softer compound, which led to several instances of blistering as temperatures rose into the fifties and the sun further heated the asphalt surface. But the Roush drivers escaped tire trouble through the first half of the race. With Martin running sixth, Kenseth seventh, Burton tenth, and Busch 15th, Roush's premonition seemed like it might be realized.

Martin's luck ran out with some fifty laps to go: His right-front tire, the one usually most vulnerable to wear, began to go down, and he was forced into a pit stop. He would finish the race ninth—and the season in 12th.

Burton liked his tires, but not his car's handling as the race wound down. Stoddard and the crew made several adjustments, but they were futile; Burton finished the race in 17th, and the season at tenth in the standings, just 12 points behind Harvick, who placed 26th in the New Hampshire 300.

Busch reached as high as 14th in the race, but he trailed away as the laps ticked off. He finished 21st, and ended the season 27th in the point standings.

With twenty-five laps to go, Matt Kenseth, the quietest of the Roush racers, had the last remaining chance at the limelight. He was running in fourth when Ricky Craven lost control and crashed on Turn Three, where Adam Petty and Kenny Irwin Jr. had died; Craven was unhurt, but his day was over.

"Yellow is out!" radioed Mike Calinoff, Kenseth's spotter.

Kenseth returned to his pit for fresh tires and fuel. With several drivers jockeying to win, the restart would be furious.

"Keep your head up," said Calinoff. "It's going to get a little wacky. Let's rock 'n' roll." Less than ten laps remained in the 2001 season. The sun was setting behind the main grandstands now, the lovely day giving way to a cold New England evening.

Kenseth passed Tony Stewart and began to work on Bobby Labonte.

"Go on buddy," said Calinoff. "You got something for him."

"Four to go, man," said Robbie Reiser. "Let's get 'em."

But Kenseth could not take Labonte, and he finished the race in fourth, giving him 13th place in the final point standings. The winner was Robby Gordon, who had touched off the big wreck at the season-opening Daytona 500.

"Beautiful!" Reiser exclaimed. "Awesome!"

"Great job, guys!" Kenseth said, a hint of uncharacteristic excitement in his voice. "Last month and a half we've had a top-ten car. Good way to end the year." It wasn't a win, but it indicated that a victory in 2002 was within close reach after Kenseth's long withdrawal.

*

The limousine crept through the midday Manhattan traffic. Inside, Jack Roush regaled Geoff Smith with a story about shooting a bird that had gotten into his hangar and soiled one of his airplanes. Jeff Burton and Matt Kenseth joked with Becky Hanson, and Kurt Busch recalled ice skating at Rockefeller Center with Melissa earlier in the week. It was Friday, November 30, and the Winston Cup banquet would begin in a few hours. But now, Roush and several of his people were bound for the headquarters of the Uniformed Firefighters Association, whose ranks had been devastated by the attacks of September 11.

The limousine stopped outside a building on East 23rd Street and the racers took an elevator to the office, where chairman of the board Jerome V. Huntzinger greeted them. On behalf of the association's Widows' and Children's Fund, Huntzinger accepted a check from Roush for $89,613, which represented a percentage of Roush Racing souvenir sales since September plus employee contributions that Roush Industries had matched dollar for dollar. Also, several Roush licensees had donated thousands of dollars in merchandise to be handed out as Christmas gifts.

Huntzinger thanked his guests for their generosity—and he told the story of how he had overturned his car driving to a firefighter's funeral. He wasn't badly hurt, he said, but he had lost his taste for motoring.

"You guys are amazing," Huntzinger said. "I watch you guys go around and around and I say: 'Not for me.' I would rather go into a burning building than get into a racecar." Risk-takers were a varied lot.

The limo brought Roush and his employees back to the Waldorf-Astoria, where one of Jeff Gordon's No. 24 DuPont racecars was parked by the front door, surrounded by a crowd of onlookers—some of whom had never seen such a strange sight in Manhattan, judging by how they gawked. Inside the grand old hotel, NASCAR fans wearing T-shirts and jeans mingled with stylishly dressed people carrying shopping bags from Saks Fifth

Avenue. The year before, Busch had been able to move virtually unnoticed through the Waldorf. Now he was besieged for autographs and pictures, as were Roush and his other drivers.

Night fell, and men in tuxedos escorting women in evening gowns began to fill the lobby. Members of the Waldorf staff were now manning the outside doors, preventing access to anyone lacking a legitimate reason to enter, but some fans had managed to breach security—and they huddled in furtive groups in the hotel's crannies, clutching their cameras and autograph pads and looking very much like the uninvited guests they were.

Private parties preceded the formal ceremony. Mark Martin had just arrived (and would leave in the morning, to watch his son race), and he joined his teammates, Jack Roush, and several of the Roush Racing managers at the Ford Motor Company suite, where two open bars were in operation, crab legs and cocktail shrimp were piled high by a glistening ice sculpture, and a lavish dinner buffet was spread over several tables. Two other Ford drivers, Dale Jarrett and Ricky Craven, mingled with Roush's men. At about eight o'clock, after a stop at a larger NASCAR party, everyone entered the grand ballroom.

Like the Academy Awards, the Winston Cup ceremony, broadcast live on TV, continued on interminably—for more than three hours. Gordon, who had appeared earlier in the week on the *David Letterman* and *Today* shows, thanked each of his many primary and associate sponsors, and also the R. J. Reynolds tobacco company—a free commercial for all, more than one guest remarked. Harvick accepted his Rookie-of-the-Year Award, which came with a $50,000 check, and NASCAR memorialized the victims of September 11. And Teresa Earnhardt spoke and Garth Brooks sang as part of a tribute to Dale Earnhardt, named posthumously as NASCAR's most popular driver. This was the last year, of course, that The Intimidator would be included in the NASCAR statistics books: Credited with a 12th-place finish at the opening Daytona 500, he was listed 57th in the point standings, with winnings of $296,833.

Bill France Jr. spoke—just once, when naming Jack Roush the recipient of the Bill France Award of Excellence, an honor bestowed only every few years. Surprised, Roush managed a moment of humor in his brief acceptance speech. "You know, fourteen years I've been doing this," he said. "I feel a lot like Winston Churchill in one of his speeches—except mine is in reverse. I feel like never in the history of Winston Cup racing has any car owner done so little with so much for so long. I apologize!" The crowd roared.

After the banquet, France would reflect on the season just ended—and the one soon to begin.

"We got an unusual amount of attention this year with the new television contract," France said. "I thought that NBC and Fox and Turner did an excellent job, all in all, of presenting the sport. I kind of like to say I predicted part of it, because of the additional money that we were receiving from them—they had to protect that investment and promote the sport."

Nielsen was just about to release the final ratings for the second half of the Winston Cup season, broadcast on NBC and TNT—and the numbers would show a 34 percent increase over the year 2000. (Nielsen had previously reported that the Fox broadcasts of the first half of the Cup season had risen 29 percent.) In an age of ever-increasing competition for viewers' attention, NASCAR was the only major sport to see overall ratings rise in 2001. And the news for NASCAR was even better in the demographic segments most dear to advertisers: 73 percent more adults between the ages of twenty-five and fifty-four who earned at least $75,000 a year were watching Cup races.

France acknowledged that Earnhardt's death had been a factor in NASCAR's popularity. "When you're on the 6:30 national news for about three days in a row with that, there's a lot more awareness going on," he said. "I'd just as soon that didn't happen, needless to say. He may have moved us along in his death—but we'd have got there anyway, and I'd rather have him back now."

According to an internal study, the number of adult NASCAR fans increased 19 percent in 2001, to 75 million. France predicted that NASCAR's popularity would continue to grow in the 2002 season. "We're going to keep on trying to climb the mountain, get to the top," he said.

But he could not quantify what the top would be.

"I don't know—and I don't want to know, because I don't want to lose the incentive to keep climbing. 'Cause once you get to the top, the other side is just coming down. Nobody wants to do that. So we'll just keep trying to make it bigger and better—improve it in every respect, safety and otherwise."

Jeff Burton received about two minutes on the grand ballroom stage. "What a scam we've got going to get paid for doing this!" he said in accepting his $363,404 bonus check for finishing the year in tenth. He soon turned philosophical—acknowledging the disappointment that many shared in his 2001 season, and then, as his audience listened intently, putting the sport of automobile racing in a larger perspective.

"In the grand scheme of things," said Burton, "I think we—and I mean we as a country, not just we in the racing world—learned that perhaps there are just some things that are more important than leading laps and winning races." Among them, Burton said, was the importance of compassion and sympathy. "From drivers to crew members to owners and sponsors, what I have seen this year is something unbelievable," he said. "I've seen so many self-less acts and so much gratitude from our entire community that it makes me proud to be involved with such a great group of people—and even more proud to be an American." Burton thanked Frank Stoddard and his crew for sticking with him all year, and then he closed on the matter dearest to his heart:

"I also learned not to take things for granted. I received some great advice from the Petty family: They said, you should never let a chance go by where you don't grab your kids and kiss them and tell them you love them. My wife, Kim, who is my biggest supporter, has made that our highest priority."

It was approaching midnight when the formal ceremony ended and workers began to prepare the ballroom for K.C. and The Sunshine Band, which would kick off the champion's party at 1:00 A.M. The Roush contingent went back to the Ford suite, where the buffet tables were now laden with desserts. Bottles of Budweiser beer in hand, Kenseth and Burton shared small talk with their wives and some friends. Busch and Melissa joined in. Busch still didn't look his age—and dressed in their formal wear, he and his girlfriend could easily have been mistaken for a couple at a high school prom. The highlight of the evening for Busch, a former Little League player and still a baseball fan, had been meeting New York Yankees manager Joe Torre.

Busch's rookie year officially ended that night at the Waldorf, but already Roush had made changes that would dramatically influence Busch's coming season. Seeking to strengthen the chemistry of two of his teams at once, on Tuesday Roush had named Jimmy Fennig crew chief for Busch—and Ben Leslie crew chief for Martin. Roush hadn't stopped there: He had swapped the crews along with their chiefs, and he planned to hire Joe Dan Bailey, a member of Dale Earnhardt's 1993 and 1994 championship teams, to be Martin's car chief. Roush could not claim credit for the moves. The idea belonged to Burton, who would likely assume a major management role at Roush Racing when his driving days ended. Burton's inspiration delighted the owner. "It's a cross-pollination that will make both flowers prettier and stronger," Roush said.

By his own measure, Busch had faltered in his rookie year. But by most other reckonings he had succeeded in his inaugural Winston Cup season. He finished second in the Rookie-of-the-

Year contest to a driver who was being compared to Dale Earnhardt, and he was 27th in the overall point standings—ahead of more than a dozen veteran drivers, including Kyle Petty and John Andretti, the sons of two racing dynasties. In his thirty-five races, Busch had recorded one pole, three top-five, and six top-ten starts—more top tens than a half dozen drivers who finished ahead of him in the point standings. Busch led for a hundred and sixty laps during his thirty-five races, the 20th best of all the drivers—more even than Kenseth, and only thirty fewer than Martin.

Busch had proved beyond any shadow of a doubt that he had speed—and a future, perhaps a great one, in Winston Cup racing.

"It wasn't a disastrous year—it just wasn't a good year," said Jack Roush. "I had hoped to trip the light fantastic."

EPILOGUE

Considering that it was the start of a new season, Jack Roush was surprisingly gloomy on the morning of the 2002 Daytona 500. He arrived at the Daytona International Speedway garage as dawn was breaking on that Sunday, February 17, checked on his four crews, then went to the lounge of Mark Martin's hauler, where recent discouraging events preoccupied him.

Daytona Speedweeks includes Craftsman Truck and Busch Grand National competition, as well as a variety of short races and time trials that determine the starting order of the Daytona 500. In Tuesday's Cup practice, Jeff Burton had demolished the left side of his car, forcing Roush to fly in a team of mechanics from Charlotte to help Burton's regular trackside crew repair it. In Friday's Truck race, young Roush driver Jon Wood ran strongly—until he was hit by Ron Hornaday Jr., who had finished the 2001 Cup year in 38th place, a showing that had sealed his return to the lesser series. And in Saturday's Busch Grand National race, Greg Biffle ran at the front of the pack and even led briefly—until he was rammed by Jimmy Spencer, who had taken Kurt Busch out in the fall Cup race at Phoenix.

But crashes were a fact of life in NASCAR racing. What weighed on Roush's mind that morning was something that evoked an unsettling feeling of deja vu.

During the off season, Roush had spent nearly a million dollars to perfect the 32 engines his teams had brought to Florida—and half a dozen of them had failed in the days leading up to the Daytona 500. The cause was an unforeseen consequence of development: an improvement in one area had inadvertently created a problem in another, but the problem had not surfaced in machine-shop testing, only on the track. It could be corrected, but not in time for the 500. Roush was forced to adopt a Band-Aid approach: adjustments in timing and carburetion that he hoped, but could hardly be sure, would prevent more failures under almost four hours of punishing operation.

"Normally I go into the races feeling that my glass is at least half full," Roush said. "I have a feeling this morning more of foreboding. I think it's at best half empty."

Roush's drivers shared his concern, and in one of their haulers on Saturday, a model racecar had mysteriously appeared on a workbench—with a toy engine hanging from a toy hoist, a sort of gallows humor that was furtively kept from the boss. But on the morning of the 500, all four drivers were in fighting trim. Jeff Burton was filled with his usual race-day energy, and he left the crowd at the hospitality tents roaring with his jokes about his brother Ward. Matt Kenseth kidded around with his wife and his crew chief, and he said that he felt rested: "That's one thing I don't have a problem with, is sleeping," he declared. Mark Martin had been one of the fastest drivers in practice, and despite starting in 39th, he was optimistic about his chances in the race ahead. He was delighted with the swap with Kurt Busch over the winter, which had brought Busch's crew chief Ben Leslie and Leslie's men to the No. 6 Viagra Ford Taurus. "The deal's perfect," said Martin as he snacked on a protein bar inside the entrance to his hauler. "I'm real excited. We're gonna be fighting tooth-and-nail." After one of the worst years of his Cup career, Martin, who had recently celebrated his 43rd birthday, believed that he and his new team could create the chemistry he needed to win races again.

Kurt Busch had spent some of his time since the Winston Cup banquet reflecting on his rookie season, and he was beginning his sophomore year with a noticeable new poise—and gratification for now being under the watchful eye of the experienced Jimmy Fennig and the rest of Mark Martin's old crew, who were his men now. "Everything just seems more comfortable," Busch said. "It's easier to go about my business." Unlike his teammates, Busch had arrived in Florida lacking the carryover provisional points that might have put him in the 500, having used them all up during the dismal end of his 2001 season. To make the race, he had needed a strong showing in Thursday's qualifying heat—and he had turned in an exceptional run, good enough to start today in 15th, best of the Roush racers.

It was approaching noon, and drivers' introductions would soon begin. Melissa had prepared Busch a lunch of pasta and marinara sauce at their motor coach, and he had returned to his hauler to dress in his fire suit. Busch was determined not to repeat last February, when he had finished second to last in his maiden Daytona 500. "I'm not going to take any 'obscene' types of moves or passes or anything," he said. "I'm trying to talk myself into being less nervous." He was succeeding: he was relaxed, and hopeful of a good finish.

"That's my gut feeling—that's what I had on Thursday. I didn't know how I was going to do it, but it just ended up happening!" Busch laughed, and then, accompanied by Melissa, he headed for pit road.

Having honored Dale Earnhardt at the July Pepsi 400 and again during Speedweeks with the unveiling of a bronze statue outside the track where The Intimidator died, NASCAR chose not to stage yet another tribute before the 2002 Daytona 500; in interviews,

Mike Helton emphasized the many safety improvements NASCAR was making, rather than the long, blood-stained road that had led to NASCAR's new resolution. A year after Black Sunday, stockcar racing fans were also moving on—many of them to Earnhardt's son, Dale Junior, who received the loudest applause during drivers' introductions.

Since his emotional victory at the Pepsi 400, Junior had emerged as more than the new NASCAR star who had completed the 2001 season in eighth place in the point standings, and who was picked by some to be the 2002 Cup champion. Junior had become a full-blown American celebrity, with appearances on *The Tonight Show*, on the cover of *TV Guide*, and in a music video. His memoir had debuted in January on *The New York Times* bestseller list, and Anheuser-Busch, which had signed him to a six-year contract estimated at more than $60 million, was featuring him in hip new television commercials. He had driven a No. 3 car in Saturday's Busch Grand National race—and he had won, adding another chapter to Earnhardt lore that Bill France Jr. himself could not have scripted better. Junior was the sentimental favorite to capture the Daytona 500, and with a fast car and a fifth-place starting position, all indications were that he stood an excellent chance.

The introductions ended and drivers went to their cars, where family and friends wished them safety and luck. Chad Holliday, chief executive officer of DuPont, the primary sponsor of Jeff Gordon's car, gave the command to start engines, and pace car driver Jay Leno led the racers on their parade laps. The green flag flew and the 44th running of the Daytona 500 was underway.

"All right, boys, they start keeping the points now," Busch radioed to his crew. His attention, as always, was on the standings in the long season just begun.

With Daytona's long history of surprises and the new aerodynamic rules that had resulted from the fall race at Talladega, the race was expected to be unpredictable—and the early going proved that expectation true. Three laps in, Tony Stewart lost his engine, and it could not be repaired; second in the point standings in 2001 and a frontrunner for the 2002 title, he would begin the new season in 43rd place. Eighteen laps after Stewart's day ended, one of Junior's tires blew, sending him into the wall. He returned to pit road for repairs, which appeared to put him out of contention. All doubt vanished further in, when Junior lost another tire and his brakes, and several laps to repairs.

The Roush racers, meanwhile, were disproving their boss's gloomy apprehensions.

Busch cracked the top ten early in the race, and Kenseth, who had started 40th, took the lead on lap 24 and held it through lap 27—a remarkably swift advance. Burton had started in 33rd— and he took the lead after Kenseth, for two laps, the first time he had ever led the Daytona 500. Martin did not head the field, but he drove quickly toward the front and stayed there. The halfway point passed, and Roush's engines were running flawlessly. The only complication for the Roush racers was a bizarre episode involving Burton: after complaining that he felt some unknown object rolling around under his feet, he lost precious seconds during a pit stop while a crew member crawled through his window to find and remove the culprit. It was a roll of electrical tape.

So far, racers had avoided the big wreck that everyone always anticipated in superspeedway racing. Stewart and Junior were no longer factors, but Gordon, Kevin Harvick, 2001 Daytona winner Michael Waltrip, and the crafty veteran Sterling Marlin continued to be.

Lap 117 found Martin in third, Kenseth in fourth, Busch in fifth, and Burton in 14th. The Roush racers so impressed the TV broadcasters that NBC displayed a graphic showing their progress from where they had started.

"Thanks for all your help," Busch radioed to Kenseth, his drafting partner of the moment. "We're hauling ass on the long run."

"That's what teammates are for," Kenseth radioed back.

A two-car spinout on Lap 138 brought out the yellow caution, and most drivers came into their pits for fuel and fresh tires. If the race continued to the checkered flag under green, this would be the last stop for many.

But the final quarter of a Daytona was always the most hair-raising. Drivers were wearying, even as they hungered for the win.

"It's about to get serious right now in Daytona," declared a radio announcer whose commentary went out over the speedway's loudspeakers. Atop Martin's pit cart, Roush was calculating fuel mileage on his clipboard.

Eleven laps later, mayhem descended.

In a dance at 190 miles per hour, Gordon was battling to pass Harvick and Harvick was blocking when their vehicles contacted, setting off a classic superspeedway chain reaction. Cars spun, smashed into the wall, and ricocheted off one another like balls in a crazed game of pool. Flames burst from beneath one car and thick smoke obscured everyone's vision. No one was seriously injured, but twenty-one cars were damaged—thirteen so severely that they had to go to the garage. Among them was Matt Kenseth's No. 17 DeWALT Ford. "Once they spin," said Kenseth, who would be credited with a 33rd-place finish, "it just makes a bunch of smoke and you just try to make it through the best you can. Sometimes you make it and sometimes you don't." Kenseth, as always, was a pragmatic sort.

As he waited for the debris to be cleared, Gordon placed a measure of blame on Busch, who had also been trying to pass at the moment hell broke loose.

"It's that damn 97, the wild man," Gordon radioed to his crew.

But Busch had not been driving wildly, nor had he caused the wreck—although he, Martin and Burton had all escaped it. When the track was finally cleaned and racing resumed, Busch was running in second, behind Sterling Marlin.

A short while later, on lap 162, Busch passed Marlin for the lead. It was a bold move, one that all but guaranteed retaliation from the veteran of more than 500 Cup races.

"Use your head," radioed Fennig.

Busch had indeed angered Marlin, who roared back and soon was sitting on Busch's bumper. His spotter warned him of the imminent danger.

But Busch was cool.

"He hasn't been able to bump me," he radioed. "We're looking good."

Jack Roush was overwhelmed by the unfolding drama; he felt as he had during the final moments of the 2001 Coca Cola 600, when Jeff Burton was closing in on victory. With conversation impossible over the thunder of the cars, Roush dashed off a few words on a writer's notebook.

I can't breathe, he wrote. *Wish at this moment I was someone else watching from a safe distance. My heart's racing, my mouth is dry.*

Busch kept the lead until Gordon overtook him 15 laps later. Gordon was at the front of a line of cars that were drafting together, and buffeted by their air, Busch was quickly shuffled back—behind Martin and Burton to the end of the small group of drivers who remained on the lead lap.

But with four laps to go, several cars collided.

Rather than conclude the Daytona 500 under the yellow caution, an anticlimactic end to any race, NASCAR decided to stage a shootout. The red flag flew, stopping the cars on the track. NASCAR rules prohibit servicing cars under a red flag—but incredibly, as nearly 200,000 spectators and a national television audience watched, Sterling Marlin climbed out of his car and began pulling back the sheet metal of his damaged right-front quarter panel. "I saw Earnhardt do it at Richmond one time," he later explained. "He got out and cleaned off his windshield, so I thought it was OK. I don't guess it was." It wasn't. For his punishment, Marlin was sent to the end of the line that would start the four-lap shootout. Gordon was similarly penalized, for pitting before the red flag (when pit road was closed). The Daytona 500 almost always held surprises, but no one could remember any quite as weird as these.

As Busch waited in tenth position to start the final laps, Fennig coached him. "Kurt, it will be green, white, checkered," the crew chief said. "Sterling's probably going to be mad. So he's going to be coming up there like a wild man."

"Let's do it, boys," Busch said, and the race resumed.

Keeping Gordon and Marlin safely behind him, Busch powered toward the front. And although time ran out before he could catch winner Ward Burton, he did finish fourth—as his new crew erupted and the cameramen moved in for closeups.

"Good job, boys!" Busch radioed. "Wooo! We got a car!"

Jeff Burton wound up in 12th, not where he'd wanted but better than the start to his 2001 season, and Mark Martin finished in sixth. Martin thanked his new crew and his son, Matt, who had given him a lucky penny before the race. "Maybe," said Martin, "this is the start of good things!"

Roush shook Busch's hand and thanked him for a great race, and Busch started back toward his hauler, where a cluster of reporters awaited him. Busch answered their questions and posed for the photographers with his arm around Melissa. Then he went inside to change into his street clothes. He was outwardly calm, but the unseen energy that had powered him at extreme speed for 500 miles was palpable.

And so was his delight at how the new year had started.

"I just couldn't wait for the season to end last year—and to miss Atlanta, that just made it twice as bad," Busch said. "That's the lowest point in my racing career. For us to come out of here fourth is exhilarating."

Only minutes from the checkered flag, and already Busch's thoughts were on the next race, at Rockingham the following weekend. More than a year had passed since he had visited Victory Lane, and more than ever, the young man craved a return.

"Winning is the ultimate feeling that you get, that you want, that you strive for every Sunday," he said.

*

He had feared the worst that morning, but Roush left Daytona that evening praising each of his drivers. "The guys were brilliant in their interpretation and their instincts in what the racetrack required," he said. He was grateful that no one had been hurt, and that his engines—five of them, including the one he had supplied to second-place finisher Elliott Sadler—had come through with flying colors. His gloom had lifted: the 2002 season had started on a far more encouraging note than 2001, and there was every reason to believe that more good things lay ahead for Roush Racing. The second race of the 2002 season, the Subway 400 at Rockingham, North Carolina, where the Roush racers had fared so poorly in February 2001, demonstrated such optimism to be sound: Matt Kenseth won, Jeff Burton took sixth, Kurt Busch finished 12th, and Mark Martin was 21st. And the third race, the UAW-Daimler-Chrysler 400 at Las Vegas on March 3, was more encouraging still: after strong finishes by all four, Burton stood third in the points, Martin fourth, Busch eighth, and Kenseth tenth. Heading to Atlanta, where the 2001 season had turned so disastrously, the Winston Cup championship that had eluded Roush for so many years no longer seemed a dream beyond reach.

In two months, Roush would turn sixty. For more than half a century, since first flying down a hill on a bicycle, he had been compelled by speed. Speed had excited him, motivated him, and served as the foundation for his racing and business empires. Winning at speed had brought acclaim and monetary rewards, and also something without price.

"When I was eleven years old," Roush said, "I remember being concerned that I would not have a life that was interesting or exciting enough to have stories that anybody would be interested to hear about. Now I don't have the time to write them all down!"

The journey that began on two wheels continued, and Jack Roush was as enthralled as ever.

SOURCE NOTES

The roots of *Men and Speed* lie in the fall of 1999, when I began to think that automobile racing would be an intriguing topic for my next book. I knew little about NASCAR except that it had become one of America's most popular sports, and it involved men (and a few women) who put themselves at great risk pursuing extreme speed. Risk-takers have always fascinated me, though as book subjects I had profiled them mostly in business and medicine.

My journey soon brought me to Matt Kenseth, who I met one frigid day in January 2000 at a car show in Providence—and then to Kenseth's boss, car owner Jack Roush, to whom I introduced myself at the first Winston Cup race I attended, in Martinsville, Virginia, in April 2000. I told Roush that I wanted to chronicle the 2001 Cup season through the lives of his drivers, and that a compelling account would require unrestricted access inside his organization, including his shops and business offices and his drivers' private lounges. Roush agreed on the spot—and I returned home, a bit stunned but nonetheless delighted. To my knowledge, no writer has ever been let loose inside a leading NASCAR operation, certainly not for two years.

True access, of course, requires more than the boss's permission. I encountered nothing but cooperation almost wherever I went—and eventually, I went virtually everywhere inside Roush's empire. Starting at New Hampshire International Speedway on the weekend in July 2000 that Kenny Irwin Jr. died, I spent untold hundreds of hours with Roush and his people at speedways, where I was welcomed inside the garage, the pits, and the private haulers of Mark Martin, Jeff Burton, Matt Kenseth, and Kurt Busch. I spent several days at the Roush Racing shops in Concord, North Carolina, and the marketing offices in nearby Huntersville, and I visited the Roush Industries headquarters and the Craftsman Truck Series shop near Detroit. I rode with Roush in his corporate jet and in the back of one of his P-51 World War Two vintage airplanes. I spent three days with Roush in the History Channel's Great Race.

In all, I attended twenty-one Winston Cup race weekends through the 2002 Daytona 500, and conducted more than seventy-five formal, taped interviews and untold dozens of shorter sessions. Because of my tight deadlines, I wrote portions of *Men and Speed* in speedway media centers, hotel rooms, airports, airplanes, and even a short passage while stuck in traffic leaving Martinsville Speedway. Unless otherwise attributed in the text or indicated here, quotes are from statements made to me or recorded by me at press conferences that I attended. I directly witnessed most of the events recounted in *Men and Speed,* and watched a few others on TV. I re-created the rest by means of interviews and press accounts.

NASCAR and its race teams tenaciously seek editorial control over books and other accounts of their operations, but neither the sanctioning body nor Roush asked for nor received it over *Men and Speed*; similarly, while royalties and licensing arrangements are the norm in NASCAR, I was not asked to pay, nor did I pay, anything. The book stands as an independent account by an independent journalist. More detailed notes follow.

PREFACE

I drove the Stage 3 Mustang on June 19, 2001.

CHAPTER 1

I was the passenger in the flight of Roush's P-51 that I have recounted. We flew on October 3, 2000.

My brief history of NASCAR came from many sources, including several of the books cited below. Also helpful were my interviews of NASCAR president Mike Helton on July 22, 2001, at New Hampshire International Speedway; and of NASCAR director of operations Kevin Triplett on May 26, 2001, at Lowe's Motor Speedway.

I interviewed Bill France Jr. on January 15, 2002. This quote is from that interview.

Geoffrey Bodine on seeing his dead father: "A matter of faith: Geoffrey Bodine's survival is a story of father, son and holy spirit," *St. Petersburg Times,* April 29, 2000.

Kurt Busch on making friends in the 2000 Daytona 250: "Wallace wins Daytona's first truck race," Associated Press, February 19, 2000, as posted on ESPN.com.

CHAPTER 2

NASCAR has not disclosed the financial terms of its TV contract, and estimates have ranged from $2.4 billion to $2.8 billion. I have gone with the higher figure because it has been published by motorsports writer David Poole of *The Charlotte Observer,* as reliable a source as any. Poole breaks the contract down as: NBC and Turner, $1.2 billion for six years; Fox, $1.6 billion for eight years.

Dale Earnhardt's "candy ass" quote: "Earnhardt blasts restrictor-plate racing," *The Charlotte Observer,* June 30, 2000.

CHAPTER 3

France's quote is from the January 15, 2002, interview.

Kurt Busch on "another rookie day" at Rockingham: the Busch race recap on roushracing.com.

Forklifter letter: on file at Roush Racing.

Busch's Gong Show audition: interviews with Busch and Rich Reichenbach.

Details of the Earnhardt tribute at Las Vegas International Speedway: speedway public relations head Jeff Motley.

Teresa Earnhardt's statement was published widely, including in the March 5, 2001, *Las Vegas Review-Journal,* from which I quoted.

I interviewed *Orlando Sentinel* editor Timothy A. Franklin by telephone on May 22, 2001.

Richard Childress's quote appeared in the Associated Press's coverage of the Cracker Barrel 500, March 11, 2001.

Busch's Cracker Barrel 500 quote: the Busch race recap on roushracing.com.

"Twilight Zone" quote: "The season of the third dimension," by contributor Bob Margolis, *The Sporting News,* March 16, 2001.

"Blowing raspberries" quote: "Burning questions: Several multi-car teams continue to struggle," sportsillustrated.cnn.com, March 13, 2001.

CHAPTER 4

Busch's "rookie day" quote: the Busch race recap on roushracing.com.

The New Hampshire medical examiner on Adam Petty and Kenny Irwin, and Helton's quote on the causes of death: "Petty, Irwin autopsy reports untouched months later," *The Orlando Sentinel,* September 14, 2000.

Dr. Steve Bohannon's statements on Earnhardt's seat belt: "Earnhardt's lap belt is a focus," *The Charlotte Observer,* February 23, 2000.

France: the January 15, 2002, interview.

"Notebook: NASCAR Spins Out," *Brill's Content,* June 2001, p. 42.

Jim McLaurin's quote: "Introducing the NASCAR translator," *The (Columbia, S.C.) State,* March 21, 2001.

Beacher Orr on his son's death: Orr testified in a hearing on a suit brought by a Florida Web site and a Florida student newspaper, and his testimony was widely published, including on sportsillustrated.cnn.com, June 13, 2001.

The Orlando Sentinel as "pond scum": "The big cover-up! By Stooge," column that appeared on stoogesracing.rivals.com, April 5, 2001.

Letter to *The Orlando Sentinel,* by Marvin Lovern, published March 18, 2001.

Kevin Harvick spoke of being aggressive since he was five during a chat conducted on MSNBC.com on August 28, 2001.

Harvick's Web site is kevinharvick.com, formerly harvickmotorsports.com.

CHAPTER 5

Julian Martin's quotes were taken from Mark Martin's illustrated biography by Bob Zeller, see below. The Locust Grove track promoter's quote was taken from the book as well.

The Viagra joke was posted on Martin's bulletin board at roushracing.com on March 20, 2001.

Busch on being pleased his car was no longer white: "Busch rebounds from spin to finish fourth," by Dave Rodman, nascar.com, posted April 1, 2001.

Ben Leslie on Busch as a great wheelman: "Taking charge: Busch's new crew chief helps rookie to top-five finish," by Mark Ashenfelter, *NASCAR Winston Cup Scene,* April 5, 2001.

Jeff Burton on starting his season at Martinsville: his press conference on April 6, 2001, statements from which appeared in a story by Jim Utter posted on *The Charlotte Observer*'s stockcar racing Web site, thatsracin.com, that day.

Teresa Earnhardt's statement read at Martinsville was widely reprinted, including in "'We just want it to end,' Teresa Earnhardt says," posted on April 8 on thatsracin.com, from which this quote was taken.

Dr. Barry S. Meyers's report: "Expert: Seat belt no factor: Doctor at odds with NASCAR over Earnhardt's fatal crash," *The Orlando Sentinel,* April 10, 2001.

Criticism in the *St. Petersburg Times*: "NASCAR silence paid for in trust," by Gary Shelton, *St. Petersburg Times,* April 11, 2001.

Darrel Waltrip's quote: "Waltrip not afraid to criticize NASCAR's lack of safety concern," by David Climer, *The Tennessean,* April 13, 2001.

The *Dutton's Dozen* column by Monte Dutton is syndicated; I found this one at icflorida.com.

CHAPTER 6

Busch's remark about topping off gas at California, and a reporter's analysis of Busch's finish: "Busch fights back," by Butch Bellah, frontstretch.com, May 2, 2001.

Busch on a lucky and wonderful day: the Busch race recap on roushracing.com.

Tommy Propst's claims: "Rescuer: Earnhardt seat belt was intact," *The Orlando Sentinel,* April 29, 2001.

France: the January 15, 2002, interview.

"Conspiracy isn't too strong a term": "The smoking gun," speedfx.com, April 29, 2001.

Sympathetic feature on Helton: "Helton's public loss, private pain," *The Atlanta Journal-Constitution,* May 13, 2001.

Early story on Matt Kenseth: "John Close: Sportsman close-up," *Midwest Racing News,* July 7, 1988.

NASCAR fan expenditures are quantified in "The Power of the NASCAR Brand," a confidential study by the research firm of Ipsos-Reid, released in January 2002.

Superman analogy: letter to *NASCAR Winston Cup Scene,* May 24, 2001.

Tony Stewart's appraisal of fans as idiots: "Silencing the critics," *NASCAR Winston Cup Scene,* May 31, 2001.

In part because racecar drivers do not want to be encumbered by data collection when they are racing, the physiology of winning at speed has been incompletely studied. I wrote my passage after interviews with Dr. Stephen E. Olvey, associate professor of clinical neurological surgery, University of Miami, and medical director of the Championship Auto Racing Teams from 1978 to 1988; Larry Couture, a part-time racer and a vice president at City of Hope National Medical Center in Los Angeles; and Jacques Dallaire, of Human Performance International in Huntersville, North Carolina. I also read these articles:

—Goldfarb, Allan H., and Athanasios, "Beta-endorphin response to exercise: An update," *Sports Medicine*, July 1997, pp. 8–16.

—Lighthall, James W., John Pierce, and Stephen E. Olvey, "A physiological profile of high performance race car driver," *1994 Motorsports Engineering Conference Proceedings*, Vol. 1: Vehicle Design Issues, Society of Automotive Engineers Inc., Dearborn, Michigan, 1994, pp. 55–63.

—Jacobs, Patrick L., and Stephen E. Olvey, "Metabolic and heart rate responses to open-wheel automobile racing: A single-subject study," *Journal of Strength and Conditioning Research*, 2000, 14(2), pp. 157–161.

Eddie Hill quote: "Brave or crazy, drag racers addicted to acceleration," *The Fort Worth Star-Telegram*, October 19, 1997.

CHAPTER 7

Paul Walker and Dale Earnhardt Jr. on NASCAR: "NASCAR is hot! Car racing steers to the mainstream as more spectators and TV viewers go along for the joyride," *Entertainment Weekly*, July 12, 2001.

Earnhardt Jr.'s column on his father: "NASCAR behind the track: Dale Earnhardt Jr.," nascar.com, October 18, 2000.

Earnhardt Jr. on growing up after his father died: "Earnhardt Jr. acknowledges the changes," *The Charlotte Observer*, March 31, 2001.

Earnhardt Jr.'s comments after the Pepsi 400: note of his press conference provided by Nancy Wager, GM Racing Communications reporter/transcriptionist.

Busch after Chicagoland: the Busch race recap on roushracing.com.

Profile of Adam Petty: adampetty.com.

The interview of Kyle and Pattie Petty on the first anniversary of Adam's death: a video session conducted on May 10, 2001, by sportsillustrated.cnn.com and found on nascar.com.

CHAPTER 8

Kyle Busch is "legendary": "Kyle Busch gets head start at topping brother's feats," by Joe Hawk, *Las Vegas Review-Journal*, July 30, 2000.

Tom Gaye's comments on Kyle being fifteen: "Kyle Busch raced under age: The promising young driver's career hits a snag when he's found to be just 15, too young to compete," *Las Vegas Review-Journal*, August 2, 2000.

Jeff Burton after the Global Crossing@The Glen: the Burton race recap on roushracing.com.

Matt Kenseth after Michigan: the Kenseth race recap on roushracing.com.

The results of the Dale Earnhardt investigation are contained within the two-volume "Official Accident Report: No. 3 car," August 21, 2001, distributed on a limited basis by NASCAR.

The complete transcript of the questions and answers from the August 21, 2001, conference was published on *That's Racin'* as part of *The Charlotte Observer*'s report: see thatsracin.com/01/theearnhardtreport.htm.

Restrictor-plate racing and TV ratings: "NASCAR offers no answers," by Jason Whitlock, *The Kansas City Star*, August 21, 2001.

Gil Lebreton's column: "Report misses chance to do good," *Fort Worth Star-Telegram*, August 22, 2001.

Mark Martin's final quote about his crew as heroes at Martinsville: the Martin race recap on roushracing.com.

Comments by Kurt Busch and Jack Roush after Busch won the pole at Darlington: a transcript of the media center interview provided by Dan Zacharias, reporter/transcriptionist for Ford Racing.

The words between Jeff Green and Kevin Harvick at Bristol were widely reported, including in "Harvick's risky move angers RCR mate Green," nascar.com, August 25, 2001.

Ricky Rudd's "love tap" quote, made in the post-race interview, was reported in many accounts, including: "Cheap shots vs. love taps," thatsracin.com, September 9, 2001.

CHAPTER 9

Mark McGwire on not playing sports in the wake of September 11: "NASCAR, IRL follow NFL's lead," ESPN.com, September 13, 2001.

Mike Helton on rescheduling the New Hampshire 300: "NASCAR postpones races," nascar.com, September 13, 2001.

The priest at Blaise Alexander's funeral: "Sorrow finds Alexander's home town again," thatsracin.com, October 9, 2001.

Felix Sabates on death: "One year's tragedy will forever linger," *Daytona Beach News-Journal,* October 14, 2001.

Jimmy Spencer's fears with the HANS: "Peer pressure could force Spencer to accept head and neck restraint," Associated Press, August 24, 2001.

"Humpy" Wheeler on safety: "Wheeler: Safety has to be a bigger priority," *The Charlotte Observer,* October 5, 2001.

Helton's frustration: from the Associated Press, as reported on October 7 at cbs.sportsline.com.

Dale Jarrett on the war in Afghanistan: post-race Ford quotes, provided by Zacharias.

Tony Stewart on Osama bin Laden: post-race Pontiac quotes, provided by Al Larsen, reporter/transcriptionist for Pontiac Racing.

H. Clay Earles and his quote: martinsvillespeedway.com.

George Pyne on mandating head restraints: "NASCAR immediately mandates restraints," nascar.com, October 17, 2001.

Stewart on being claustrophobic: "Stewart still has issues with head restraints," nascar.com, October 17, 2001.

The comments of drivers, owners, and Jim Hunter after Talladega were reported in several publications, including "NASCAR assailed after big wreck," *Richmond (Va.) Times-Dispatch,* October 22, 2001.

Helton on change: "Helton said rules would not have changed without Talladega accident," Associated Press, posted on thatsracin.com, November 2, 2001.

Roush and Burton at Phoenix: post-race Ford quotes, provided by Zacharias.

CHAPTER 10

Todd Bodine on Harvick: post-race Ford quotes, provided by Zacharias.

Bobby Hamilton on Harvick: his statement was made in the post-race interview, and reported, among other places, in "TNT making strides in its race coverage," *The Sporting News,* October 17, 2001.

Harvick on Hamilton: "Harvick's rough week highlights pressures of unique rookie season," RacingServer.com, October 20, 2001.

Fans increase: the Ipsos-Reid study.

Harvick needing IV fluids: "Kevin Harvick: Into the Spotlight," by Marty Smith, nascar.com, January 26, 2002.

France: the January 15, 2002, interview.

Kenseth on his finish: the Kenseth race recap on roushracing.com.

Jeff Gordon's characterization of Busch as a "wild man": from a tape of the NBC broadcast of the race.

Roush wrote his thoughts during the race in my notebook.

Sterling Marlin on getting out of his car: press conference with Marlin after the race at Daytona International Speedway.

THESE BOOKS PROVED USEFUL:

Assael, Shaun. *Wide Open: Days and Nights on the NASCAR Tour.* New York: Ballantine, 1999.

Burt, Bill. *Behind the Scenes of NASCAR Racing.* Osceola, Wisc.: MBI, 1997.

Dutton, Monte. *At Speed: Up Close and Personal with the People, Places, and Fans of NASCAR.* Washington, D.C.: Brassey's, 2000.

Earnhardt, Dale, Jr., with Jade Gurss. *Driver #8.* New York: Warner, 2002.

Hagstrom, Robert G. *The NASCAR Way: The Business That Drives the Sport.* New York: Wiley, 1998.

Hemphill, Paul. *Wheels: A Season on NASCAR's Winston Cup Circuit.* New York: Berkley, 1998.

Higgins, Tom, and Steve Waid. *Junior Johnson: Brave in Life.* Phoenix: David Bull, 1999.

Howell, Mark D. *From Moonshine to Madison Avenue: A Cultural History of the NASCAR Winston Cup Series.* Bowling Green, Ohio: Bowling Green University Popular Press, 1997.

Huler, Scott. *A Little Bit Sideways: One Week Inside a NASCAR Winston Cup Race Team.* Osceola, Wisc.: MBI, 1999.

Irvan, Ernie, and Peter Golenbock. *No Fear.* New York: Hyperion, 1999.

Latford, Bob. *Built for Speed: The Ultimate Guide to Stock Car Racetracks.* Philadelphia: Courage, 1999.

Martin, Mark. *NASCAR for Dummies.* Foster City, Calif.: IDG, 2000.

Montville, Leigh. *At the Altar of Speed: The Fast Life and Tragic Death of Dale Earnhardt.* New York: Doubleday, 2001.

Sowers, Richard. *Stock Car Racing Lives.* Phoenix: David Bull, 2000.

Zeller, Bob. *Mark Martin: Driven to Race.* Phoenix: David Bull, 1997.

I also made extensive use of NASCAR's official media guides for its Winston Cup, Busch Grand National, and Craftsman Truck Series; of the weekly media updates provided by NASCAR's fine Statistical Services division; and of the media track guides that speedways on the Cup circuit prepare for their every race.

Finally, in addition to relying on thatsracin.com and nascar.com, I made extensive use of the Winston Cup insider's Web site at jayski.com. And I was a regular weekly reader of *NASCAR Winston Cup Scene.*

ACKNOWLEDGMENTS

A book like this requires the cooperation, goodwill, and patience of a large cast of characters. I was fortunate on every step of my journey.

My gratitude first and foremost to Jack Roush, who opened his world to me and imposed no preconditions other than that I get it right—if I didn't, the fault is entirely mine. When I began this book, Jack and I expected that I would be chronicling a championship season for one of his drivers and a rookie title for another. It speaks volumes to Jack's character that when a very different kind of year began to unfold, he did not withdraw the unlimited access that he had granted me; win or lose, Jack was a man of his word. Ironically, just as this book is being put to bed, it appears that Roush will have in 2002 the season many expected in 2001.

All of the Roush drivers welcomed me from the start—and then graciously allowed me to hang out with them as they traveled the Cup circuit. My thanks to Matt Kenseth, whose quiet manner belies a fine sense of humor and a ferocious racing talent; Mark Martin, as genuine and nice a person as you're likely ever to meet; Kurt Busch, a young man with a fine heart, spirit, and future; and Jeff Burton, who is as close to a resident philosopher as the sport of NASCAR offers. My gratitude also to the women in these drivers' lives: Arlene Martin, Kim Burton, Katie Kenseth, and Melissa Schaper. And my thanks to the remaining Roush Racing drivers: Greg Biffle, who races in Busch Grand National; and Jon Wood, of the Craftsman Truck Series.

Great thanks to Geoffrey L. Smith, the president of Roush Racing, a subsidiary of Jack's larger company: Geoff is the consummate professional, and his wry insights were invaluable. Great thanks also to Stephanie E. Smith, the director of sponsor relations, an equally wry and knowledgeable student of the sport of auto racing. And great thanks to James S. Rodway, the manager of licensing; like Geoff and Stephanie, Jamie cheerfully answered my million-and-one questions, and smoothed the way at every turn. Without the support of these three people, this book would have been a shadow of what I had hoped. A growler of Ipswich Ale to all three!

Also at Roush Industries or Roush Racing, my gratitude to: Evan D. Lyall, Douglas E. Smith, Brenda Stricklin, Robin Johnson, John Miller, Jeff Godkin, Harry McMullen, Buddy Parrott, Tom Ghent, Bob P. Rinaldi, Kenneth C. Fackender, Nick Ollila, Steven C. Stropes, Randy Duncan, Max Jones, Randy Goss, Rich Reichenbach, Steve Loyd, Amy Rowell, and Shelley Leslie. Thanks to account managers, present and former: Rebecca Hanson, Lori Halbeisen, Kathryn Kalin, Patrick Rogers, Erin Hunter, Kevin Woods, Sheri L. Herrmann, and Hope Bunker.

Roush Racing's Cup crew chiefs proved accommodating, and I thank them all: Frank Stoddard, Jimmy Fennig, Robbie Reiser, and Ben Leslie. Special thanks to five guys on Jeff Burton's team who always went out of their way to accommodate me: Pierre Kuettel, Mike Messick, Dave Ballard, Joseph Wernert, and Sherman Forrester, who also drives Burton's motor coach. And special thanks to the Nos. 97 and 17 shop foreman, Wayne Gaudet; Dave Dunlap, manager of the Roush chassis shop; and Jeff "Junior" Paxton, who enhanced my understanding of engines.

Thanks to these remaining members of Jeff Burton's 2001 team: Mark Armstrong, Michael Brill, Phil Carpenter, Bobby Christensen, Cory DeMarco, Chris Farrell, Kim Fisher, Todd Foster, Hal Ralston, Donnie Ratledge Jr., Steve Wedvick, Chuck White, and Chip Goode.

Thanks to these folks with Mark Martin in 2001: Brian Alley, Robert Benfield, Scott Chinn, Rich Dupuis, Cindy Feliciano, Mark Full, Steve Gardner, Jeff Gonynor, Chuck Goode, Rick King, Tom McCrimmon, Donnie McManus, Chris Morris, Doug Newell, David Oliver, Bob Osborne, Alice Owens, Shawn Parker, Scott Radel, Rick Rausch, Dennis Ritchie, Bobby Sada, and Paul Southworth.

On Matt Kenseth's 2001 team, thanks to: Jeff Vandermoss, Todd Millard, Dave Smith, Mark Demarco, Brent Swim, Ed Young, Justin Nottestad, Bryan Dunaway, Dave Paronto, Matt Millard, Chris Hunley, Jim Smith, Darrin Fabinso, Michael Armstrong, Jeremy Brickhouse, Benjy Grubb, Jim Gudette, Daniel Walkup, Kevin Steinmetz, Scott Kurtz, Mark Tillson, Scott Russell, Trace Conchan, Chris Becker, Jim Crowell, Chip Bolin, and Mike Calinoff.

Thanks to the Kurt Busch 2001 team: Mark Bieberich, Mike Janow, Chris Webb, Nick Bailey, Chris Hladik, David Buckelew, Rich Machcinski, Scott Kurtz, Will Smith, David Weiss, Greg Tester, Jeremy Brickhouse, Dan Ecklund, Scott St. John, Bruce Hayes, Kevin Steinmetz, Dave Bullock, Larry Judd, Phil Cook, Chris Becker, Karen Gilbert, and Kristy Cloutier.

My gratitude to these former Roush employees: Kevin Radvany, T. Kirk Lowry, Elizabeth Patterson, Matt Chambers, Ryan Young, and Mark Price. Thanks to Eddie and Len Wood, and to three folks whose pre- and post-race interview transcriptions saved me countless hours of work: Dan Zacharias, Al Larsen, and Nancy Wager. My education in auto racing was abetted by several motorsports writers, notably David Poole and Jim Utter of *The Charlotte Observer* and thatsracin.com; Mike Harris of the Associated Press; Mark Schmeidel of *The Providence Journal*; and Mike

Mulhern of the *Winston-Salem Journal*. Thanks to help from Dustin Long of the *Greensboro (N.C.) News & Record*.

Thanks to Jay Selle and his Charlotte infield friends; Chad Little, the first NASCAR driver I met; Kevin Lepage; and the Great Race team, including Victor Vojcek, Rod Girolami, Tom Donoghue, Wayne Stanfield, Andy Massimilla, and Susan and Dale McClenaghan, Jack Roush's daughter and son-in-law. Thanks to Jud Preece, Russ Branham, W. A. DeVore, George J. Harris, Jim Miller, Julie-Ann V. Ransom, Robyn A. Leibold, Jon Howland, and Carol Hall. Also, Tamara Lightner and Judi Battles.

A sincere thank you to the many current and former speedway officials who assisted me, including Angela Clare and Cheryl Hamilton, Atlanta Motor Speedway; Ben Trout and Sonya Moore, Bristol Motor Speedway; Ray Burns and Donna Freismuth, Daytona International Speedway; John Dunlap and Pam Cramer, Dover Downs International Speedway; Deb Taylor, Indianapolis Motor Speedway; Dawn McDow and Jeff Motley, Las Vegas Motor Speedway; Scott Cooper, Myra Faulkenbury, and Jerry Gappens, Lowe's Motor Speedway; Karen Parker and Mike Smith, Martinsville Speedway; Crystal Collier and Kelly Goodin, Michigan International Speedway; Frederick J. Neergaard, New Hampshire International Speedway; Patti Angeloni, Pocono Raceway; and Ken Patterson, Talladega Superspeedway.

I was helped by several at NASCAR, including: Bill France Jr., Mike Helton, George Pyne, Kevin Triplett, Danielle Humphrey, Herb Branham, Bill Greene, Kelly Crouch Brook, and Tim Packman. Also helping me were Jack Roush's parents, Charles and Georgetta Roush, and his brother, Frank; Matt Kenseth's sister and father, Kelley Maruszewski and Roy Kenseth; and Gaye, Tom and Kyle Busch.

Several librarians and historians were there for me, and I am grateful to Martha Macon, of the Kannapolis History Foundation; Linda Henderson, *Providence Journal* head librarian; Suzanne Wise, Stock Car Racing Collection, Belk Library, Appalachian

State University, Boone, N.C.; Sandra Mundy and Lynda Rivet, Jesse Smith Memorial Library, Harrisville, R.I.; and Judy Grimsley, editorial research manager, *The Orlando Sentinel.*

I am indebted to a bunch of folks at my new publisher, Public-Affairs: publisher Peter Osnos, executive editor Paul Golob, assistant editor David Patterson, marketing manager Nina Damario, marketing director Lisa Kaufman, production editor Melanie Peirson Johnstone, copy editor John Thomas, indexer Robert Swanson, and jacket designer Jamie Keenan. I am similarly indebted to several people at *The Providence Journal*: publisher Howard G. Sutton, executive editor Joel P. Raws on, metropolitan managing editor Thomas E. Heslin, sports editor Art Martone, photographer Connie Grosch, and executive assistant Carol Montrond. And I cannot forget Jon Karp, who began this journey with me.

On my weekends in New Hampshire, I was a house guest of my mother, Mary Miller, and my sisters, Mary Wright and Linda Twombly. Thanks, folks.

And, as always, Kay McCauley was with me from the command to start writing! Thanks once again, my dear.

Finally, I owe the biggest debt of all to my immediate family, who had endured varying degrees of my absence for my five earlier books—but never anything like the schedule I kept for the more than two years that I chased men and their speed. Alexis, Rachel, Katy, and Cal, I love you guys forever.

INDEX

ABOUT THE AUTHOR

G. Wayne Miller is a senior staff writer at *The Providence Journal,* where he has worked since 1981. Miller specializes in long-term narrative journalism—stories of people and places ordinarily off-limits to writers, and several of his newspaper series have served as the basis for his critically acclaimed nonfiction books. *The Work of Human Hands* (1993) chronicles the life and work of Hardy Hendren, the pioneering chief of surgery at Children's Hospital in Boston; *Coming of Age* (1995) takes readers inside the lives and adventures of two typical American teenagers and how they cope with growing up in today's fast-moving world; *Toy Wars* (1998) is a business saga about the highly competitive toy industry, where the makers of Barbie and G.I. Joe fight their own life-or-death struggles; and *King of Hearts* (2000) profiles the unconventional medical visionaries who thought it was possible—and desirable—to operate on the human heart when the medical establishment considered such ideas not only unrealistic, but dangerous. Miller is also the author of a novel, *Thunder Rise* (1989), and is a recipient of the American Society of Newspaper Editors' prize for feature writing.

Men and Speed, Miller's sixth book, is the product of nearly two full years of research and hundreds of interviews with drivers, crew members, business-side people, and fans. More information on the book and many more photographs are available at www.menandspeed.com, and Miller's author site is www.gwaynemiller.com.

PublicAffairs is a publishing house founded in 1997. It is a tribute to the standards, values, and flair of three persons who have served as mentors to countless reporters, writers, editors, and book people of all kinds, including me.

I. F. STONE, proprietor of *I. F. Stone's Weekly,* combined a commitment to the First Amendment with entrepreneurial zeal and reporting skill and became one of the great independent journalists in American history. At the age of eighty, Izzy published *The Trial of Socrates,* which was a national bestseller. He wrote the book after he taught himself ancient Greek.

BENJAMIN C. BRADLEE was for nearly thirty years the charismatic editorial leader of *The Washington Post.* It was Ben who gave the *Post* the range and courage to pursue such historic issues as Watergate. He supported his reporters with a tenacity that made them fearless and it is no accident that so many became authors of influential, best-selling books.

ROBERT L. BERNSTEIN, the chief executive of Random House for more than a quarter century, guided one of the nation's premier publishing houses. Bob was personally responsible for many books of political dissent and argument that challenged tyranny around the globe. He is also the founder and longtime chair of Human Rights Watch, one of the most respected human rights organizations in the world.

For fifty years, the banner of Public Affairs Press was carried by its owner, Morris B. Schnapper, who published Gandhi, Nasser, Toynbee, Truman, and about 1,500 other authors. In 1983, Schnapper was described by *The Washington Post* as "a redoubtable gadfly." His legacy will endure in the books to come.

Peter Osnos, *Publisher*